Second Edition

BEST Behavior

Jeffrey Sprague
Annemieke Golly

Building Positive Behavior Support in Schools

Cambium LEARNING Group | Sopris LEARNING

Cambium LEARNING Group | Sopris LEARNING

ISBN 13: 978-1-60697-991-4
ISBN 10: 1-60697-991-4
JDE #: 310295/07-12

1 2 3 4 5   B&B   16 15 14 13 12

Printed in the United States of America
Published and Distributed by

4093 Specialty Place • Longmont, Colorado 80504
303-651-2829 • www.soprislearning.com

Acknowledgments

The research, techniques, and ideas in this guide represent many years of hard work in schools for us, first as classroom teachers, and later as consultants, trainers and researchers. We are gratefully indebted to many of our mentors, colleagues, and friends for their support, innovative ideas, and enthusiasm for helping school personnel, families and students lead happier and more successful lives during their school years and beyond.

We have had many mentors at the University of Oregon. We thank Hill Walker for his superb expertise as a researcher and mentor of so many leaders in our field, and for being an excellent friend and colleague. His mentorship, quiet guidance, and passion for improving the lives of children is a beacon for all of us.

We also thank Rob Horner and George Sugai for their amazing leadership and insight regarding methods and systems for implementing schoolwide behavioral support and functional behavioral assessment. The opportunity to collaborate with them to develop and refine many of the methods in this guide has been an honor and pleasure, and we look forward to many more years of collaboration and shared learning. Rob has also been a special mentor and friend to Jeff for more than 30 years and continues to dramatically influence his career and thinking.

We give special thanks to Geoff Colvin for his superb work on defusing behavioral escalation, and for his ability to help us interpret and solve complex teacher-student interactions in ways that make them seem simple.

One of the markers of the outstanding research success at the University of Oregon is our superb colleague group. We work with several amazing colleagues who provide new ideas and shape our thinking and practice daily.

We would also like to give special recognition to our colleagues and trainers in the Netherlands, in particular Monique Baard and Inge Reijnders, who have contributed significantly to enriching and expanding the implementation of *Best Behavior*.

We would also like to give special thanks to Kevin Boling, principal of Bertha Holt Elementary School (a model PBIS school). Kevin and Annemieke were teaching colleagues for 20 years and successfully implemented many of the *Best Behavior* strategies during that time. While writing the second edition, Kevin not only provided us with numerous ideas and examples but he assisted in editing the book.

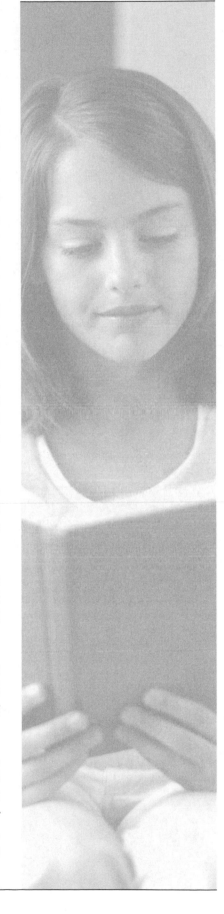

Finally, we wish to thank our colleagues in schools across the United States and the world for their commitment to improving behavior support systems, and to the lives of students. They also guide our work and help us make it as good as it can be!

About the Authors

Jeffrey Sprague, Ph.D., is a professor of special education and director of the University of Oregon Institute on Violence and Destructive Behavior. He directs federal, state, and local research and demonstration projects related to positive behavior interventions and supports, response to intervention, youth violence prevention, alternative education, juvenile delinquency prevention and treatment, and school safety. His research activities encompass applied behavior analysis, positive behavior supports, behavioral response to intervention, functional behavioral assessment, school safety, youth violence prevention, and juvenile delinquency prevention.

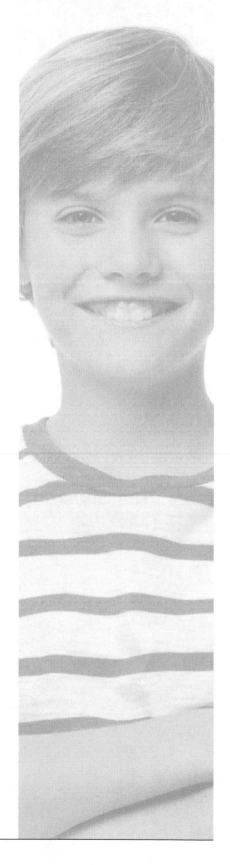

Dr. Sprague began his career as a teacher of students with low incidence cognitive disabilities, and his early career research was focused primarily in this content area. In 1990 and 1997, Dr. Sprague coauthored the first guide to Functional Behavioral Assessment (O'Neill et al., 1997). He is a contributor to "Early Warning, Timely Response," and the 1998, 1999, and 2000 *Annual Reports on School Safety*. He has written a book on crime prevention through environmental design for school administrators. Dr. Sprague has authored a book on school safety with Hill Walker for Guilford Publications (Sprague & Walker, 2005), and in 2008 he published a book on response to intervention and behavior supports (www.shoplrp.com). He has published over 150 journal articles and book chapters.

Dr. Sprague currently directs a research project from the National Institute in Drug Abuse to conduct the first evaluation of the effects of positive behavior supports in middle schools. He is also co-principal investigator on five Institute of Education Sciences Goal 2 development projects focusing on positive behavior supports, response to intervention for behavior, classroom management, student self-management, and PBIS implementation in juvenile justice settings.

Annemieke Golly, Ph.D., born and raised in the Netherlands, is a certified special education teacher who has taught children with behavior and conduct disorders for two decades. Dr. Golly received her Ph.D. in special education at the University of Oregon. Her areas of expertise are early and preventive intervention, behavior management, and classroom and schoolwide management. She is a research scientist at the Oregon Research Institute and works at the Institute on Violence and Destructive Behavior at the University of Oregon as a teacher trainer and behavioral consultant.

Dr. Golly is a co-author for the First Step to Success Program (PreK–3rd grade) and has been a coordinator for designing, implementing, and conducting nation-wide research on this program for the past decade. She has trained hundreds of teachers and consultants to implement school and home interventions for young students who are dealing with challenging behaviors.

Dr. Golly has worked as a consultant/trainer to implement behavior management strategies in the United States, Canada, the Virgin Islands, Germany, South Africa, and Turkey. For the past three years, she also has been training, coaching, and providing technical assistance to school and youth services staff in the Netherlands to implement *Best Behavior* nation-wide. She has authored and co-authored books on practical strategies for dealing with challenging behaviors, including *Why Johnny Doesn't Behave: 20 Tips and Measurable BIPs* and *Five Universal Principles of Positive Behavior Support and the Story of my Life*. She has taught several university courses and has written numerous research articles.

Contents

Note From the Authors

The first edition of *Best Behavior* was published in 2005. Since then, thousands of teachers, administrators, and *Best Behavior* implementation teams throughout the United States and across the world have been using this book as their staff development guide to implement schoolwide systems for creating a positive, pro-active and effective school climate. We believe a large part of the popularity of this book is its simple language, and easy to adopt evidence-based behavioral and organizational strategies. Furthermore, the intervention techniques included here are the result of more than 30 years of research in the area of school discipline from the fields of education, psychology, and criminology.

Why *Best Behavior* Is Important

Researchers and practitioners have intensified their efforts to understand how to induce school personnel to adopt, implement, and sustain effective prevention practices (Fixsen, Naoom, Blase, Friedman, & Wallace, 2005; Mihalic & Irwin, 2003). We know that our goals for prevention of violent and antisocial behavior will not be met until this is achieved. Researchers are now focusing intensely on this matter.

Implementation appears most successful when the following occurs.

- The whole school community receives coordinated training, coaching, and frequent performance assessments.
- School organizations provide the infrastructure necessary for timely training, skillful supervision and coaching, and regular process and outcome evaluations.
- Communities are fully involved in the selection and evaluation of programs and practices.
- Funding sources, policies, and regulations create a hospitable environment for implementation and program operations.

(Fixsen et al., 2005)

What's New in the Second Edition?

While providing training and technical assistance over the past few years to schools implementing *Best Behavior*, we have learned a great deal from incredibly experienced, creative, and innovative school personnel. We have incorporated their ideas, experiences, and practical adaptations into this new edition, which has greatly enhanced the *Best Behavior* approach.

The first edition of *Best Behavior* provided an essential foundation and starting point for the second edition. Retaining our uniquely accessible language, we have responded in this second edition to the need to provide schools with additional recipes, strategies, and ideas for success as they adopt, implement (and adapt), and maintain PBIS techniques for schoolwide discipline, classroom management, individual student support, and communication and collaboration with families.

To illustrate that point, we have added the following to this second edition:

- A new chapter on aggression, harassment, bullying, and cyber bullying, and integrated *Best Behavior* with antibullying and social skills curricula
- Expanded strategies, tips, scripts, templates, and sample expectations, lesson plans, letters, and forms to allow schools to use and customize a variety of effective PBIS approaches
- Detailed examples, case studies, and ideas from schools that have successfully implemented *Best Behavior*
- More clearly outlined steps and forms for developing and enacting RTI procedures for dealing with students who are in need of Tier II and Tier III behavior interventions
- Greater support for home/school collaboration, including research-based teacher tips and numerous tools, such as a good-news note, a sample newsletter, a model note and letter for caregivers, and a sample schedule and calendar suggesting when and what to communicate
- Increased focus on sustaining a dynamic and responsive system, using problem-solving and data-driven review to respond to changes in school or student needs

We believe that you will find these new features to be a critical component to building and sustaining a successful *Best Behavior* system in your school.

Sincerely,

Jeff Sprague
Annemieke Golly

List of Reproducibles

SECTION 1

Schoolwide Positive Behavior Interventions and Supports

Welcome to *Best Behavior*: Building Positive Behavior Interventions and Supports in Schools

Why *Best Behavior*?

Positive Behavior Interventions and Supports (PBIS) is a significantly different, yet very simple, approach to problem behavior (Sugai & Horner, 2010). At its heart is this very different assumption: Students may not be doing what you want because they aren't sure of what you want or don't believe that you care if they do it or not. It is positive, not because there are no consequences for inappropriate behavior, but because the focus of the teacher's work shifts from noticing and punishing inappropriate behavior to teaching and noticing desired behavior. This kind of shift isn't easy, but the reason for it is important to understand.

Core Principles

Simply stated, the core PBIS principles are:

1. **Develop clear expectations:** Decide what behaviors you want to see and hear.

2. **Communicate and teach the expectations:** Systematically teach and reteach students what those behaviors look like and what they don't look like.

3. **Reinforce and recognize when students are following the expectations:** Systematically notice students for engaging in the desired behaviors.

4. **Minimize attention:** Don't give attention to minor inappropriate behaviors (don't make mountains out of molehills).

5. **Have clear and consistent consequences:** Deal with unacceptable behavior in predictable ways. "Big stick" punishments never work in the long run, and actually can make things worse (Mayer, 1995).

OBJECTIVES

- ▶ Provide an introduction to *Best Behavior*

- ▶ Describe what *Best Behavior* provides for schools, students, and families

- ▶ Describe why *Best Behavior* is needed to improve discipline and student well-being in schools

- ▶ Discuss how *Best Behavior* supports staff members, students, and families

With these principles at its core, this integrated system of schoolwide, classroom management, individual student, and family supports is designed to give you simple but effective tactics and strategies to improve behavioral outcomes for the students you serve and their families. Furthermore, this guide will help you gain a variety of new skills and knowledge that are based on the best research available.

Challenges

Two issues are constant challenges to effective education: academic achievement and discipline. Students who are not safe, respectful, and responsible in schools impede the learning process for others and for themselves. School personnel who do not work together and focus on critical outcomes will be frustrated (even burned out), inconsistent, and ineffective. Parents who are not supported and encouraged to collaborate will feel left out, and their children will not do as well in school (Walker, Ramsey, & Gresham, 2004). In this guide, we will spend time together learning the most recent research-validated and evidence-based techniques for establishing a positive school climate where no child is left behind, no teacher is left unsupported, and strong home-school connections between teachers and caregivers are created and sustained.

How Schools and Adults Contribute to the Problem

Many school practices inadvertently contribute to the development of antisocial behavior and the potential for violence in schools. Because it has been common to place responsibility for behavior change on individual students or their families, school practices are often overlooked as factors in a behavior problem. These practices include:

- Ineffective instruction that results in academic failure.
- Failure to individualize instruction to adapt to individual differences.
- Inconsistent and punitive schoolwide, classroom, and individual behavior-management practices.
- Lack of opportunity to learn and practice prosocial interpersonal and self-management skills.
- Unclear rules and expectations regarding expected behavior in all school settings.
- Failure to correct rule violations in a firm but fair manner that emphasizes teaching rather than retribution.
- Failure to help students from at-risk backgrounds adjust to the schooling process.
- Failure to encourage active collaboration and cooperation with parents and families.
- Failure to sustain and consistently implement positive behavior support practices.

These factors are *all* amenable to change with a broad-based, preventive approach. Unfortunately, school personnel have a long history of applying simple and unproven solutions (e.g., office discipline referrals, suspensions) to complex behavior problems, and they express understandable disappointment when these attempts do not work as expected (Walker et al., 1996). This practice is sustained by a tendency to try to remove the student who is displaying the inappropriate behavior via office referrals, suspension, or expulsion, rather than finding a way to change the administrative, teaching, and management practices that have contributed to the problem.

Background: Misbehavior in Schools

A child is misbehaving . . . A classroom is "out of control" . . . Hallways are chaotic . . . Learning is suffering. What can we do?

The most common response to the above question is some sort of consequence or punishment. As a society, we tend to believe that if we can just find the correct punishment, then people will start doing the right thing (Biglan, Hallfors, Spoth, Gottfredson, & Cody, in press). This approach doesn't work well, yet we find ourselves doing the same thing over and over again or increasing the severity of punishments.

In school, this problem manifests itself by increasing the numbers of students who experience office referrals, suspensions, or other punishments that take them out of the classroom on a regular basis. It is hard to achieve academically when you are not in the classroom (Kellam, Mayer, Rebok, & Hawkins, 1998). Maybe we should try something different. We need to re-aim our work (Glasgow, Vogt, & Boles, 1999).

> "Insanity is doing the same thing again and again and expecting different results."
>
> Albert Einstein

Researchers and practitioners have intensified their efforts to understand how to get school personnel to adopt, implement, and sustain effective prevention practices (Fixsen, Naoom, Blase, & Wallace, 2007; Mihalic & Irwin, 2003). We know that our goals for preventing disruptive and antisocial behavior will not be met until this is achieved. Researchers are now focusing intensely on this matter and exploring the challenge from a cultural perspective as well.

Implementation appears to be most successful when all of the following conditions are met (Fixsen, et al., 2007).

- The whole school community receives coordinated training, coaching, and frequent performance assessments.
- School organizations provide the infrastructure necessary for timely training, skillful supervision and coaching, and regular process and outcome evaluations.

- Communities are fully involved in the selection and evaluation of programs and practices.
- Funding sources, policies, and regulations create a hospitable environment for program implementation and operations.

How Does *Best Behavior* Address the Challenge?

Best Behavior provides structured and evidence-based training and support to representative teams of educators and families in schools over a 2- to 3-year period, as well as training and technical assistance to adopt, implement, and maintain a collection of effective schoolwide, classroom, and individual student interventions. These school teams work to complete initial and ongoing needs assessment, choose interventions (e.g., school rules, reward systems, systematic supervision), and use student- and staff-level data to refine and evaluate their efforts. Schools using *Best Behavior* to support the implementation of systemic behavior improvement can be found across the United States and in other countries, such as Norway, Iceland, the Netherlands, Denmark, and Chile.

This book builds from the original *Best Behavior* book by providing schools with additional details (ideas, variations, and expansions) for success as they adopt, implement (adapt), and maintain PBIS techniques for schoolwide discipline, harassment, including bullying and cyber bullying, classroom management, individual student support, and communication and collaboration with families.

We believe a large part of the popularity of this book is due to its simple language and its easy-to-adopt, evidence-based behavioral and organizational strategies. *Best Behavior* provides an essential foundation and starting point. These "recipes" originated in schools that have successfully implemented *Best Behavior,* and this added level of detail provides what is reflected in the new chapter subtitle: Building Positive Behavior Interventions and Supports in Schools.

Summary of Measurable Outcomes

Best Behavior and similar models have been replicated by other researchers using similar, or the same, techniques. The effects of the intervention are documented in a series of studies implemented by researchers at the University of Oregon (Biglan, Metzler, Rusby, & Sprague, 1998; Sprague et al., 2001; Sugai & Horner, 2010; Taylor-Greene et al., 1997) (see also www.pbis.org for the latest research studies and reports). Studies have shown reductions in office discipline referrals of up to 50%, with continued improvement over a 3-year period in schools that sustain the intervention (Irvin, Tobin, Sprague, Sugai, & Vincent, 2004). In addition, school staff report greater satisfaction with their work, compared to working in schools that did not implement *Best Behavior.* Comparison schools show increases (or no change) in office referrals, along with general frustration with the school discipline program.

To what extent has the prevalence of risk behaviors been prevented and protective factors, or assets, been increased? Studies are underway now to relate the quality of implementation to changes in student and staff behavior, as well as to document changes in student attitudes, self-reported problem behavior, and academic achievement.

> Research indicates that practices like those taught in *Best Behavior* are related to positive outcomes, ranging from decreased discipline problems to increased academic achievement and teacher satisfaction.

In studies employing the components included in the *Best Behavior* program, reductions in antisocial behavior (Bradshaw, Mitchell, & Leaf, 2010; Sprague, et al., 2001); vandalism (Mayer & Butterworth, 1995); aggression (Grossman et al., 1997); later delinquency (Kellam at al., 1998; O'Donnell, Hawkins, Catalano, Abbott, & Day, 1995); and alcohol, tobacco, and other drug use (Biglan, Holder, Brennan, & Foster, 2004) have been documented. Positive changes in protective factors such as academic achievement (Kellam et al., 1998; O'Donnell et al., 1995) and school engagement (O'Donnell et al., 1995) have also been documented as using a positive school discipline program, such as *Best Behavior*, in concert with other interventions.

What *Best Behavior* Provides

Best Behavior provides proven, effective management methods for students in school common areas (*all* students), for those at risk of behavior problems (*some* students), and for the (*few*) students in your school who are already disruptive and exhibit undisciplined behavior. This integrated approach has been shown to be effective in research (Walker et al., 1996) but has only recently been broadly adopted by schools and school systems. Without an integrated approach to melding school, classroom, and individual student supports, schools often use effective strategies in a piecemeal and inconsistent fashion, thereby reducing their impact.

Best Behavior provides a standardized staff development program aimed at improving school and classroom discipline and reducing associated outcomes, such as school violence and alcohol, tobacco, and other drug use. It is based on the Positive Behavioral Interventions and Support (PBIS) approach (Sugai & Horner, 2010; Walker, et al., 1996) developed at the University of Oregon and the National Center on Positive Behavioral Interventions and Supports (www.pbis.org), an Office of Special Education Programs–funded research center.

> *Best Behavior* provides:
> - Proven practices that support schools and the healthy development of students
> - A comprehensive program for delivery and improvement cycles
> - An integrated, tiered approach to meet all student needs

The goal of *Best Behavior* is to facilitate the academic achievement and healthy social development of children and youth, in a safe environment that is conducive to learning.

Best Behavior addresses schoolwide, classroom, and individual student interventions, as well as family communication and collaboration. It is one of the few programs that offers supports for *all* students in the school, *some* students with additional needs, and the *few* students who need the most intensive supports (as outlined in Chapter 3). Figure 1 shows the interconnection of each of these areas.

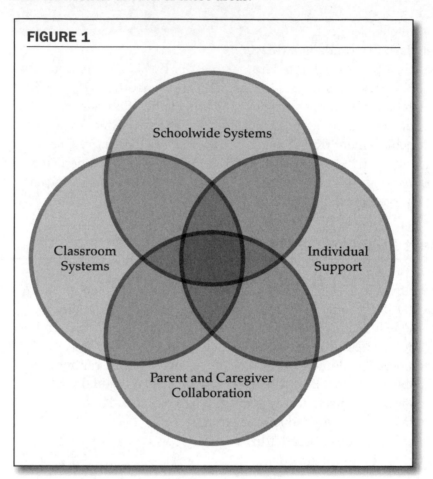

FIGURE 1

Schoolwide Systems

Classroom Systems

Individual Support

Parent and Caregiver Collaboration

Changes to the New Edition

As noted above, the first edition of the *Best Behavior* book gave school personnel tools to support *all* students in the school (whole school methods), *some* students who are at risk for academic and behavioral failure, and a *few* students who present the most serious challenges. This revised edition adds a range of new examples and advanced "recipes" for implementing PBIS procedures that were not included in the original book. *Best Behavior* has been attractive to educators because it is both simple and comprehensive, and this new version continues that tradition.

The following material is included in this updated book.
- Companion and supplemental materials providing advanced examples and detailed scripts for implementing key aspects of the *Best Behavior* approach.
- Checklists to guide program implementation.
- New materials for students and families.
- A new chapter on bullying and harassment with critical information about cyber bullying.
- A case study of one school's experience using the *Best Behavior* system.

How *Best Behavior* Will Help You

☑ Improve Schoolwide Practices

You will learn to:
- Carry out strategies for improving the consistency and the effectiveness of school discipline systems. We recommend that every school employ a representative team to implement each strategy in this guide.
- Assess the current status and needs of your school regarding discipline and safety and use that assessment to set goals. Interventions are more effective if they are based on a comprehensive and representative needs assessment.
- Develop a plan for choosing and teaching school rules and behavior expectations. Schools should use a small number of clear, positively stated rules to guide both students and teachers.
- Develop a plan to directly teach expected behavior in your school. Students must be regularly taught expected behavior to assure maintenance. Complete teaching scripts are included.
- Develop a plan to actively supervise all students in common areas such as hallways, cafeterias, and playgrounds. Much problem behavior occurs in common areas of the school. *Best Behavior* outlines a simple but powerful strategy for improving common-area supervision.
- Develop a plan for preventing harassment, bullying, and cyber bullying. Such plans should include creating lesson plans outlining correct behavior and pairing interventions with *Best Behavior* strategies.
- Use office discipline referral patterns and other data to continuously improve and share success with all adults in the school. School personnel perform better and buy in to program improvement if they get regular feedback on discipline patterns in the school.
- Work to build and sustain effective management practices in your school. Improving school discipline and academic achievement is an ongoing process.
- Achieve consistency between classroom and schoolwide discipline procedures. As schoolwide procedures are established, you will link them to your classroom management routines and practices and to your students' academic performance.

Figure 2 provides a visual of the chain events that occur before, during, and after behavior support takes place.

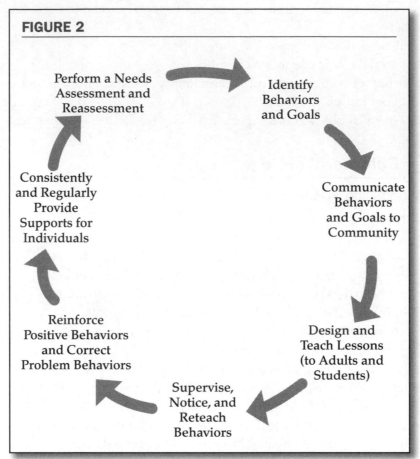

FIGURE 2

Perform a Needs Assessment and Reassessment → Identify Behaviors and Goals → Communicate Behaviors and Goals to Community → Design and Teach Lessons (to Adults and Students) → Supervise, Notice, and Reteach Behaviors → Reinforce Positive Behaviors and Correct Problem Behaviors → Consistently and Regularly Provide Supports for Individuals

☑ Improve Classroom Management Effectiveness

You will learn to:

- Decrease student misbehavior in the classroom and prevent problems before they start by using your behavior strategically.
- Effectively and consistently gain student attention. Using clear signals in the classroom minimizes disruption.
- Use effective systems to reward and maintain expected social and academic behavior. Students need clear, consistent encouragement.
- Foster cooperative, respectful, and responsible behavior between students by directly teaching and providing positive and corrective feedback. Predictable problems in classrooms can be solved by preventive teaching.
- Directly teach and support positive student social skills in the classroom. Expected behaviors need to be taught and reviewed.
- Avoid power struggles.

☑ **Improve Support Systems for Individual Students**

You will learn to:

- Objectively assess the reasons for student misbehavior and develop universal positive support plans tailored for individual students. Thinking functionally about behavior will increase your effectiveness.
- Respond effectively to bullying and harassment (including cyber bullying), noncompliance, and escalating behavior. Use your behavior to defuse these challenges.
- Teach students to self-manage their behavior and learning. Self-control and intrinsic motivation are taught using simple procedures.

☑ **Collaborate Effectively with All Parents and Caregivers**

Parents are valuable partners in promoting student success.

You will learn to:

- Develop strategies for positive communication with families. It is critical to inform families of your schoolwide and classroom procedures.
- Collaborate with parents to support healthy and safe behavior at home and at school.
- Support parents to prevent and respond to bullying and cyber bullying.

The materials included in this guide are designed to be used for both your practice and for the support of team-based training. The best results are obtained when all the adults in the school use the practices, all students are affected, and data are used continually to improve and sustain each school system (e.g., schoolwide, classroom, individual student) and intervention method (e.g., school rule teaching, self-management). Chapter 2 will outline our approach to providing team-based staff development.

How This Guide Is Organized

Best Behavior is organized into four sections: (1) Schoolwide Positive Behavior Interventions and Supports, (2) Classroom Management, (3) Individual Student Supports, and (4) Family Support and Conclusions. Each chapter is designed to be used to support team-based staff-member development at the building or school district level.

Section 1: Schoolwide Positive Behavior Interventions and Supports

Chapter 2: **Best Behavior** *Staff Development: What It Looks Like.* This chapter describes the logistics of the staff development and technical assistance program. We outline recommended start-up procedures and tasks and provide sample training agendas to illustrate the approach.

Chapter 3: Introduction to the Challenge of Antisocial Behavior: The Three-Tiered Approach. We begin this chapter by outlining the challenge of school violence and discipline problems. It is critical for educators to understand the prevalence of destructive life outcomes for children who are antisocial if they are not given positive behavior supports. We close by providing a review of evidence-based, effective practices. Knowledge of what works and what doesn't can guide you and your school's team as you build and implement your interventions.

Chapter 4: Building Positive Behavior Interventions and Supports: One School's Story. In this chapter, we describe the components of a schoolwide positive behavior support system. Conducting a needs assessment is the first step in the program development, and we present a self-assessment of the essential practices in your school and ask you to identify priorities for intervention. You will also develop three to four annual goals into an action plan.

Chapter 5: Defining Schoolwide Behavior Expectations. In this chapter, you will learn how to define behavior expectations (e.g., compliance to adult requests, positive peer-to-peer interactions, academic effort, and school safety) for your school and communicate them to all adults and students.

Chapter 6: Communicating and Teaching Schoolwide Behavior Expectations. In this chapter, you will learn the basics of teaching and communicating behavioral expectations and develop a sample lesson plan for teaching them. We present practical methods for increasing consistency of rule teaching and making it fun for both adults and students. As you consider the adoption of research-validated social-skills curricula, such as the Second Step Violence Prevention Curriculum (Committee for Children, 1997) or the Life Skills Training (Botvan, 1979), you will find that the recommendations in this chapter provide an excellent foundation for maximizing their effectiveness.

Chapter 7: Schoolwide Recognition and Reward Systems: Creating a Positive School Culture. In this chapter, we list the components of effective reward systems, discuss facts and fictions about positive reinforcement, and present ideas for increasing consistency among the adults in the school. You also have the opportunity to build a schoolwide recognition and reward system. We will discuss a continuum of recognition systems that cover the array from external systems to intrinsic motivational systems.

Chapter 8: Systematic Supervision of Common Areas. Common areas, such as cafeterias, playgrounds, and hallways are often overlooked as the source of many behavioral problems in schools. In this chapter, we present four essential techniques of active supervision: (1) positive contacts with students, (2) positive reinforcement, (3) scanning and movement, and (4) correcting behavioral errors. We present a method for planning a strategy to make your common areas safer and more positive.

Chapter 9: Preventing and Responding to Aggressive Social Behavior, Bullying, and Harassment. No matter what their experiences or background in growing up, most adults can remember at least one or two occasions during childhood where they were picked on, made fun of in front of peers, humiliated in some way, threatened, intimidated, or perhaps even beaten up . Most can clearly recall the student or students who did these things, as well as details and circumstances surrounding the incident(s), even though they may not be able to remember much else from this period in their lives. This chapter describes the background of various forms of aggression, bullying, and harassment in schools (including cyber bullying) and lists the components of an effective response to these aggressive behaviors. We also discuss how a schoolwide bullying prevention strategy can integrate with *Best Behavior.*

Chapter 10: Using Data to Diagnose Schoolwide, Classroom, and Individual Student Systems. Larry Irvin and his colleagues (Irvin, et al., 2004) suggest that analyzing office discipline referral patterns in schools provides a simple but useful source of data to make decisions about the effectiveness of schoolwide, classroom, common area, and individual student interventions. In this chapter, we describe features of a good discipline referral system, provide model discipline referral forms, and offer a set of decision rules to detect school program improvement needs.

Section 2: Classroom Management

Chapter 11: Classroom Organization: The Foundation of Classroom Management. Classroom organization is the beginning of a comprehensive and evidence-based approach to improving classroom management effectiveness. The techniques are simple and powerful when implemented consistently across classrooms in your school. We describe the organization of an effective classroom and provide a checklist to evaluate your classroom environment. You will be asked to set goals for improving your classroom environment.

Chapter 12: Designing and Teaching Classroom Behavioral Expectations. We recommend linking schoolwide behavior expectations and routines to those used in your classroom. As a teacher, you have unique routines and expectations that fit your classroom and teaching practices. In this chapter, we guide you to develop a few positive classroom rules that are linked to the schoolwide system. We also describe how teaching and encouraging compliance to classroom rules contribute to effective classroom management.

Chapter 13: Preventive Interactions. If we want to change a student's behavior, then we must change our own behavior. This chapter presents some very useful preventive interactions that can minimize problem behavior in your classroom. You will learn to use a consistent attention signal for the whole class and to use direct speech when giving instructions to students. We will teach you how to stay out of power struggles and to present a specific, predictable request sequence to noncompliant students. We will show you how to teach an on-task routine, called the Concentration/Focus Power Game, to increase on-task behavior and to use during disruptions.

Chapter 14: Using Positive and Corrective Consequences to Change Behavior. Effective teachers use a combination of positive reinforcement for expected behavior and firm but fair corrections for behavioral errors. In this chapter, you will identify positive consequences to use in your classroom as well as effective corrective consequences as we will discuss the importance of neutral positive statements and neutral corrective statements. You will also design integrated motivational systems to teach and reinforce positive behavior change.

Section 3: Individual Student Supports

Chapter 15: Responding to Escalating Behavior and Power Struggles. Escalating behavior and power struggles exhibited by students seriously impact the proper functioning of a school and classroom. Behaviors such as aggression, bullying, severe disruption, and acting-out can cause major problems for adults and students, in terms of personal safety and stress, and significantly disrupt the teaching and learning processes in school. In this chapter, we identify common assumptions that get teachers into power struggles, and we suggest procedures to both avoid them and deescalate behaviors.

Chapter 16: Thinking Functionally About Behavior. Behavioral approaches to school and classroom management provide some of the most effective solutions to reducing problem behavior. Functional Behavioral Assessment (FBA) methods (O'Neill et al., 1995) provide an easy way to assess the motivation behind problem behavior and link our response logically to that motivation. In this chapter, you will learn to define functional behavioral assessment, list the outcomes of a complete functional behavioral assessment, describe information needed for a functional behavioral assessment, and discuss the logical link between functional behavioral assessment outcomes and positive support plan procedures that can be adapted. Thinking functionally works for students in special education as well as for those in mainstream education.

Chapter 17: Building Positive Behavior Support Plans for Individual Students. We need to develop positive support plans that fit our skills, values, and resources. In this chapter, you will learn to describe the logical link from functional assessment results to positive supports and discuss what changes adults can make to bring about change in student behavior. Positive behavior support plans help us make problem behaviors irrelevant, ineffective, and inefficient by teaching and encouraging replacement behaviors. Most common chronic behaviors that require individual interventions can be dealt with through the development of schoolwide templates that can be individualized for students requiring Tier II interventions. Universal positive behavioral support plans that can be adapted for individual students are included.

Chapter 18: Adapting Curricula to Prevent Problem Behavior. One of the principal reasons why students misbehave in school is due to instruction that is too difficult or poorly adapted. In this chapter, you will learn to use instruction and curriculum adaptation to help students become more successful and behave better. You will learn to describe classes of adaptation that can prevent problem behavior, outline a process for adapting curricula and instruction, and develop and adapt a classroom lesson to prevent problem behavior.

Chapter 19: Teaching Students Who Are at Risk to Self-Manage Their Behavior. Many of us hope that our students will become self-directed, intrinsically motivated learners. H.M. Walker (1995) indicates that teachers value compliance to reasonable requests and students who are prepared for class and do their best to complete assigned work. Safe, respectful, and responsible students learn to self-manage their behavior. In this chapter, we describe the purposes and benefits of teaching self-management, describe the core features of self-management programs, and illustrate how to design and teach a self-management program.

Section 4: Family Support and Conclusions

Chapter 20: Working with Families and the Community for Best Behavior. Parents and caregivers are key partners in supporting school success and encouraging expected behaviors from children. This chapter provides you with ideas and resources to communicate and work cooperatively with parents and/or caregivers. The first part of the chapter provides tips and effective strategies for teachers. The second part outlines effective parenting practices and includes reproducible sheets for family use.

Chapter 21: Planning to Sustain and Improve Your Success with Best Behavior. In the conclusion, we ask you to reflect on your learning and set goals for the continued improvement of practices in your school. This chapter provides you with ideas and resources to sustain positive practices in your school.

Reflection

Personalizing Your Learning From *Best Behavior*

Please take a few minutes to write down your thoughts before you begin *Best Behavior*.

1. Things I would like to learn about effective positive behavior support practices are . . .

   _____

   _____

2. The most frustrating behavior I encounter is . . .

   _____

   _____

3. If I could have any resources for supporting a student, they would be . . .

   _____

   _____

4. Things that work when dealing with problem behavior are . . .

   _____

   _____

5. Things that don't work when dealing with problem behavior are . . .

   _____

   _____

6. Some ways to improve discipline consistency in my school are . . .

   _____

   _____

7. Some roadblocks to gaining discipline consistency in my school are . . .

   _____

   _____

CHAPTER 2

Best Behavior Staff Development: What it Looks Like

Background: Supporting Change

Educators in today's schools and classrooms must be supported if they are to adopt and sustain effective, cost-efficient practices, such as those that improve challenging behavior (Sugai & Horner, 2010; Walker et al., 1996).

Effective approaches to preventing the onset and development of antisocial behavior include the following (Sprague, Sugai, & Walker, 1998; Sugai, 2007).

- Systematic and sustained social skills instruction.
- Academic and curricular restructuring.
- Positive, behaviorally based interventions.
- Early screening and identification of antisocial behavior patterns.
- Schoolwide rules for teaching and recognition systems.

These, then, are the approaches that educators and staff members must undertake. This chapter will describe how to support educators in improving schoolwide and classroom behavior using these approaches.

How *Best Behavior* Supports PBIS Adoption, Implementation, and Maintenance

Best Behavior is based on the Schoolwide Positive Behavior Support (SWPBIS) (Sugai & Horner, 2010) approach, which was developed and tested at the University of Oregon and the National Center on Positive Behavioral Interventions and Supports. The mission of the *Best Behavior* program is to facilitate the academic achievement and healthy social

> ### OBJECTIVES
>
> ▶ Describe the format and logistics of *Best Behavior* staff development
>
> ▶ Outline time requirements for successful implementation
>
> ▶ Illustrate a sample staff development schedule

development of children and youths in a safe environment conducive to learning. This mission starts with educator training and continues with the ongoing support of educators as they carry out the systemic elements of the program over time.

The program includes intervention techniques based on over 30 years of rigorous research regarding school discipline from education, public health, psychology, and criminology. Program components address the whole school, the common area, the classroom, and individual student interventions. They are intended to be used in combination with other evidence-based prevention programs, such as the Second Step Violence Prevention Curriculum (Committee for Children, 2007).

Representative school team members are trained to develop and implement program elements, including the following:
- Positive school rules.
- Rule teaching.
- Positive reinforcement systems.
- Data-based decision making at the school level.
- Effective classroom management methods.
- Curriculum adaptation to prevent problem behavior.
- Functional behavioral assessment.
- Positive behavioral intervention.

What are the Critical Elements for Implementation?

The critical elements are addressed in the materials provided to schools and to trainers. Staff development materials are included in this attractive and easy-to-read book. These materials were initially developed and field tested in Mississippi and Oregon (social validity data are available). *Best Behavior* training initiatives are underway in several school districts in Oregon as well as in multiple school districts in California, Arkansas, Arizona, Connecticut, Montana, Nebraska, New Mexico, Oregon, Texas, Washington, and Wyoming; the Bureau of Indian Affairs schools; and schools in Norway, Iceland, the Netherlands, and Chile.

How Much Time Is Involved?

The training sessions associated with each chapter are designed to last approximately 1 to 1.5 hours. There are 21 chapters designed to be delivered sequentially, for a total approximate time of 20–30 hours for initial training. Each segment can be delivered alone or as part of an all-day or multiday training event. In this chapter, the times for each training segment are specified.

Training is designed to be delivered in three to four one-day sessions, or it can be delivered in separate, distributed training sessions. Figure 3 provides a sample four-day agenda. Our experience is that longer sessions (half or full day) are most productive for school discipline teams. Checklists outlining the tasks and activities for the team to complete are reviewed during the training events.

We recommend that, while participating in training (and after completing the basic material), school discipline teams, consisting of building administrators, representative teachers, and other stakeholders, meet approximately once per month to review the training content, as needed. The teams should also set up a regular process of reviewing and refining the school discipline plan (as initial goals are developed during training) and other site-based activities. A format for these meetings is specified, and each meeting should last between 20–60 minutes.

In the first year of implementation, the staff development and team-meeting activities will require an estimated 20–30 hours. We also suggest that the entire building staff (faculty members, administrators, and classified staff members) and family members receive informational updates and an initial presentation on the components of the model, the expected benefits, and the staff responsibilities.

How Much Does It Cost to Implement?

Costs include trainer time, curriculum purchase, and other costs related to implementing a quality, schoolwide positive behavior support plan. These could include staff compensation (if not using regular staff release days), stipends for school discipline teams for additional meeting times, student incentives, food and beverages for meetings, travel to visit model sites, stipends for the additional work that in-building facilitators and coaches may perform, and so forth. Actual costs will vary, depending on how the activities are funded and on whether personnel resources are already available in the district or school (Blonigen et al., 2008).

> "Never doubt that a small group of thoughtful, committed citizens can change the world. Indeed, it is the only thing that ever has."
>
> Margaret Mead

What Roles Do Stakeholders Play?

The school team should represent each major stakeholder group. Once implementation goals are set, all stakeholders should receive training and information. The dates and format for schoolwide training need to be planned during normal staff release days, or funding will need to be provided to support these activities.

A recommended option is to appoint a school-based facilitator who can oversee the scheduling of meetings and the general functioning, as well as the tasks of the school discipline team. We also recommend appointing a coordinator at the school district level who supports the building-level coaches.

Coaching assistance is available from the Institute on Violence and Destructive Behavior (IVDB) staff members and by school discipline team members who are responsible for supporting and informing their colleagues in the school. IVDB staff members will offer telephone, Internet, and on-site technical assistance. We recommend 2–5 days of follow-up technical assistance each year after the initial training is completed. In addition, our research indicates that additional improvement will be achieved if the school team continues to carry out the program for at least three years. As such, a maintenance dose of training and technical assistance will be required past the initial year.

IVDB staff members are also available to train district-level or building-level personnel to deliver the training content after each component is modeled by IVDB staff. At this point, we aim to train local personnel to assume the trainer's position and the coach's roles and responsibilities. Thus, train-the-trainer is provided using clearly delineated instructions.

Does the Training Use Adult Learning Techniques?

The training is based on the recommendations of the Association for Supervision and Curriculum Development (ASCD) guidelines and includes elements such as lectures, discussions, reflections, work tasks germane to the intervention, and jigsaws. The training is designed to be active, and the school discipline teams work on tasks that will be immediately usable in their school.

How Do We Know If It Is Working?

Participating school teams are asked to develop and present an annual plan with measurable goals and objectives to the remaining school staff members and to the school's site-based management council. The goal-setting session is conducted early in the training and is refined over the course of the remaining days of training (or during in-building meetings). Review of these goals, including an annual data gathering and assessment, provides improvement tracking.

We have a full evaluation model developed, and an essential feature of the program is providing staff members with data-based feedback on essential outcomes. Student measures include knowledge change on social skills teaching, discipline referral patterns, achievement test scores, and attendance. We also use staff and student surveys to measure progress. The evaluation model maps directly to the content and process of the model. A sample evaluation packet is available from the IVDB.

How Does *Best Behavior* Fit in the Big Picture of School Improvement?

The schoolwide PBIS team must represent all school stakeholders. We also recommend that schools include the improvement of discipline and safety as a top priority for their improvement and that at least 85% of staff members formally indicate a commitment to the training and implementation process.

Administrative leadership is emphasized throughout the process. The building administrator is required to be part of the school discipline team and participate in all the planning and staff development activities.

Where Can I Find Additional Information?

Everything you need for implementing the *Best Behavior* program is in this book. However, Sopris Learning (www.soprislearning.com) provides other products that may support your endeavors, such as *The Stop and Think Social Skills Program* and the *Bully-Proofing* series.

FIGURE 3 Sample *Best Behavior* Training Agenda

Day 1

Schoolwide Positive Behavior Interventions and Supports

1—Welcome to *Best Behavior*: Building Positive Behavior Interventions and Supports in Schools

2—*Best Behavior* Staff Development: What It Looks Like

3—Introduction to the Challenge of Antisocial Behavior: The Three-Tiered Approach

4—Building Positive Behavior Interventions and Supports: One School's Story

5—Defining Schoolwide Behavior Expectations

Day 2

Schoolwide Positive Behavior Interventions and Supports and Classroom Management

6—Communicating and Teaching Schoolwide Behavior Expectations

7—Schoolwide Recognition and Reward Systems: Creating a Positive School Culture

8—Systematic Supervision of Common Areas

9—Preventing and Responding to Aggressive Social Behavior, Bullying, and Harassment

10—Using Data to Diagnose Schoolwide, Classroom, and Individual Student Systems

Day 3

Classroom Management and Individual Student Supports

11—Classroom Organization: The Foundation of Classroom Management

12—Designing and Teaching Classroom Behavioral Expectations

13—Preventive Interactions

14—Using Positive and Corrective Consequences to Change Behavior

Day 4

Individual Student and Family Supports and Conclusions

15—Responding to Escalating Behavior and Power Struggles

16—Thinking Functionally About Behavior

17—Building Positive Behavior Support Plans for Individual Students

18—Adapting Curricula to Prevent Problem Behavior

19—Teaching Students Who Are at Risk to Self-Manage Their Behavior

20—Working with Families and the Community for *Best Behavior*

21—Planning to Sustain and Improve Your Success with *Best Behavior*

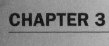

CHAPTER 3

Introduction to the Challenge of Antisocial Behavior: The Three-Tiered Approach

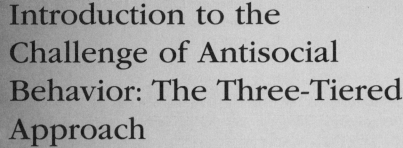

A Preventive Approach

This chapter describes a fully integrated, comprehensive approach to preventing problem and challenging behavior in schools—an approach that may have a better chance to work than other, more traditional approaches. Specifically, we outline a school-based approach to the prevention of challenging, aggressive behavior patterns that is:

- **Comprehensive:** targets the entire school site as well as individual students for assessment and intervention.
- **Flexible:** matches the intensity and nature of interventions with the severity of students' adjustment problems.
- **Prosocial:** emphasizes the fostering of prosocial and safe learning environments for all students.

Background: Antisocial Behavior in Schools

Children and youths in the United States are at an increased risk for developing and displaying challenging behavior, resulting in negative school and life outcomes. This increased risk is largely due to the changing social, economic, and cultural conditions of our society over the past several decades (Loeber & Farrington, 2001; Sprague & Walker, 2005). Growing numbers of children and youths are exposed to a host of risk factors such as poverty, abuse, neglect, criminal activity or substance use by parents, harsh and inconsistent parenting practices, and limited exposure to language and reading prior to the beginning of their school careers (Patterson, Reid, & Dishion, 1992; Reid & Patterson, 1989). At the same time, the number of children and youths exhibiting aggressive,

OBJECTIVES

- ▶ Outline the need for positive behavior interventions and supports in schools

- ▶ Describe how challenging behavior develops through a student's life

- ▶ Outline an integrated approach to addressing the problem of challenging behavior in schools

noncompliant, and acting-out behaviors in schools has been rising steadily (Loeber et al., 2001). These students are entering the public school system unprepared for the experience of schooling, and they often bring emerging antisocial behavior patterns with them (Loeber et al., 2001). Antisocial behavior and high levels of aggression evidenced early in a child's life are among the best predictors of academic failure and delinquency in later years (Patterson, et al., 1992).

In *Best Behavior*, we use the term **antisocial behavior** to represent any form of challenging behavior (e.g., defiance, noncompliance, aggression, bullying, harassment, drug use, or violence) that would cause a teacher or other school adult to implement a disciplinary or behavior-management response. A student's behavior can be considered challenging (antisocial) if his or her behavior in school interferes with the student's learning or with the learning of other students.

The statistics cited above leave little doubt that the declining social conditions in American society have spilled over into the process of schooling in very unfortunate ways. Thousands of students today enter school with a history of exposure to multiple and overlapping risks, such as the limiting factors described above, in addition to poverty, divorce, and domestic violence. These risk factors negatively affect today's students in family, school, neighborhood, and community contexts.

Effects and Outcomes

The cumulative effect of these risks is to place vulnerable children and youths on a pathway to destructive outcomes that are manifested in adolescence and young adulthood (e.g., drug and alcohol abuse, delinquency, violent acts, and criminal behavior). If children are not supported to change these patterns in the early grades, then it is likely that they will continue to struggle with school success throughout adolescence and into adulthood (Biglan, Holder, Brennan, & Foster, 2004). Indeed, these individuals will likely require continued supports and services throughout their lives to reduce the ongoing harm they cause to both themselves and others.

These noted problems compete directly with the instructional mission of schools. The result is decreased academic achievement and a lower quality of life for students and staff members alike. These outcomes illustrate the clear link that exists between declining safety in schools, school violence, and academic achievement. It is not possible to achieve national educational goals and meaningful reform without addressing these disturbing conditions (Elias et al., 1997).

Early Identification of Students Needing Extra Support

Students who display chronic challenging and violent behavior are on a risk pathway for short- and long-term negative outcomes. Figure 4 outlines a classic pattern of challenging behavioral development and illustrates the complexity of the pathway, as conceptualized by Gerald Patterson and his associates (Patterson, et al., 1992).

When children go to school, the development of challenging behavior is actually increased because children encounter additional structures, demands, and peer interactions. We have also learned that, without intervention and ongoing supports, children with the most serious problems do not simply "grow out of it." Instead, they tend to become challenging adults who continue to have adjustment problems.

The root of these problems often originates in the family and community through chronic and long-term exposure to key risk factors—experiences that make negative outcomes more likely for a child. Although these risk factors are not the only causes of maladaptive behavior and negative outcomes, they are worth a closer look. We can see a similar pattern of development for students with developmental disabilities such as autism, or with learning disabilities, ADHD, and so on. (It is beyond the scope of this book to address the many and diverse patterns of development that may be observed for students with these disabilities.)

FIGURE 4   The Risk Path to Antisocial Behavior and Negative Life Outcomes

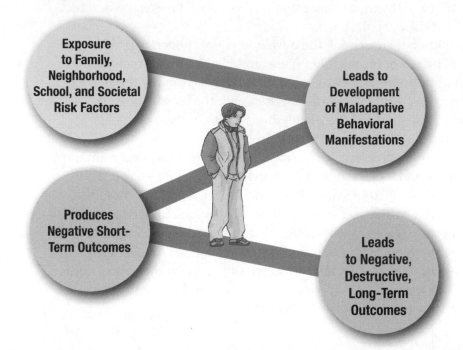

Exposure to Family, Neighborhood, School, and Societal Risk Factors	Leads to Development of Maladaptive Behavioral Manifestations	Produces Negative Short-Term Outcomes	Leads to Negative, Destructive, Long-Term Outcomes
• Poverty, abuse, and neglect • Harsh and inconsistent parenting • Drug and alcohol use by caregivers • Emotional and physical or sexual abuse • Modeling of aggression • Media violence • Bullying • Negative attitude toward schooling • Family transitions (death or divorce) • Parent criminality	• Defiance of adults • Lack of school readiness • Coercive interactive styles • Aggression toward peers • Lack of problem-solving skills	• Truancy • Peer and teacher rejection • Low academic achievement • High number of school discipline referrals • Large numbers of different schools attended • Early involvement with drugs and alcohol • Early age of first arrest (less than 12 years)	• School failure and dropout • Delinquency • Drug and alcohol use • Gang membership • Violent acts • Adult criminality • Lifelong dependence on welfare system • Higher death and injury rate

Used with permission from the Institute on Violence and Destructive Behavior.

Our Challenge: Effective Response

Having a clear understanding of the causes and development of problem behavior helps guide us toward a comprehensive response to the problem. Often, discipline is meted out to students to "teach them a lesson" or to punish their actions. Research has shown that, although this may stop the behavior for a short time, chronic punishment coupled with school failure actually makes the problem worse (Mayer, 1995). Therefore, the challenge for schools is to develop interventions and supports that are evidence-based, to implement them, and to sustain them over time.

Punishment Is Not the Solution

The dominant response to challenging, violent, and potentially violent behavior by children and youths in schools has been overwhelmingly characterized by the use of sanctions and punishing consequences such as referrals to the office, suspension from school, and even expulsion. Although these practices are common, the paradox is clear.

Typically, we wait until youths who are at risk fail school, drop out, and start offending before we seriously begin addressing the problems and challenges they present.

These youths come to our attention through their contacts with public safety, law enforcement, juvenile court, and corrections officials. In far too many cases, especially with children and youths who are severely at risk, such delayed reactions are insufficient to effectively address the myriad problems posed by such behavior. Despite their exposure to multiple sanctions, including incarceration, many youths continue along the path to oftentimes violent adult criminality.

> **Reflection**
>
> **Risk Path Review**
>
> Think about the following questions as you review the risk path:
> - What practices or conditions present in my school may make behavioral problems worse?
> - Does the discipline process in my school help students accept and focus on restoring academic achievement, social relationships, and the learning environment?

> It is clear that punishing problem behaviors without a schoolwide, positive support system results in increased:
> - Aggression
> - Vandalism
> - Truancy
> - Dropouts
>
> (Mayer & Sulzer-Azaroff, 1991; Skiba & Peterson, 2000; Skiba, 2002)

Generally, the warning signs of exposure to environmental risks are evident early on in the lives and school careers of children and youths. These warning signs vary substantially in terms of how well they predict or are associated with juvenile violence; all should be of serious concern, however. The greater the number of these signs a student manifests, the greater the risk and the greater the urgency for appropriate intervention.

The persistence of these behaviors over time is strongly associated with a host of negative developmental outcomes, including delinquency, school failure and dropout, drug and alcohol abuse, peer rejection, and sometimes violence (Loeber & Farrington, 2001). It is difficult and often impossible to reduce the environmental risk factors and conditions that produce these behaviors in children and youths who are at risk, but it is very important that the resulting behaviors be reduced, eliminated, or buffered by exposure to well-designed interventions (Walker et al., 1996).

FIGURE 5 What Works in School and Classroom Discipline?

- School capacity to carry out interventions and keep them going.
- Clear communication of behavior norms.
- Positive school rules.
- Consistent enforcement of behavioral expectations.
- Positive reinforcement for expected behavior.
- Communication of norms through school-wide campaigns.
- Effective classroom management.
- Comprehensive social skills programs.
- Instruction for improving problem-solving and impulse-control skills.
- Instruction in responsible decision making (limit setting).
- Positive behavioral support plans based on functional behavioral assessment.
- Group behavior contingencies for expected behavior.
- Instruction in self-management.
- Differential reinforcement of expected behavior.
- Token economies (class or schoolwide).
- Teacher approval or disapproval.

(Gottfredson et al., 2000)

What Works

Keeping students engaged with learning for as long as possible is one of the best things schools can do to prevent them from exhibiting problem behaviors and becoming involved with disruptive peer groups during school hours. Research on school discipline gives new insight into what is effective in doing this. Although intuition may tell us that punishment or counseling approaches will work, other approaches actually show the most promise. The list in Figure 5 outlines best practices in school and classroom discipline. You will learn about many of these techniques as we progress through the book.

Now that we have reviewed effective practices in school and classroom discipline, we will demonstrate how to implement some of them.

A Three-Tiered Model of Discipline Strategies

Effective schools approach problem behavior using a three-tiered model of discipline strategies. This model is based on extensive research about different types of children and their needs.

The three-tiered model depicted in Figure 6 defines the discipline challenge for schools as one that addresses the needs of three groups of students. The goal is to link each of these groups to a different level of discipline intervention: universal interventions (for *all* students), selected interventions (for *some* students), and targeted interventions (for a *few* students). One single discipline strategy

> For interventions to work, the **prevention** of problem behavior needs to be a priority.

designed to fit *all* students will not work for the entire school population. Rather, schools need to use at least three (*all*, *some*, and *few*) different discipline efforts.

Best Behavior addresses schoolwide, classroom, and individual student interventions, as well as family collaboration. It is one of the few programs that offers supports for *all* students in the school, *some* students with additional needs, and the *few* students who need the most intensive supports. Although a single intervention or approach will not meet all the discipline and student support needs within a school, the model in Figure 6 shows why student needs can be met in a tiered approach.

Interventions for *All*

The assumption is that one group of students (85 to 90%) will arrive at school already having learned important social and academic readiness skills. An important part of any schoolwide discipline and prevention program is to ensure that the skills of these students are embedded in the daily workings of the school. This can be accomplished through strategies aimed at *all* students. These interventions attempt to prevent problems before they start, and they must be efficient, at a low cost to deliver, and provided to *all* students without prior individual assessment.

Interventions for *all* elementary and middle school students can take the form of direct social skills training in class; rules instruction for specific settings (e.g., playgrounds); positive reinforcement systems; consistent consequences; lessons to teach expected school behavior; or alcohol, tobacco, and other drug resistance programs. These students must be inoculated against exposure to school, peer, and community risk factors and able to model positive social skills for their peers who are considered at risk. The foundation of all effective schoolwide discipline efforts lies in the attention to universal training, adult modeling, monitoring, and reinforcement of expected social behavior for all students.

> We believe that schools must closely monitor and teach *all* students, including those who currently are not engaging in problem behavior.

Interventions for *Some*

Not all students, however, respond as well to schoolwide approaches. Students with chronic patterns of problem behavior require either more selected support or highly individualized and targeted support. The level and intensity of support is dictated by the level and complexity of the behavior problem. Interventions for *some* students (7 to 10%) may require support from counselors, special educators, school psychologists, and so forth and focus additional resources on the needs of small groups of students. Programs involving extra academic support, greater adult attention (school-based mentors), scheduling changes, self-management, and more frequent access to rewards can be used to improve the overall likelihood of school success and to reduce levels of problem behavior.

Interventions for a *Few*

For the *few* students (3 to 5%) who do not respond even to extra support, intensive, targeted intervention based on functional behavioral assessment procedures is required. These students will test the capacity of any school's staff and will require intensive social skills training, individual behavior management plans, parent and/or caregiver training and collaboration, and multi-agency (wrap-around) service coordination.

Tiered Model for Behavior

Best Behavior focuses on each of the three tiers of behavior supports and on new and improved strategies for implementing them. A continuum of behavior support comprising three very different levels of intervention is needed. The intensity of the intervention must match the intensity of the problem behavior and the complexity of the context in which problem behavior occurs.

Interventions for *all* students focus on improving the overall level of appropriate behavior of most students but are not sufficient for *some* students and will have limited impact on the *few* students (3 to 5%) who exhibit chronic patterns of problem behavior. Therefore, interventions are identified for the students needing more intensive interventions as well.

> "Most people don't plan to fail; they fail to plan."
>
> –John L. Beckley

FIGURE 6　Three-Tiered Model of Schoolwide Discipline Strategies

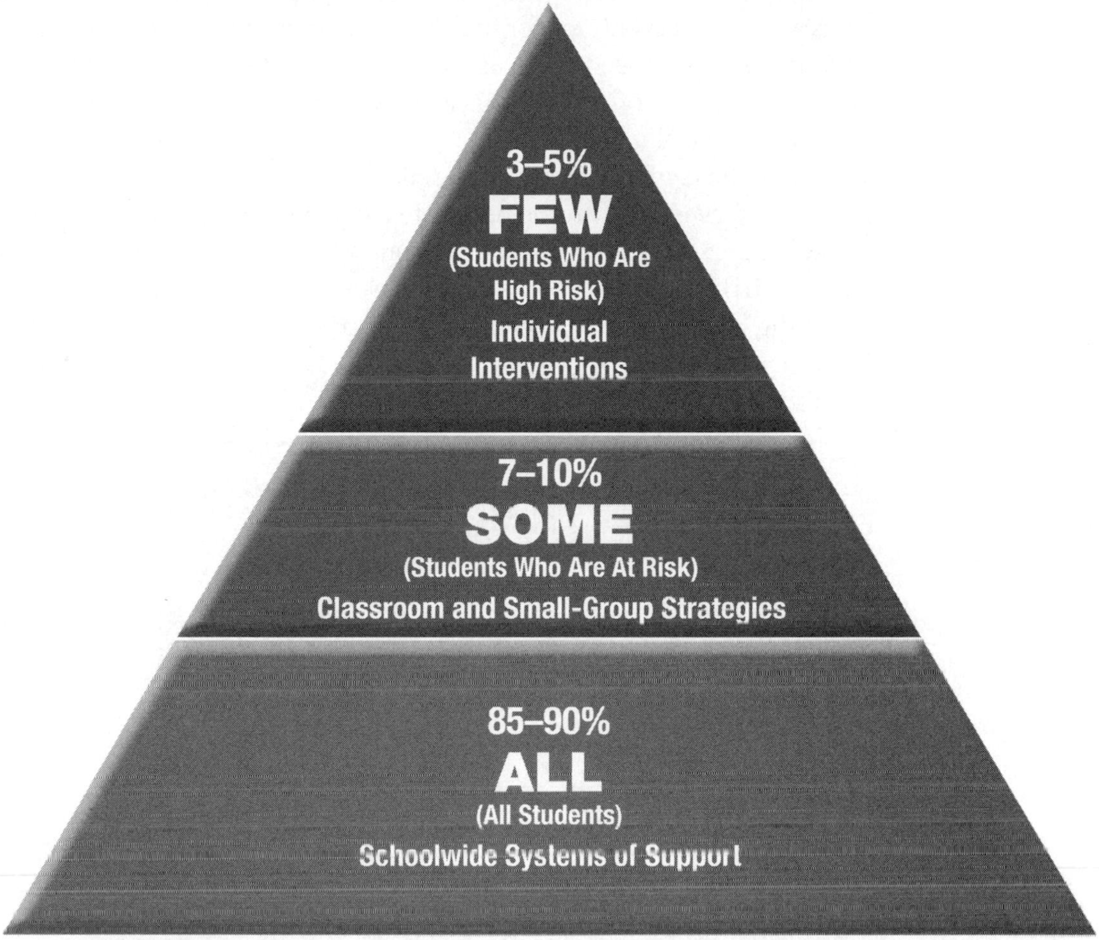

3–5%
FEW
(Students Who Are
High Risk)
Individual
Interventions

7–10%
SOME
(Students Who Are At Risk)
Classroom and Small-Group Strategies

85–90%
ALL
(All Students)
Schoolwide Systems of Support

FEW	*SOME*	*ALL*
• Intensive academic support • Functional assessment • Individual behavior management plans • Parent training and collaboration • Multi-agency collaboration (wrap-around) • Alternatives to suspension and expulsion • Community and service learning	• Intensive social skills teaching and support • Self-management programs • School-based adult mentors (checking in) • Increased academic support • Alternatives to out-of-school suspension	• Effective academic support • Social skills teaching • Effective classroom management • Teaching school behavior expectations • Active supervision and monitoring • Positive reinforcement for *all* students • Firm, fair, and corrective discipline • Data-based decision making

Adapted from Sprague, J., & Walker, H. (2000). Early identification and intervention for youth with antisocial and violent behavior. Exceptional Children, 66(3), 367–379.

Activity: Build Your Own Tier Model for Behavior Support

In the RTI era, we have observed many schools building a three-tier triangle of interventions for their reading and mathematics curricula. As student support needs increase, the intensity of support must rise to match it. We believe strongly that this is the case for organizing support for behavior as well.

Use the example menu provided as a reference (you will not use all of the interventions on the list). After reviewing it, go to the blank table and list behavior support interventions at each level of intensity (Tiers I, II, and III) that you use or wish to implement. Also define the criteria for moving between each level of intensity or support. This is just a start; after you have read all the way through this book, come back and rework your tiered intervention plan.

Behavior Support Menu: Sample Interventions

Intensity	Intervention	Indicator
Targeted/Intensive FEW	• **Sample Tier III Interventions in** *Best Behavior* • **Multidimensional Treatment Foster Care** • **Adolescent Transitions Program (ATP)** • **Family Check Up** • **FBA to PBIS** • **Multisystemic Therapy** • **Systematic Screening for Behavior Disorders (SSBD)**	Lack of response to lower tier supports, documentation of a specific symptom or disease (e.g., depression)
Selected SOME	• **Sample Tier II Interventions in** *Best Behavior* • **Adolescent Transitions Program** • **Family Check Up** • **Check and Connect (University of Minnesota)** • **First Step to Success (K–2)** • **Cognitive Behavioral Intervention for Trauma in Schools (C-BITS)**	Teacher nomination, office referral rates, normative behavior ratings

Universal
 	
ALL
	• ***Best Behavior:***
	  – Set and teach rules
	  – Positive reinforcement systems
	  – Systematic supervision
	  – Firm but fair behavior corrections
	• **Good Classroom Management**
	• **Websites for interventions:**
	  – Consortium for Academic Social and Emotional Learning (www.casel.org)
	  – Improving the Wellbeing of Adolescents in Oregon (www.earlyadolescence.org)
	• **Sample Tier I Interventions:**
	  – Triple P (Positive Parenting Program)
	  – The Strengthening Families 10–14 Program
	  – Positive Action (PA) Classroom Management and Social Skills
	  – Project Towards No
	  – Tobacco Use
	  – Life Skills Training
		Applied to *all* students, regardless of risk status

Behavior Support Menu

Intensity	Intervention	Indicator
Targeted/Intensive FEW		
Selected SOME		
Universal ALL		

Building Positive Behavior Interventions and Supports: One School's Story

Background: Challenges to Discipline

From shrinking budgets to inconsistent discipline, educators are faced with a variety of challenges to school and classroom discipline, including.

- Doing more with less—fewer resources
- Coping with increased diversity (abilities, needs) in the classroom and school
- Managing students with severe problem behavior
- Multiple competing initiatives
- Low implementation priority
- Low staff member involvement, agreement, and commitment
- Keeping the good stuff going
- Achieving consistency among the adults in the school
- Lack of administrative leadership
- Inefficient operation and decision making
- Lack of knowledge and fluency in behavior management

Use the following reflection to think about the challenges to effective school discipline that you may face in your school.

OBJECTIVES

▶ Outline the components of an effective and efficient schoolwide behavior support system

▶ Learn about a successful *Best Behavior* school

▶ Use a self-assessment survey to identify priorities for change in your school and classroom

▶ Identify the top three or four priorities for improving discipline systems in your school

▶ Set an action plan for the year, with goals and objectives

Reflection

What are some general challenges to achieving good behavior in your school?

1. _____

   _____

   _____

2. _____

   _____

   _____

3. _____

   _____

   _____

What are some challenges that you face in making your schoolwide PBIS team work effectively?

1. _____

   _____

   _____

2. _____

   _____

   _____

3. _____

   _____

   _____

Foundations of a Comprehensive, Schoolwide PBIS Plan

One of the major problems in schools is that we have been unable to fit effective practices into the daily operations of our classrooms and common areas (Sugai & Horner, 2010; Zins & Ponte, 1990). It's not that the practices we use are bad, it's that we often don't attend to the *processes* and *systems* necessary to get good programs and practices off the ground and keep them going. In order to create an effective and efficient schoolwide discipline plan, we need to build a strong foundation using the following practices.

- **Integrate the plan with school improvement.** School discipline goals should be an integral part of school improvement planning.
- **Ensure that the principal is an involved and active leader.** In our experience, no schoolwide PBIS plan will be effective without active and substantive principal leadership (Fixsen, Naoom, Blase, Friedman, & Wallace, 2005).
- **Use standardized curriculum materials (for students and adults).** Simple, standardized materials will ease the effort of implementation, increase consistency, and provide an onsite resource for current and incoming staff members. In this case, we don't mean curriculum that you purchase, but rather using the information and activities in *Best Behavior* to build your local curriculum. For example, only you and your colleagues can design a school-level agreement about what problems are to be handled in the classroom, versus the office. Similarly, the protocol and routines for your cafeteria and hallways will need to be designed by your schoolwide PBIS team.
- **Make sure all adults help implement the program.** It makes good sense that we would want to work as a schoolwide PBIS team, with all adults, students, and family members following the same routines and pursuing a shared set of values about how the school should be operated. It's natural for some people to "lag," but in the long run, those are only harmful to the larger goals of the school (Rogers, 1995).

> It is essential that most, if not all, adults in the school teach, prompt, and recognize expected behavior.
>
> (Sugai & Horner, 2010)

- **Make sure that *all* students are affected (even the tough ones).** Universal intervention means just that: *all* students! We can consider universal strategies as "vertical," meaning they are provided to all students, regardless of their level of risk. *Some* students will need support beyond the universal strategies, and these are applied "horizontally" in Tier II or III in an RTI model (Domitrovich et al., 2010). See Chapter 3 for more detail on interventions for *all*, *some*, and a *few* students.

- **Make sure behavior and social skills are taught or reviewed about once per week.** Research from many perspectives indicates that learning social behavior is like exercise—we need to do it often and regularly to acquire and maintain essential skills and behaviors.
- **Include frequent, positive communication with families.** Some of us feel frustrated with a perceived lack of parent involvement, but we often do not take the time to implement simple, yet effective methods to work with parents as partners. Chapter 20 illustrates these methods.

"Coming together is a beginning; keeping together is progress; working together is success."

–Henry Ford

A Case Study of Success: How One School Implemented *Best Behavior*

Before we begin the step-by-step work of *Best Behavior,* we have found it useful to read a story about a successful *Best Behavior* school. One of the ways to achieve broader adoption and implementation of *Best Behavior* is if all the adults in the school can tell the story of how it all fits together. Sharing the following case study is a very powerful way to learn that story and to begin envisioning your own!

A Successful PBIS Middle School

Big Ideas

School Specifics Prevention Middle School is located in a suburban community in southwestern Oregon. There are 625 students in grades 6–8. Approximately 40% of the students in the school qualify for free and reduced-cost lunch. In the summer of 2010, staff from Prevention agreed upon the need for improving discipline in the school. They formed a team of grade-level teachers (one from each grade), a special education teacher, a parent from the school, and the building administrator. They developed a plan for reducing problem behaviors in the school and in the classrooms and implemented that plan during the 2010–2011 school year.

Rules Identified The school team met monthly and developed a set of school rules. They decided on behaviors that were important to the school staff.

Be respectful.

Use put ups, not put downs.

Cooperate with others.

Solve problems peacefully.

They developed lessons for teaching these school rules and agreed to consistently enforce the rules.

Positive Recognition The school also implemented a schoolwide system called "Success Tickets." The tickets listed all of the school rules, and teachers were given stacks of tickets. Teachers and other staff agreed to "catch kids being good" and reward them by giving out a Success Ticket and indicating the school rule that they were demonstrating. Students could then place the ticket in a bucket in the school cafeteria for a door-prize drawing at the end of the week. The staff monitored how many tickets were distributed and who was receiving them. The team designed several other ways to recognize and reward good behavior in the school, as well.

Feedback The staff was given feedback on reductions in discipline referrals at the monthly staff meeting. In addition, students and staff were asked each quarter to complete a survey indicating their opinions on the new discipline system.

Family and Community Involvement Finally, parents and the community were also involved as much as possible. Parents were given information about the new program and expectations for students. Local businesses gave incentives, such as coupons and small items, to give away in the weekly drawings.

Results In the first year, discipline referrals were reduced by 35% and an additional 20% in the subsequent school year. Suspensions were reduced by over 55%. Students and staff also reported feeling safer and happier in the school under the new program.

The Details

The School Intervention The school intervention involved assisting the school in implementing a Schoolwide Positive Behavior Interventions and Support (PBIS) system to increase appropriate social behavior in all school settings by:

- Defining a set of clear rules and expectations.
- Teaching the expected behaviors to students.
- Providing increased levels of praise and rewards for appropriate social behaviors.
- Monitoring students' behavior to provide consistent enforcement of the rules.
- Utilizing frequent summary data about student behavior to evaluate progress and further develop intervention plans.

Beginning the Process The school intervention process began with a faculty forum where problem behavior, communication with parents, and the process of the PBIS implementation were presented and discussed. Following the faculty forum, a Schoolwide Positive Behavior Interventions and Supports (PBIS) team was formed with three teachers (each representing one of the inner-school teams), the vice-principal, one of the school counselors, project staff (a school intervention specialist and two research scientists), and an expert on PBIS from the local county educational cooperative. This team met on a monthly basis to develop the intervention plan. The first three meetings provided training for the team, consisting of an introduction to the PBIS approach, facts on problem behavior, schoolwide behavior intervention, and using discipline referral data to make intervention planning decisions.

> **The goals of improving the social behavior of students and the school climate were consistent with the school improvement plan.**

The meetings then transformed into work sessions on developing interventions, where the team developed goals, brought back ideas from the inner-school teams regarding target behaviors, defined the rules and expectations for the school, defined the reward systems, selected and developed the evaluation assessment tools, developed the lessons for teaching the behavioral expectations to the students, and worked out the logistics of implementing the lessons.

During the summer before implementation, teachers and other school staff were invited to attend a lunch session to share ideas and create a vision for the school. The objective for these sessions was to ensure that all teachers had the opportunity to participate in building a common vision and collaborative framework to help youths be successful at the school and in the community. Those who attended these sessions were asked to imagine themselves two years in the future and think about how they might view their progress. They agreed that the middle school had really improved in how it guides young people's development. From this perspective, attendees were asked to share their ideas on:

- What more the students should be doing
- What more the teachers should be doing
- What more the parents should be doing
- What more the community should be doing

Participants also described positive roles for students to facilitate skill development and gave feedback on the PBIS team's target behavior expectations and on ideas for rewarding worthwhile student behavior. The ideas from these visioning sessions were summarized, presented, and discussed during a staff inservice at the onset of the school year.

Defining and Teaching Behavioral Expectations The Schoolwide Positive Behavior Interventions and Supports (PBIS) team reviewed discipline referral summaries from previous years to help determine the areas in which student behavior could be improved. The predominate discipline difficulties that the team wanted to address were verbal and physical harassment of students, fighting, obscene language, and class disruption. Student behavior was most troublesome in the hallways during passing times between classes. Based on these targeted behaviors, the team defined the student behaviors that they wanted to see increase at the school. These behavior expectations were further refined into four separate rules. A small set of topics under each rule was established and lesson plans to teach students the behavioral expectations were developed for each topic (see Table 1 for a list of the rules and topics).

Table 1. The Behavioral Expectations Developed for Prevention Middle School

Rule		Lesson Topic
1. Be respectful.		• Use appropriate language. • Understand roles and responsibilities for students and teachers. • Respect others' space and belongings.
2. Use put ups, not put downs.		• Compliment others. • Respond appropriately to put downs.
3. Cooperate with others.		• Work together to peacefully share a locker. • Work together and help each other.
4. Solve problems peacefully.		• Make appropriate responses regarding rumors. • Give up harassment and name calling. • Use appropriate physical contact.

For each rule and topic, the lesson plans included specific elements, teaching strategies, and behavior-specific guidelines for preventing problem behaviors. These common lesson components are outlined in Table 2.

Table 2. Lesson Components

Lesson Elements	Teaching Strategies	Preventing Problem Behavior
• What students were expected to do. • How to teach students the expected behavior. • How to prevent problem behaviors. • How to give both positive and corrective feedback to students. • How to review the behavioral expectations with students regularly.	• Explain the importance of the rule. • Examples. • Non-examples. • Practice (brainstorming, games, discussion, role playing).	• How, where, and when supervision is most important for this behavior. • How to provide reminders of the expected behaviors.

These teaching strategies utilize effective teaching practices based on instructional design for teaching concepts, as well as a proactive approach for teaching social behavior.

These lessons were taught schoolwide at the beginning of the school year. Teachers of 6th and 7th grade students taught all the lessons within the first three weeks of the school year, and 8th grade students received one lesson per week for a total of 10 weeks. Booster lessons were implemented throughout the year to specifically address the issue of harassment in the hallways.

Environmental Issues Addressed In addition to the lessons, the school altered the class schedules. To decrease the number of students in the hallway at one time, the passing times between classes for 6th grade students were different from those of 7th and 8th grade students. Additionally, three lunch periods were scheduled—compared to the previous year where only two different lunch breaks were scheduled—so that students went to lunch with their grade level. This decreased the number of students in the cafeteria at one time.

Systems for Positive Reinforcement One of the goals for the school intervention was to increase the positive recognition of students who were engaged in appropriate and expected behaviors at school. During the implementation year, the token economy system in which students received Success Tickets was modified and revitalized. Additionally, the following new schoolwide recognition systems were implemented:

- Good-news referrals
- Praise notes
- Good-news bureau
- Phone calls home by teachers

Problem Solving the Reinforcement System During the previous school year, Success Tickets were given to students for engaging in prosocial behavior at the school. Students would turn the tickets in to a drawing for prizes (usually for soda or snacks). According to school personnel, the system was not working well, as students were not receiving the tickets consistently and students were not turning in the tickets for the prize drawings. By the end of the school year, Success Tickets were not being handed out and no drawings were taking place.

The PBIS team decided to revitalize the Success Tickets program with the following changes.

- Tickets were given to students for following the four school rules (specific behavior expectations related to these were defined and taught schoolwide).
- Teachers, other school personnel (administration, office staff, counselors), and students (with a teacher's signature) could give out Success Tickets.
- Businesses within the community were solicited for donations for the prizes (to get better prizes and to increase the value of the tickets for students).
- Drawings occurred on a weekly basis with announcements of winners held during lunch.
- A tracking system was implemented to count who was giving out and receiving the Success Tickets.

A total of 14,219 Success Tickets were given to students throughout the implementation year, averaging 395 per week. These numbers may be an underestimate, as counts were done once students turned their tickets in for the weekly drawings (some students held onto their tickets and turned a bulk of them in at once to increase their chances of winning

> "Action is the foundational key to all success."
>
> **Pablo Picasso**

a prize in the drawings). The weekly counts tended to increase when valued prizes were offered in the drawing; for example, a total of 700 tickets were counted during the week that a boom box was offered as a prize. In addition, after the second trimester, the school decided to change the color of the Success Tickets to invalidate the old tickets so that students would turn in their tickets. A total of 2,659 tickets were counted during the last week for which the old tickets were valid.

Using a Variety of Recognition Strategies

Good-News Referrals A new method for providing recognition and rewards for students at the school was through the good-news referral system. Traditionally, teachers and other personnel would send discipline referrals to the school office for students' misbehavior. These discipline referrals were followed up by either one of the school counselors, the vice-principal, or the principal. Some of the discipline referrals would result in a phone call home to parents. During the implementation year, the middle school added good-news referrals to this system. Teachers gave the vice-principal or principal positive good-news referrals for students who did something especially notable (above and beyond following the behavior expectations). For example, good-news referrals were given for marked improvement in behavior or academics over an extended period of time, taking a leadership role in helping other students, and preventing conflict by demonstrating good problem-solving skills. The principal or vice-principal would then call the student's parents to notify them of their child's positive behavior. A total of 222 good-news referrals were given out over the course of the school year.

Praise Notes In addition, a "praise notes" computer program was developed for teachers so that they could send students home with notes of praise. Once teachers entered their class rosters into the computer, they could select a praise note, click on the name of the student, and print a personalized note (with or without a border and graphics) for the student to take home to his or her parent(s). Teachers could select a praise note from a menu, or they had the option of creating their own praise message.

Good News!

_____is being recognized!

WHY? _____

Signed_____

Thank you for helping your son on his homework assignments. He has shown real improvement.

Because the program ran slowly on some of the older computers, actual usage of the program was not as high as the original interest in it. In the fall of 2010, fourteen teachers had the praise notes program installed on their classroom computer. A total of 269 praise notes were given to students during the school year.

Good-News Bureau Another system of providing positive recognition was through the good-news bureau. The goal of the bureau was to collect information about the good things that people have done in support of middle school students and dispersing the information through various media channels such as the student newspaper, the school newsletter, the school PA system, bulletin boards at the school, the local newspaper, and the local radio station.

Monitoring Progress Monthly data about student behavior were summarized to evaluate progress and to drive the further development of intervention efforts. Patterns of discipline, good-news referrals, student survey data, and Success Ticket tallies were charted and discussed at the monthly PBIS team meetings. The following week, a summary of the data was presented to the inner-school teams where teachers had the opportunity to provide feedback and ideas to the PBIS team. This summary also presented good news about teachers, where teachers were recognized and praised for their efforts towards schoolwide effective behavior support and community building. The goal of this data-based feedback was to provide positive reinforcement for school personnel and to aid in decision making regarding the PBIS intervention.

School Staff Feedback In addition, school faculty was surveyed on mid-year progress towards school improvement. They were asked about school safety, student behavior, effectiveness of specific intervention strategies, student progress toward writing goals, and the frequency in which they implemented the lessons and engaged in activities for student behavior support. Students were also surveyed about the Success Ticket system. The results of these surveys were presented and discussed during a faculty forum in February. Overall, the majority of school staff agreed that the school was a safer place for students and that student behavior had improved, compared to the previous year. Furthermore, 100% of the faculty surveyed agreed that providing recognition to students for positive behavior had a positive impact on their behavior. The majority of students from all grade levels wanted the Success Ticket system to continue, and many thought that more teachers should consistently give them out.

> "Don't tell people how to do things. Tell them what to do and let them surprise you with their results."
> **General George S. Patton**

Finally, at the end of the school year, school personnel were given a survey to evaluate the current schoolwide behavior support systems to determine whether they were working well or needed improvement. During a faculty meeting, the results of this survey were summarized and discussed. The PBIS team then utilized the input from the survey and discussion during a planning session to prepare for the next school year.

Activity: Needs Assessment and Goal Setting

To begin your journey toward a more effective schoolwide behavior support program, we recommend that you complete the following needs assessment: the *Best Behavior* **Self-Assessment Survey**. Although we strongly recommend that all adults in the school complete this assessment, you can also reflect on your views about your school's status on each item.

Once you have identified areas needing improvement, use the **Setting Goals** table that follows the assessment to write goals and set concrete action steps for a few schoolwide priority areas. Your PBIS team will refer to these goals often and modify them as you gather key data regarding their effectiveness. Data relevant to these goals may be gathered from sources such as office discipline referrals or observations of rates of inappropriate behavior on the playground. We will cover data-based decision making in Chapter 10.

Refer to the reflection below after you've completed your tasks in this chapter.

Reflection

- What foundation pieces are needed to make *Best Behavior* implementation work?
- What is the role of the school administrator?
- Who is our *Best Behavior* coach?
  - What is the role of the *Best Behavior* coach?
  - What skills are needed to be a *Best Behavior* coach?
- If you are on the *Best Behavior* team:
  - What impact do you expect to make as a *Best Behavior* team member?
  - What are my concerns about being a *Best Behavior* team member?

Best Behavior Self-Assessment Survey

School: _____ Date: _____

Your Role (please choose one)	
Administrator	
Teacher	
Classified	
Special Education Teacher	

Related Service Provider	
Parent	
Student	
Other	

	In place	Working on it	Not in place	Target as a goal?
School Capacity				
1. A representative PBIS team is formed to guide program implementation and the evaluation of effectiveness.				
2. The school administrator is an active member of the PBIS team.				
3. School personnel (80% or more) have committed to improving school discipline and safety by implementing, supporting, and agreeing to use positive behavioral support systems.				
4. A needs assessment has been conducted to guide intervention selection.				
5. An action plan with clear goals and objectives has been developed to improve school discipline.				
6. Regular schoolwide PBIS team meetings are scheduled for training and planning.				
7. Schoolwide behavior support has a budget for rewarding students (and staff), regular team meetings, teaching activities and materials, and data collection and analysis.				
8. A coach has been identified to provide assistance to teachers and staff, organize team meetings, and facilitate data review.				
Whole School Behavior Teaching				
9. Three to five schoolwide behavior expectations have been defined (e.g., be safe, respectful, responsible).				
10. Positive behavior expectations have been defined for each school setting (e.g., What does "safe, respectful, responsible" look like in the cafeteria, gym, restrooms?).				
11. Lesson plans have been developed for teaching all behavioral expectations in all school settings.				

	In place	Working on it	Not in place	Target as a goal?
12. Rules are posted and visible in all school settings (e.g., hallways, classrooms, cafeteria, gym, etc.).				
13. Staff have been trained to teach behavioral expectations.				
14. Staff teach behavioral expectations.				
15. Behavioral expectations for each rule are taught and reviewed at least ten times per year.				
16. Expected behaviors for each setting are taught in that setting at least two times a year.				
Dealing with Problem Behavior				
17. Problem behaviors are clearly defined and explained to all students.				
18. Consequences for problem behaviors are clearly defined and explained to all students.				
19. Staff use consistent consequences for inappropriate behavior.				
20. Staff consistently correct and reteach students who exhibit problem behavior.				
Data-Based Decision Making				
21. Data (discipline referrals, surveys) are collected to guide decision making.				
22. Data are regularly summarized (at least monthly) by the discipline and behavior support team.				
23. Staff receive regular (at least monthly) reports on key discipline outcomes (e.g., information about referrals, suspensions, etc.).				
24. Intervention decisions and strategies are evaluated regularly (at least once per term) based on behavior data.				
Classroom Management				
25. Expected student behavior and routines in classrooms are stated positively and defined clearly.				
26. Problem behaviors are defined clearly.				
27. Expected student behaviors and routines in classrooms are taught directly.				
28. Expected student behaviors are acknowledged regularly (positively reinforced; > 4 positives to 1 negative).				
29. Problem behaviors receive consistent consequences.				

	In place	Working on it	Not in place	Target as a goal?
30. Procedures for expected and problem behaviors are consistent with schoolwide procedures.				
31. Classroom-based options exist to allow classroom instruction to continue when problem behavior occurs.				
32. Instruction and curriculum materials are matched to student ability (math, reading, language).				
33. Students experience high rates of academic success (> 75% correct responses).				
34. Teachers have regular opportunities for access to assistance and recommendations (observation, instruction, and coaching).				
35. Transitions between instructional and noninstructional activities are efficient and orderly.				
36. The school has defined systems of classroom behavior management.				
37. Curriculum and instruction match student ability (students have high rates of academic success; > 75% correct responses schoolwide).				
38. Transitions within classrooms, between activities, and between settings are planned for, taught to students, well-established, and orderly.				
Individual Student Support				
39. Teachers can easily get assistance with problem students in their classroom.				
40. Behavioral assessments are used to identify students exhibiting problem behavior.				
41. A PBIS team member attends promptly (within 2 school days) when a student exhibits chronic problem behavior.				
42. Teachers are trained in and use effective methods to prevent behavioral escalation.				
43. Teachers are trained in functional behavioral assessment and positive behavioral intervention for students with chronic problem behavior.				
Family Support and Collaboration				
44. Families are active participants in supporting whole school discipline systems.				

	In place	Working on it	Not in place	Target as a goal?
45. The school supports good parenting practices by providing information and support to families.				
46. The school has defined systems for regular, positive contacts with families.				
47. At least one parent is a member of the whole school positive discipline team.				
Common Areas				
48. There are adequate staff on playgrounds, during recess and free time, and in other common areas to effectively supervise the number of students present.				
49. A system of positive reinforcement is in place in all common area settings.				
50. Recess, free time, playground, and common areas are easily observable (unobstructed views) from any given position in the area.				
51. Supervisors maintain close contact with students in all recess, free time, playground, and common areas.				
52. Playground, recess, and recreational equipment are safe.				
53. Access to and from the playground, recess, and free-time areas is supervised.				
54. Formal emergency and crisis procedures for students and staff on playgrounds, during recess, and in other common areas have been developed and are practiced at least twice a year.				
55. Common-area supervision staff have been trained in active supervision techniques and methods this year.				
56. A system for addressing minor problem behaviors in recess, playground, and other common areas is in place and is practiced by common-area supervision staff.				
57. A system for addressing serious or major problem behaviors in recess, playground, and common areas is in place and is practiced by all common-area supervision staff.				
58. Off-limits areas are clearly identified, taught to students and staff, and known by all.				
59. All staff members have received training in active supervision of common areas.				

Setting Goals

Review the results of your self-assessment and identify the top three or four priorities for improving school discipline systems. List a clear goal statement on the left side of the table below, and then use the right side to set concrete action steps. For example, an improvement goal might be to improve hallway behavior outside of the gym. Relevant action steps for this example might include reviewing staff availability during transition times, making comparisons to the lunch line schedule (areas overlap), adjusting transition times, and assigning time slots for supervisors.

Improvement Goal	Action Steps
Goal 1	
Goal 2	
Goal 3	
Goal 4	

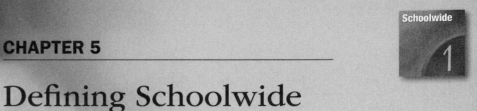

CHAPTER 5

Defining Schoolwide Behavior Expectations

Background: Behavior Expectations and Discipline

Developing school and classroom behavioral expectations is an important first step in building an effective positive discipline plan. Clearly stated expectations convey to students what teachers want. In addition, they tend to guide student behavior and strengthen teacher awareness and monitoring (Emmer, Evertson, & Worsham, 2000; Marzano, Pickering, & Pollock, 2001). It is critical to develop and secure agreement from all school adults on schoolwide behavior expectations before the start of the school year. We recommend that you teach these expectations on the first day of school and reinforce the expected behavior throughout the school year. (In Chapter 6, you will learn to develop lesson plans to teach the expectations and see a sample weekly teaching and review schedule that can be adapted for your school.)

> If the adults in the school agree upon and can state all specific behavior expectations, minor inappropriate behaviors diminish significantly.
>
> (Sprague et al., 2001)

OBJECTIVES

▶ Describe the importance of defining clear and positive behavior expectations for your school

▶ Outline the features of effective schoolwide expectations

▶ Define three to five positive behavioral expectations for your school

▶ Define what those behaviors look like across multiple school settings

Simply developing and posting school behavior expectations alone does not guarantee appropriate behavior (Becker & Engelmann, 1978). Schools need to develop the rules, post them throughout the school, teach them directly to students via role plays and practice, and provide frequent monitoring and positive feedback.

You may be wondering, "Does this really work?" Researchers have demonstrated that these types of programs, when paired with monitoring and a system of positive reinforcement, can reduce problem behavior and improve school climate (Bradshaw, Mitchell, & Leaf, 2010; Sprague, et al., 2001).

Why Do We Need Positive Schoolwide Behavior Expectations?

Research has shown that teachers who are less effective at classroom management tend to rely on punishment (e.g., reprimands, criticism, and discussion) or removal from the classroom when students misbehave. A consistently reactive approach actually makes the problem behaviors worse, however, because the teacher gives most of his or her attention to inappropriate behaviors (Hagan-Burke et al., 2002; Shores, Wehby, & Jack, 1999). Another error is using many different approaches without clear definition for adults or for students. If different teachers in the school use dramatically different approaches or have different expectations, then students will be confused because expectations vary so much from class to class and setting to setting. For example, one teacher may allow students to be unsupervised while making the transition to recess, and those students may run, push, or shove their classmates. However, another teacher may actively supervise and monitor students as they exit the classroom.

Additional research tells us that educators prefer to consider positive attributes of children (e.g., follows directions) as opposed to negative ones (e.g., bullies others) when observing or rating children. We also tend to watch how children respond to us, as well as to their peers. Positive student-teacher relationships emerge when students comply with teacher requests, get their work done, do their best, and so forth. Similarly, children who get along well with their peers and who solve problems tend to adjust the best in schools—academically and behaviorally.

> A focus on positive behavior improves teacher experience, as well as students experiences with their teachers, peers, and school adjustment.

Hill Walker (1995) created a set of "teacher preferred" behaviors based on extensive longitudinal research, and this list of teacher- and peer-preferred behaviors gives us a good place to start defining a comprehensive list of positive behavior expectations for our schools. Review Figure 7 and consider what words you might use to help define these behaviors for your students. You can use these ideas when writing your behavior expectations.

FIGURE 7 Social Behavior Competence

Teacher-Related Adjustment
Related Behavioral Correlates

Adaptive

1. Comply promptly
2. Follow rules
3. Control anger
4. Make assistance needs known appropriately
5. Produce acceptable-quality work
6. Work independently
7. Adjust to different instructional situations
8. Respond to teacher corrections
9. Listen carefully to teacher

Maladaptive

1. Steal
2. Defy or provoke teacher
3. Engage in tantrums
4. Disturb others
5. Damage property
6. Cheat
7. Cuss or make lewd gestures
8. Aggress toward others
9. Ignore teacher

Outcomes

Positive

Teacher acceptance

School achievement and success

Negative

Teacher rejection

Referral for specialized placements

School failure and/or dropout

Low performance expectations

Peer-Related Adjustment
Related Behavioral Correlates

Adaptive

1. Cooperate with peers
2. Support peers
3. Defend self in arguments
4. Remain calm
5. Achieve much
6. Lead peers
7. Act independently
8. Compliment peers
9. Affiliate with peers

Maladaptive

1. Disrupt the group
2. Act snobbishly
3. Aggress indirectly
4. Start fights
5. Display short temper
6. Brag
7. Seek help constantly
8. Achieve little

Outcomes

Positive

Peer acceptance

Positive peer relations

Friendships

Negative

Social rejection or neglect

Low self-esteem

Weak social involvement or engagement

How Do We Choose and Define Our School Rules?

School and classroom rules should state exactly what you expect from the students and target specific areas within the school setting. For example, students may be able to sit where they want at lunch but not in the auditorium. Use the following reflection to assess consistency at your school. Take a moment to reflect on the schoolwide expectations in place now. Ask some of your colleagues what they think. Is there consistency?

Reflection

A Lesson in Consistency

To the best of your ability, list all of the school and classroom rules in place in your school and classroom. Do this by yourself and then share with your colleagues.

School Rules

_____

_____

_____

_____

_____

_____

Classroom Rules

_____

_____

_____

_____

_____

_____

Did you and your colleagues produce the same list of rules? If your rules and their rules don't match most of the time, then your school needs to work on consistency!

What Do We Know About Designing Effective Behavioral Expectations?

The following list presents the big ideas about developing and communicating schoolwide behavioral expectations. Each item is then explained in more detail.

- They create a culture of consistency.
- They include *all* students.
- They use positively stated expectations.
- They target all forms of behavior (safe, respectful, responsible).
- They are regularly taught and reviewed.
- They are known by all students and adults (ask them!).

Create a Culture of Consistency It is essential that all adults in the school, including paraprofessionals, parents, and noninstructional staff, know what is expected. Consistent expectations create a predictable and less stressful school environment and allow for effective correction of behavioral errors that teach students the right way to behave.

Include All Students It is necessary to include *all* students in the schoolwide plan. For students developing typically, communicating consistent expectations creates predictability, reduces the general level of disruption, and fosters a sense of belonging. When students know what is expected, it is easier for them to make good choices (e.g., comply with adult requests and get along with peers). Students who exhibit challenging behaviors will benefit even more from this consistent, clear environment, and teachers will have more opportunities to provide them with positive feedback and react less to the problematic behavior.

Use Positively Stated Expectations Research clearly indicates that students are much more likely to comply with *do* requests than *don't* requests. For example, "Walk in the hallway" is more likely to promote compliance than "Don't run in the hallway." The negatively stated expectation may even prompt running! If the expectation is stated positively, then teachers will be able to give positive feedback when they see the behavior they want, and they will be able to more effectively correct a behavioral error. Stating expectations positively helps adults attend to what they want rather than what they don't want. Expectations should be stated in behavioral terms, that is, as what the behavior looks like. For example, instead of stating "Students will behave in school" or "No running," phrase the expectation as "Students will walk in the hallway."

> If we can help students be safe, responsible, and respectful, then they will be more likely to succeed in school and remain engaged in the schooling process.

Target All Forms of Behavior "Be safe" implies a feeling of social, emotional, and physical safety and creates a feeling of belonging. "Be respectful" relates to compliance to teacher requests and positive peer and adult relationships. "Be responsible" addresses school efforts such as being ready for class, completing work, and keeping the school and classroom clean and orderly. All expectations must be regularly taught and reviewed.

Rules Are Known by All Students and Adults It is common for schools to have a long list of rules in the student handbook and then assume that all students and adults know them. The rules in the school handbook (e.g., no weapons) are often required for administrative purposes to meet due process requirements for serious actions, such as suspension. Schools should also develop a simple list of expectations, however, such as "be safe, be respectful, and be responsible." In this chapter, you will define your school's rules and what the expected behaviors look like in all settings of the school. You should be able to ask any student or adult in the school about these expectations and get a consistent answer. If students can't quickly state what is expected, then they won't know what to do in the moment. If teachers are not clear about what they want students to do, then they are more likely to punitively correct students, thus setting up noncompliance or behavioral escalation.

Developing School Rules

The first step in this process is to select three to five "umbrella," or universal, rules. From our experience, we have found that most expectations can fall under these three rules:

- Be Safe
- Be Responsible
- Be Respectful

These rules provide continuity to students who move from school to school and are easy to teach and remember.

After the expectations have been taught and consistently reinforced, they become internalized by students. Students can reflect on what is respectful, responsible, and safe about their behavior. The entire staff team needs to agree on the umbrella rules before proceeding to the next step of defining behavioral expectations in all settings.

Sometimes, staff like to use the first letter of the school mascot or a slogan as their umbrella rules. Here is one such example.

R Respect	Raise hands to talk. Interact with sincerity and enthusiasm.
O Others	Refrain from side talk. Turn cell phone to silent. Support and encourage each other.
S Self	Move around if needed. Ask a question if you have one!
E Environment	Keep walkways clear. Reuse and recycle. Clean up area before leaving.

Creating a Schoolwide Behavior Matrix

Individual teachers have been implementing these strategies on their own for generations, with great success. This is nothing new. We all know one of these teachers. What we don't often see, however, is an entire school with these strategies in place. This is why schools often have the most difficulty in common areas, like the cafeteria and the playground, and less so in the classroom.

Teachers like to be very independent. However, if we are to impact the entire school, all staff members need to collaborate. They need to agree on what the desired behaviors look like both schoolwide and in specific settings (e.g., hallways, locker areas, bathrooms, cafeteria, playground).

Importance of the Behavior Matrix

If *Best Behavior* is new to your school, then you must pay very close attention to the development of the schoolwide expectations matrix. The matrix is the heart of the program and has several functions:

1. All adults in the school are involved in the development of the matrix.

2. The matrix sets the tone for a positive school climate.

3. The matrix defines what the school climate looks like.

4. The matrix is a tool to help design and teach behavioral expectations (Chapter 6).

5. The matrix provides positive examples when behaviors need correcting.

6. The expectations can be communicated efficiently to parents, guest teachers, new students, and the community (Chapters 20 and 21).

Defining Universal Behaviors

After the entire staff team has agreed on the umbrella rules, define a few behavioral expectations that you want to see across settings and at all times. The following example relating the universal rules "be safe, be respectful, and be responsible" to specific behaviors may be useful.

You are being safe, respectful, and responsible when we see you doing the following everywhere in and around the school.

▶ Walk on the right side.

▶ Walk with a purpose.

▶ Respect personal space.

▶ Keep hands, feet, and objects to yourself.

▶ Use appropriate language.

▶ Report accidents and spills to an adult.

▶ Keep areas free from litter.

Defining Behaviors for Specific Areas

After universal behavioral expectations are set, define the expectations in specific areas. An example of strategies on how to develop the school matrix is presented here.

- Brainstorm all the areas in the school that need to be addressed. List these on the left side of a large piece of chart paper.
- On the right side of the paper, define the behavior expectations for each area.

Areas in Our School	Behavioral Expectations
Hallways	
Stairs	
Bathrooms	
Office Area	
Cafeteria	
Arrival	
Dismissal	
Bus Area	
Nurse's Office	
Playground	
Locker Area	

It is important that all the specific areas are identified, not only problem areas, in order to be proactive and preventive in your approach. Sometimes, staff members don't feel the need to develop behavioral expectations for areas that are not problematic at this time. However, we cannot assume that this desired behavior will continue as staff and students change. In the case of current nonproblem areas, it will be easy to write down the expectations, as students are already doing what we want to see and hear.

The areas in a school where expectations need to be defined are site specific. Some schools may have unique spaces where behavioral expectations are needed. This may be a garden area, a courtyard, bicycle storage, boiler room, or others.

We recommend that you take some time to develop school rules and behavior expectations that are unique to your school. This will work best if you use the sample chart provided with a team representing all stakeholders in your school (see Chapters 2 and 4 on PBIS team development).

For your review, Figures 8 through 10 provide sample behavioral expectations matrices for:

- Elementary schools
- Middle schools
- High schools

You may need to adapt this format, depending on the age level of your students, the local norms, and your values about expected behavior.

Finalizing Your School Matrix

The following steps are a guideline.

1. Review the **Defining Schoolwide Expectations Worksheet** provided on page 63.

2. Decide on three to four umbrella rules (e.g., be safe, be responsible, be respectful).

3. Make a list of all the common areas in your school.

4. Define the expectations and complete the matrix for each setting.

5. When the matrix is completed, share with all of the adults in the school (and with students, as appropriate) and obtain agreement regarding the expectations.

FIGURE 8 Elementary School Matrix
Rules and Behavioral Expectations for Common Areas (Sample)

Common Area	Be Safe	Be Respectful	Be Responsible
All Common Areas	• Walk facing forward. • Keep hands, feet, and objects to yourself. • Get adult help for accidents and spills. • Use all equipment and materials appropriately.	• Use kind words and actions. • Wait for your turn. • Clean up after self. • Follow adult directions.	• Follow school rules. • Remind others to follow school rules. • Take proper care of all personal belongings and school equipment. • Be honest.
Cafeteria	• Keep all food to self. • Sit with feet on floor, bottom on bench, and facing table.	• Allow anyone to sit next to you. • Use quiet voices.	• Raise hand and wait to be excused. • Get all utensils, milk, etc., when first going through the line.
Playground and/or Recess	• Walk to and from the playground. • Stay within boundaries. • Be aware of activities and games around you.	• Play fairly. • Include everyone.	• Use hall or bathroom pass for leaving the area.
Passing Areas, Halls, Breezeways, Sidewalks	• Stay to the right. • Allow others to pass.	• Hold the door open for the person behind you. • Use quiet voices.	• Stay on sidewalks.
Bathrooms	• Keep feet on floor. • Keep water in sink. • Wash hands. • Put paper towels in garbage can.	• Knock on stall door. • Give people privacy. • Use quiet voices.	• Flush toilet after use. • Return to room promptly. • Use a bathroom pass.
Arrival and Dismissal Areas	• Use bike lane. • Use sidewalks and crosswalks. • Wait in designated areas.	• (See All Common Areas)	• Arrive on time. • Leave on time. • Get teacher permission to use the classroom phone.
Library	• (See All Common Areas)	• Use quiet voices.	• Use hall pass for leaving the area.
Special Events and Assemblies	• Wait for arrival and dismissal signal.	• Use audience manners. • Sit on bottom.	• (See All Common Areas) • Clap to show appreciation.

**FIGURE 9   Middle School Matrix
Rules and Behavioral Expectations for Common Areas (Sample)**

Common Area	Be Safe	Be Respectful	Be Responsible
Cafeteria	• Walk at all times. • Eat only your own food.	• Wait in line patiently. • All food and drinks stay in cafeteria. • Place recyclables in proper containers.	• Use good manners. • Clean up your area.
Gym	• Sit properly in bleachers and chairs. • Use equipment properly. • No food, drink, or gum.	• Show good sportsmanship. • Return equipment to designated area.	• Be a team player; encourage others. • Use home court.
Assemblies and Special Events	• Sit quietly during presentation. • Wait for dismissal instructions.	• Focus on presentation.	• Listen responsibly. • Applaud appropriately.
Media Center	• Keep hands and feet to yourself. • Use chairs and tables appropriately.	• Return materials to proper places on time. • Use Internet appropriately; print only what's needed. • No food, drink, or gum.	• Use kind words and actions. • Respect property—yours and others'.
Hallways	• Walk at all times. • Keep hands and feet to yourself. • Arrive to class on time.	• No food, drink, or gum. • Use drinking fountains appropriately.	• Use kind words and actions. • Respect property—yours and others'.
Main Office	• Keep hands and feet to youself. • Use chairs and tables appropriately.	• State your purpose politely. • Obtain permission to use phone. • No food, drink, or gum.	• Use kind words and actions. • Keep hands and feet to yourself.
Bathrooms	• Keep water in sink. • Wash hands. • Put towels in garbage.	• Flush toilets. • Inform adults of vandalism.	• Give people privacy. • Respect property—yours and others'.
Bicycle Parking	• Walk and ride bikes safely. • Wear helmets. • Secure bicycles to racks. • No loitering.	• Touch others' property only with permission. • Pick up litter.	• Use kind words and actions. • Respect property—yours and others'.
Bus Area	• Do not block front doors. • Stay behind yellow line.	• Wait in line patiently. • No gum. • Pick up litter.	• Use kind words and actions. • Keep hands and feet to yourself.

FIGURE 10 **High School Matrix**
Rules and Behavioral Expectations for Common Areas (Sample)

Common Area	Be Safe	Be Respectful	Be Responsible
Classroom	• Keep hands and feet to yourself. • Ask permission to leave assigned areas. • Follow directions and safety procedures. • Keep walkways clear.	• Treat others' property with respect. • Follow directions and classroom assignments. • Actively listen to designated speaker. • Use appropriate voice and words.	• Be prepared and on time. • Stay on task. • Resolve attendance issues before class. • Sign in and out. • Clean up after self.
All Common Areas	• Follow adult directions the first time given.		
Bus Area	• Keep hands and feet to yourself. • When buses are present, remain on sidewalk. • Walk at all times.	• Treat others and property with respect. • Use appropriate voice and language. • No harassment.	• Pick up your trash. • Remind others to follow rules.
Eating Areas	• Keep hands and feet to yourself. • Walk at all times. • Keep walkways clear.	• Treat others and property with respect. • Use appropriate voice and language.	• Clean up after self. • Remind others to follow rules.
Assemblies	• Keep hands and feet to yourself. • Enter and exit in an orderly fashion. • Keep walkways clear.	• Be attentive. • Listen with an open mind. • Remove hats when requested. • Applaud appropriately.	• Sit quietly. • Remind others to follow rules.
Hallways	• Keep hands and feet to yourself. • Keep walkways clear. • Walk at all times.	• Treat others and property with respect. • Use appropriate voice and language.	• Pick up your trash. • Inform staff of spills and wait for help.

Defining Schoolwide Expectations Worksheet

Name of School: _____

Common Area	Be Safe	Be Respectful	Be Responsible

When all areas have been listed and defined, present the worksheet to all staff via an LCD projector or whiteboard for discussion and editing. Soon thereafter, finalize the process and give a copy to each staff member, including a cover letter and a place to sign.

Strategies and Tips

The following general strategies and tips may help you develop your matrix.

- Involve the whole staff team in deciding on site-specific areas.
- Include areas that are not listed in the matrix examples but that apply to your unique school setting.
- Employ small groups to decide on rules for specific areas.
- Have abundant examples of positive behaviors in each area.
- Have an individual type the expectations into a template as you go along.
- Discuss and edit the completed matrix as a whole.
- Refine the matrix and send it with a cover letter to each staff member.
- Obtain sign-off from each staff member who reviews the matrix by having him or her return a signed copy to the PBIS coordinator (or other assigned person).
- The PBIS Team will collate and finalize the site-specific rules based on your school's individual feedback.
- Present revised matrix during a staff meeting and accept it as a final copy (project for whole-group viewing).

A Couple of Common Issues

There are certain controversial issues that come up at schools. There are many ways that these problems can be solved so that everyone can live with the eventual decision about behavior expectations. It is most important that staff agree on a decision, teach it to the students, and reinforce compliance. If, for some reason, the decision turns out to be a bad one that doesn't work very well, then it can be changed. Nothing is marked in stone. The PBIS team will examine the data and suggest changes.

In working with a large number of schools, we have found that staff often disagree on two issues: gum and hats. We would like to provide some examples of how certain schools solved these problems.

Chewing Gum

In several middle schools, many of the teachers did not have a problem with students chewing gum. These teachers felt that students often had a long way to get to school and that chewing gum was better than smoking or chewing tobacco. However, most teachers agreed that they didn't mind students chewing gum outside of school, but couldn't tolerate it in school. In addition, custodians spent $7,000 a year of their time cleaning gum off carpets, desks, and other areas. The first proposal was to ask the student council if it would be willing to put $7,000 in escrow at the beginning of the school year to insure funding for the removal of gum. The student council didn't think this was a good idea. The solution, then, was an idea that came from a PE teacher, who used this method in the gym. Each morning, the custodian would staple a large sheet of paper around a wooden pole in front of the school. This became the gum pole. When students arrived at school, they would stick their gum to the gum pole. As soon as students were in class, the custodian would remove the gum-filled paper and replace it with a clean sheet. This way, students were taught not to chew gum inside the building.

Wearing Hats

At many schools, the disagreement about wearing hats in class is very controversial. One school came up with the following solution. There would be "no hat zones" around the school, identified by a poster depicting a hat in a red circle with a slash through it. The cafeteria and playground supervisors didn't want students to wear hats because they became a safety issue, as students flipped hats off of other students' heads. Sometimes, the stealing of someone else's hat would be a trigger to a fight. Therefore, the cafeteria and playground became no hat zones. Staff had to agree upon a place where the hats would be kept during these times. Some teachers decided that they didn't want students to wear hats in their classroom, so they put up a no hat zone sign on their door and taught students where they could safely store their hats.

Making the Behavioral Expectations Public

After the matrix has been finalized, plans can be made on how to make the expectations public, where and how to post them, and how to teach them to all students. It is important that:

- Every student receives a copy of the matrix.
- Every student is taught the specific behavior expectations.
- Every parent receives a copy of the matrix.
- Every parent reviews, provides feedback (if desired), and returns a signed copy of the matrix to school.
- The behavioral expectations for each area are printed on a poster or displayed in that area.
- A plan is made to teach and reteach the expectations via specific lesson plans (Chapter 6).

Depending on the time a school has to design and print posters, it is not necessary to wait until the final, "fancy" posters are ready in order to teach expectations. Simple posters can be used for initial teaching.

Communicating and Teaching Schoolwide Behavior Expectations

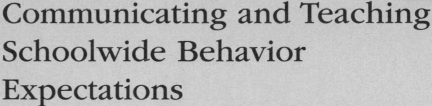

Background: Teaching the Culture of School

Once faculty and staff have defined schoolwide expectations, these must be taught directly to students. Students today arrive at school with a more diverse experience of behavioral norms. Some may not arrive with the basic social skills needed for school success. They may not have learned alternatives to hitting, pushing, or name-calling to resolve conflict, or how to comply with reasonable adult requests. To counter these behavior patterns, students must be directly taught appropriate school behavior and given ample opportunity to practice.

To review, positive school behavioral expectations have the following features.

- Expectations are positively stated.
- Expectations are posted in hallways, around classrooms, in the school handbook, on agenda planners, and so forth and are specific to their locations.
- Expectations are taught directly to students with formal lessons.
- Expectations are taught and reviewed at least 10–20 times per year.

> **OBJECTIVES**
>
> ▸ Describe methods for teaching and encouraging desired behavior
>
> ▸ Develop a school lesson plan
>
> ▸ Set a schedule to teach and review expected behavior lessons

> To maximize effectiveness, a system of positive reinforcement and recognition—at all times, by all adults—for following the expectations is in place throughout the building.

How to Communicate the Rules

Posting the expectations, or rules, is important for a number of reasons, including integrating them into the school culture, providing visual reminders at point of need, and referencing them as teaching tools. The following are guidelines to improve the effectiveness of posting rules.

- Keep the poster of rules/expectations simple.
- Make a template in your word-processing program to enter the rules and expectations into.
- Assign someone to make the posters immediately.
- For teaching purposes, make temporary posters to use right away.
- If you want a really fancy (e.g., laminated) poster, hold off until after initial teaching.
- Final posters should be large and easily read.
- Posters should include only the rules specific to the site where they are posted (e.g., cafeteria, bathroom).
- The schoolwide universal rules should be posted in each classroom.
- Classroom expectations should be based on the schoolwide expectations.

How to Teach Schoolwide Expectations

The expectations can be taught in a variety of ways. Many schools use audiovisual technologies, such as student-made DVDs, raps, songs, plays, and so forth (Smith & Sprague, 2004). The most important features are that the skills are modeled and that examples and nonexamples of the skills are presented for the different settings required for your school (e.g., hallway, bathroom, cafeteria, playground).

Social-skills instruction increases in intensity, specialization, and individualization as problems become more chronic. Teaching expectations involves demonstrating and modeling, rehearsal and guided practice, corrective feedback, and regular reviews. To ensure that students clearly understand the expectations, give examples and nonexamples of what they mean.

For the expectation "When the teacher asks you to do something, do it right away," students should be shown how to do it the right way (quickly) as well as examples of the wrong way (slowly and with complaining). Students should be asked to demonstrate only positive behavior; negative examples should be modeled only by adults. The reason for this is that students enjoy watching their teachers doing the wrong thing, and they should also not practice inappropriate behavior themselves. Figure 11 presents the big ideas about teaching social behaviors.

FIGURE 11   Teach Social Behavior Like You Teach Academic Skills

- Teach in the location where the problems are occurring (or where you anticipate them occurring).
- Give frequent practice opportunities.
- Provide useful corrections.
- Provide positive feedback.
- Monitor for success.

Reteaching Schoolwide Behavior Expectations

Reteaching the behavior expectations lessons (which you will create in this chapter) is expected during the school year and will be a part of your school's schedule. Again, formal teaching or reteaching of behavioral expectations (rather than simple error correction) should be almost a weekly occurrence.

Additionally, teachers can review rules in mini sessions at the beginning of class (for a few minutes only), or they can incorporate the rules into other teaching time. For example, a middle school home room could play a Jeopardy-style game for rule review, or a word search of rules could be available for when work is done during elementary school literacy blocks.

Finally, but certainly not least, reteaching occurs when students are corrected for not exhibiting the expected behaviors. These are learning opportunities. Consistent expectations provide the tools to reteach when things don't go well. Take for example a student running through the hallway. An adult stops the student and asks:

> *"What are the hallway rules?"*
>
> **Student response:** *"Walk on the right side with hands and feet to yourself."*
>
> **Adult:** *"That's right! Show me?"*
>
> Student walks. Adult responds, *"You are walking just right. You're showing responsible and safe behavior!"*

If a student is running in the hallway and an adult stops him and asks:

> *"What are the hallway rules?"* and the student doesn't know, the adult can simply refer to a poster on the wall or say, *"Walk at all times with a purpose, keep hands and feet to yourself, and turn voices off. What are the expectations?"*
>
> (Student responds correctly.)
>
> **Adult:** *"That's right! Show me?"*
>
> Student walks. Adult responds, *"You are walking just right. You're showing responsible and safe behavior!"*

Teach Expected Behaviors Just Like Other Subjects

Strategies for teaching and managing social behavior are the same as strategies used to teach reading, math, physics, music, and other subjects. Both social and academic management strategies must be integrated within and across the curricula. In each classroom and in every area of the school, it is important to do the following.

- Target specific times to teach the expectations. This may be done during the first few days of school. Staff may decide to have teaching stations (e.g., cafeteria, playground, hallway, and bathroom) and rotate all students through each station. It is important that the staff members who supervise in the cafeteria and on the playground present the lessons in those areas.
- Reteach the skill when it's not exhibited, using the language of the lessons. For example, if a student is running in the hall, say, *"What is the rule about all hallways? Please go back and walk."*
- Watch for students who are using the expected behaviors and give them positive feedback. Review and recall expected behaviors regularly.
- Model the expected behaviors in all of your interactions with students and adults.

Some schools provide a "passport" upon completion of each station: Students receive a stamp and go on to the next station. Middle and high schools may decide to have staggered starting days for each grade level. Each grade level would spend one entire day learning about each teaching station. A school may decide to make a video of the expectations and show it during a schoolwide assembly.

Lesson Plans for Behavior Expectations: A Model

Figure 12 presents the components of a model school's expectations lesson plan for teaching behavior expectations throughout the school. We will use this format to develop some specific behavior expectation lesson plans for your school. You may wonder why you can't just copy from another school. It is important to consider that each school is unique and that, although you should use lessons from other schools as models, you need to develop the plans to fit your unique school.

FIGURE 12   School Expectations: Lesson Plan Components

- What do we expect students to do?
  - Teach the expected behaviors.
  - Tell why it is important.
  - Give positive and negative examples.
  - Provide opportunities for additional practice and fluency building.
- Prevent problems from occurring.
  - Actively supervise students.
  - Provide reminders of expected behavior(s) before they occur.
  - Give positive feedback for expected behavior.
  - Reteach when problem behavior occurs.
  - Review behavioral expectations.
  - Measure for success.

Activity: Develop a Lesson Plan

Take a moment to practice developing a lesson plan for one of your schoolwide behavior expectations.

1. Review the sample lesson plans provided. There are a variety of general and specific samples.

2. Select one of your schoolwide behavior expectations (from Chapter 5), and develop a lesson plan. The goal is to develop multiple lesson plans, so consider assigning your rule list from Chapter 5 to your Schoolwide PBIS team members.

3. Work with your team members to develop a complete lesson using the samples and forms in Figure 13: **Schoolwide Behavior Expectations Lesson Plan**.

4. We recommend that you practice teaching your lesson by doing a role play.

FIGURE 13   School Focus Area: Schoolwide Behavior Expectations (Sample)

Rule: Be respectful

What do we expect students to do?

1. Speak respectfully to adults and peers.

2. Use respectful words to resolve conflicts.

3. Keep hands and feet to themselves in common areas.

How will we teach the expected behaviors?

1. Explain why following the rule is important.
"It is important to be respectful to your peers and adults in the school. Using words or actions to harass, tease, or bully another person is inappropriate and can hurt others physically and emotionally. Negative interactions in school interfere with learning and can cause problems at school and in the community."

2. List examples and nonexamples of the expected behaviors (at least three each).
Ask students to identify examples and nonexamples of each part of the rule. Ask them to identify both and tell why it is a good or bad example of expected behavior. These are examples you might use.

a. *A positive example*: You bumped into Mary in the hallway, and her books fell to the ground. She was upset because she would be late to class, and she started to call you names. You recognized that you were not paying attention and decided to apologize and help Mary pick up her books. Your teacher gave you a positive referral, and Mary thanked you for resolving the problem with respect.

b. *A nonexample*: You bumped into Mary in the hallway, and her books fell to the ground. She was upset because she would be late to class and called you a "jerk." You got angry and told Mary she was ugly and stupid. You walked away, and Mary was late for class. Mary was mad and began to spread untrue rumors about you to her friends.

Teachers should prompt students to (a) identify the problem, (b) think of one or more respectful solutions to the problem, (c) choose one of the solutions, (d) carry it out, and (e) evaluate the solution.

Provide opportunities to practice and build fluency.

1. Set aside a few minutes at the beginning of each period to practice the rule.

2. As the teacher models, have individual students demonstrate examples of following the rule (role play).

3. Tell students about the consequences for following and not following the rule.

School Office (Sample)

Step 1: Introduce Rule

A. Outline the focus of the lesson: "Today we are going to learn about being safe, respectful, and responsible in the office."

B. Check for student understanding: "What are we going to learn about?"

Step 2: Demonstrate Rule

- Model (or provide a story) positive and negative examples of an adult or a child being safe, respectful, or responsible in the office.

- Have students label the situation as safe or unsafe, respectful or not respectful, responsible or not responsible.

Safe (free from harm)	Respectful (polite, cooperative, and empathetic)	Responsible (dependable, trustworthy, and makes positive choices)
Role Plays—Some Examples to Use • Your teacher sent you to the office. What is the safe thing to do? (Have a pink office pass.) • You need to ask the secretary something. What is the safe thing to do? (Stay in front of the counter.) • You see someone else in the office who is poking another student. What is the safe thing to do? (Keep hands and feet to self.)	**Role Plays—Some Examples to Use** • You need to use the telephone. What is the respectful thing to do? (Ask permission to use the phone.) • Someone is using the phone. What is the respectful thing to do? (Wait your turn.) • There are a lot of students in the office and only one secretary. What is the respectful thing to do? (Listen and follow directions the first time.)	**Role Plays—Some Examples to Use** • You are talking to your friend in the office. What is the responsible thing to do? (Use a Level 2 = neighbor voice.) • You are in the office asking for something. What is the respectful thing to do? (Use polite and kind words, please and thank you.) • An adult is talking on the phone in the office and you need to make a call. What is the responsible thing to do? (Use good manners; wait for him or her to finish.)

Step 3: Provide Monitoring and Feedback

Discuss the role play.

- Ask students to indicate or show more examples of how they could be safe, respectful, or responsible when in the office.

- Encourage and support appropriate discussion and responses. Minimize attention to inappropriate responses.

- When you see students being safe, respectful, and responsible in the office, preferably use their first name and provide specific and immediate praise. Use *Caught Being Good*.

- When you see students who are not being safe, respectful, or responsible in the office, stop them, state the rule and redirect, ask the students to state the expected behavior, watch the students, and give them feedback.

Focus Area: General Behavior Expectations (Sample)

Rule: Be Respectful

Respectful: To be polite and cooperative with others

What do we expect students to do?

1. Use quiet voices.

2. Be respectful to others.

3. Set all electronic devices to silent and conceal them during school hours (cell phones, mp3, CD).

Explain why following the rule is important.

1. To promote a safe and respectful environment where all individuals feel accepted and welcome.

2. Learning of others is not disrupted.

3. Being respectful means being polite and cooperative with others.

Here are some positive and unacceptable examples to discuss with students.

1. **A Positive Example:**

   When your locker was stuck, you said, "I'm going to be late!" and walked to class.

   An Unacceptable Example:

   Your locker wouldn't open and class was about to start. You say, "_____" and punch the locker with your fist. Other people in the area feel uncomfortable and look at you.

2. **A Positive Example:**

   You bumped into Mary in the lunchroom and her tray fell to the ground. She was upset because she would have less time to eat and started to call you names. You recognized that you were not paying attention and decided to apologize and help Mary pick up her tray and food. Your teacher gave you a positive referral, and Mary thanked you for resolving the problem with respect.

   An Unacceptable Example:

   You bumped into Mary in the lunchroom and her tray fell to the ground. She was upset because she would have less time to eat and called you a "jerk." You got angry and told Mary she was ugly and stupid. You walked away and Mary had less time to eat. Mary was mad and began to spread untrue rumors about you to her friends.

3. **A Positive Example:**

   You are in an assembly and the lights are dimmed. People around you start giggling. You do the respectful thing and are silent while the lights are out.

   An Unacceptable Example:

   You are in an assembly and the lights are dimmed. People around you start giggling. You begin talking and pushing your friend in front of you.

Provide opportunities to practice and build fluency.

1. Tell students about the consequences for following and not following the rule.

2. As the teacher models, have individual students demonstrate examples of the rule (role play).

3. Encourage students to make it their goal for the next two weeks to be respectful to others by _____.

Focus Area: General Social Expectations (Sample)

Rule: Be Responsible

Responsible: To be dependable and trustworthy at all times

What do we expect students to do?

1. Follow school policies (dress code, tobacco, alcohol, drugs).

2. Use G-rated language in school.

3. Come prepared for all classes.

4. Be on time.

5. Show appropriate affection, such as hand holding and friendship hugs.

6. Take proper care of all personal belongings and school equipment.

7. Remind others to follow rules.

8. Use wastebaskets for trash.

Explain why following the rule is important.

1. Prevents injury, provides a safe and orderly learning environment.

2. Being responsible means being dependable and trustworthy at all times.

Here are some positive and unacceptable examples to discuss with students.

1. **A Positive Example:**

   You are in a hurry to get on the bus. There are several younger students ahead of you. You do the responsible thing and wait your turn.

   An Unacceptable Example:

   You are in a hurry to get on the bus. There are several younger students ahead of you. You shove your way to the front.

2. **A Positive Example:**

   Your friends want you to take them to the store real fast. You know that if you leave, you will be late to class. You choose to remain in school and go to your next class on time.

   An Unacceptable Example:

   Your friends want you to take them to the store really fast. You know that if you leave, you will be late to class. You decide to go ahead and take the tardy.

3. **A Positive Example:**

   You see a locker where the lock is not securely attached. You lock the lock.

   An Unacceptable Example:

   You see a locker where the lock is not securely attached. You open it, take a look at what is inside, and leave it open for others to see.

Provide opportunities to practice and build fluency.

1. Tell students about the consequences for following and not following the rule.

2. Have individual students identify and demonstrate examples of the rule (role play).

3. Encourage students to make it their goal for the next two weeks to look for ways to demonstrate responsibility by _____.

Focus Area: General Social Expectations
SCHOOL RULE LESSON PLAN

Rule: Be Safe

Safe: Free from harm of any kind

What do we expect students to do?

1. Report all concerns that may lead to unsafe situations to staff members immediately.

2. Keep hands and feet to themselves.

3. Walk at all times.

Explain why following the rule is important.

1. Prevents injury.

2. Provides a safe and orderly learning environment.

Here are some positive and unacceptable examples to discuss with students.

1. **A Positive Example:**

 You see a container of spilled milk in freshman hall. You proceed to class and report the spilled milk to your teacher.

 An Unacceptable Example:

 You see a container of spilled milk in freshman hall. You kick the container of milk, watch it splash across the floor, and proceed to class.

2. **A Positive Example:**

 When entering a crowded area during passing time, you keep your hands, feet, and materials to yourself and patiently enter traffic to get to your destination.

 An Unacceptable Example:

 You enter into freshman hall, shoving your way through so that you can get to your locker.

3. **A Positive Example:**

 You get out of class late and want to get lunch, so you patiently walk to the line so that you don't run into other students.

 An Unacceptable Example:

 You get out of your fourth-period class and run to the lunch line so that you can be first to get lunch. In the process, you knock into several people who are patiently walking to the lunch line.

Provide opportunities to practice and build fluency.

1. Tell students about the consequences for following and not following the rule.

2. As the teacher models, have individual students identify and demonstrate examples of the rule (role play).

3. Encourage students to make it their goal for the next two weeks to pick up things in the hall and to try and make this a better environment for everyone.

Focus Area: Assemblies and Special Events
SCHOOL RULE LESSON PLAN

Rule: Display or Use Appropriate Behavior for Assemblies and Special Events

Respectful: To be polite and cooperative to others

What do we expect students to do?

Be Safe:

1. Arrive and depart in an orderly fashion.
2. Move from class with your instructor. Fill bleachers from the top down.
3. Wait for dismissal instructions.
4. Bring no food or drink.

Be Respectful:

1. Show appreciation appropriately. Applaud appropriately.
2. Focus on the presentation.
3. Keep hands and feet to yourself.
4. Demonstrate self-control and maturity.
5. Treat the speaker and audience with respect.

Be Responsible:

1. Sit with your class.
2. Listen for and follow directions.

Explain why following the rule is important.

"We need to gather as a large group for information, entertainment, and celebration. Each speaker deserves the respect of your attention and polite acknowledgement."

Here are some positive and unacceptable examples to discuss with students.

1. **A Positive Example:**

   "It was easier to find my seat at the assembly; I did not have to climb over everyone."

   An Unacceptable Example:

   "It was so stupid. I had to climb clear to the top of the bleachers," or, "I fell over someone and had to step on them. They got upset."

2. **A Positive Example:**

   You listen to the speaker and participate in the assembly.

   An Unacceptable Example:

   You sit with your friends and not with your class. You talk through the entire assembly and don't hear that you have won a door prize.

3. **A Positive Example:**

   You leave food in your locker—it is not taken away during the assembly, and you get to eat it later.

   An Unacceptable Example:

   You bring a soda to the assembly, spill it on someone, and she threatens to knock you out.

Provide opportunities to practice and build fluency.

1. Have students role play the positive examples.
2. Have students brainstorm more examples—perhaps with a partner.
3. Lead a class discussion.

Alternative topics to discuss.

1. Discuss out-of-school group gatherings (e.g., movies, funerals, weddings, etc.).
2. What should students do if the assembly isn't very good?
3. What if a student is being good, but someone close by him or her is not?

Focus Area: Bus Stop
SCHOOL RULE LESSON PLAN

Rule: Be safe, be respectful, be responsible

What do we expect students to do?

Be Safe:

1. Walk to the bus stop.

2. Stand back from the bus until given permission to board.

3. Keep hands, feet, and objects to yourself.

Be Respectful:

1. Follow directions from the person on duty.

2. Keep your hands off others.

3. Use your manners.

Be Responsible:

1. Get to the bus on time.

Explain why following the rule is important.

"You can be seriously injured or harm others if you do not pay attention in the bus loading area."

Here are some positive and unacceptable examples to discuss with students.

1. **A Positive Example:**

   You are anxious to get on the bus, but there are students in front of you. You are patient and wait your turn.

   An Unacceptable Example:

   You are anxious to get on the bus, and there are students in front of you. You begin pushing your way to the front of the line while calling your peers' names.

2. **A Positive Example:**

   The person on duty asks you to step back while the buses pull up. You wait for the students behind you and follow the directions.

   An Unacceptable Example:

   The person on duty asks you to step back while the buses pull up. You turn around, start pushing the line back, and use inappropriate verbal responses.

3. **A Positive Example:**

   You are walking to the bus line, and the person in front of you stops. You wait a moment and then politely ask to get past.

   An Unacceptable Example:

   You are walking to the bus line, and the people in front of you stop. You grab one person's backpack, making him or her fall to the ground.

Provide opportunities to practice and build fluency.

1. Ask students to give examples of how they can be safe, responsible, and respectful while waiting for or walking to the bus.

2. Role-play students standing in line, and show an adult displaying positive and negative ways to respond to a situation.

3. Review ways students can get injured around vehicles.

4. Demonstrate positive ways to get around students who are in the way by using proper manners and respect.

5. Discuss how flying objects can distract students who are waiting for the bus, which causes them to not pay attention to oncoming buses.

Alternative topics to discuss.

1. Student Handbook—transportation page.

2. Discuss students who drive and inform them of their responsibilities and behavior when arriving to and leaving school.

Cafeteria (Sample)

Step 1: Introduce Rule

A. Outline the focus of the lesson: "Today we are going to learn about being safe, respectful, and responsible in the cafeteria."

B. Check for student understanding: "What are we going to learn about?"

Step 2: Demonstrate Rule

- Teacher models (or provides a story for) positive and negative examples of an adult or child being safe, respectful, or responsible in the cafeteria.

- Have students label the situation as safe or unsafe, respectful or not respectful, responsible or not responsible.

Safe (free from harm)	Respectful (polite, cooperative, and empathetic)	Responsible (dependable, trustworthy, and makes positive choices)
Role Plays—Some Examples to Use - A friend is not going to eat her hamburger. You would like to have it. What is the safe thing to do? (Don't eat it. Eat only your own food.) - Your friend was sitting on his knees at the table. His feet were sticking out. Someone walked by and bumped his feet. What is the safe thing to do? (Sit facing table with feet still.) - You are doing an errand for the teacher before lunch. When you arrive at the cafeteria, your class is almost through the lunch line. You are very hungry and want to run to catch up with your class. What is the safe thing to do? (Walk.) - You have gone through the lunch line and are carrying your tray back to the table. What is the safe thing to do? (Carry the tray with both hands, walk carefully, and watch out for others.)	**Role Plays—Some Examples to Use** - A kid comes to your table to sit down, but one of your friends does not want the kid to sit with your group. What is the respectful thing to do? (Allow anyone to sit next to you.) - You are done with lunch. What is the respectful thing to do? (Talk with your neighbor with a voice level of 2 = neighbor voice.) - The teacher signals for your attention. What is the respectful thing to do? (Listen to the quiet signal, voices off, stop, look, and listen.) - Your neighbor is eating something that he brought from home, and it smells good. What is the respectful thing to do? (Say, "Your food looks good.")	**Role Plays—Some Examples to Use** - You are in the back of the line, and the line is moving slowly. What is the responsible thing to do? (Wait your turn.) - You get hit on the head with a tater tot. What is the responsible thing to do? (Keep objects to yourself, continue eating, and tell a teacher.) - You have finished eating. What is the responsible thing to do? (Clean up your space and the space around you.) - You are going to dump your tray. What is the responsible thing to do? (Recycle first, then throw away garbage.)

Step 3: Provide Monitoring and Feedback

Discuss the role play.

- Ask students to indicate or show more examples of how they could be safe, respectful, or responsible when using the cafeteria.

- Encourage and support appropriate discussion and responses. Minimize attention to inappropriate responses.

- When you see students being safe, respectful, and responsible when using the cafeteria, preferably use their first name and provide specific and immediate praise. Use *Caught Being Good*.

- When you see students who are not being safe, respectful, or responsible in the cafeteria, stop them, state the rule and redirect, ask the students to state the expected behavior, watch the students, and give them feedback.

Expected Behavior Lesson Plan

The Rule: _____

What do we expect students to do?

1.

2.

3.

How will we teach the expected behaviors?

Explain why following the rule is important.

List positive examples and unacceptable examples of the expected behaviors (two to three each).

a. Positive examples:

b. Unacceptable examples:

Provide opportunities to practice and build fluency.

1.

2.

3.

4.

Schedule Lesson Times

Once your sample lesson plans are developed, it is critical to set a schedule for teaching the lessons. It is common to review or teach expected behavior at the beginning of the year, but expected behavior will be maintained only when the lessons are reviewed regularly. We recommend that a lesson or other activity regarding expected behavior be provided weekly.

Figure 14 provides a sample year-long lesson teaching schedule. Take some time to review this plan, and then set a time for the PBIS team to schedule your school's lessons across the school year.

FIGURE 14 Behavior Expectations Lessons Schedule (Sample)

Week 1 (Sept 5)
Basic Behavior Expectations, Classroom, Playground, Bus, Library, Zero Tolerance, and Guest (Substitute) Teacher

Week 2 (Sept 11)
Repeat of Week 1

Week 3 (Sept 18)
Repeat of Weeks 1 and 2

Week 4 (Sept 25)
All Common Areas

Week 5 (Oct 2)
Cafeteria

Week 6 (Oct 9)
No lessons/3-day week

Week 7 (Oct 16)
Playground

Week 8 (Oct 23)
Passing Areas

Week 9 (Oct 30)
Bathrooms

Week 10 (Nov 6)
No lessons/3-day week

Week 11 (Nov 13)
Arrival and Dismissal

Week 12 (Nov 20)
No lessons/conferences and no school

Week 13 (Nov 27)
Bus Safety

Week 14 (Dec 4)
Common Instructional Areas and Library

Week 15 (Dec 11)
Special Events and Assemblies

Winter Break (Dec 18)

Week 16 (Jan 2)
Review Basic Behavior Expectations, Classroom, Playground, Bus, Library, Zero Tolerance, and Substitute Teacher

Week 17 (Jan 8)
Repeat of Week 1

Week 18 (Jan 16)
Repeat of Weeks 1 and 2

Week 19 (Jan 22)
All Common Areas

Week 20 (Jan 30)
Cafeteria

Week 21 (Feb 5)
Playground

Week 22 (Feb 12)
Passing Areas

Week 23 (Feb 19)
No lessons/3-day week

Week 24 (Feb 26)
Bathrooms

Week 25 (Mar 5)
Arrival and Dismissal

Week 26 (Mar 12)
Bus Safety

Week 27 (Mar 19)
Common Instructional Areas and Library

Spring Break (Mar 26)

Week 28 (Apr 2)
Special Events and Assemblies

Week 29 (Apr 9)
Restricted Areas

Week 30 (Apr 16)
Zero-Tolerance Behaviors

Week 31 (Apr 23)
No lessons/conferences

Week 32 (Apr 30)
Lesson Review

Weeks 33–36
Lesson Review

CHAPTER 7

Schoolwide Recognition and Reward Systems: Creating a Positive School Culture

Background: Focusing on the Positive Versus the Negative

It is common to focus on punishing or on stopping disruptive behavior, but students with challenging behaviors will not make meaningful educational progress unless they are taught skills that increase their ability to function successfully in school. Hill Walker (1995) showed that posting rules alone had no effect on student misbehavior, but when teachers were instructed to teach school rules, catch students being good, and ignore minor inappropriate behaviors, problem behaviors dropped dramatically.

To begin, it is important to discuss issues and concerns regarding the use of positive reinforcement methods in schools. The following reflection presents some issues that others have raised regarding use of positive reinforcement (Webster-Stratton & Herbert, 1994). Please take a moment to think about each of these issues and identify your opinions and values regarding them. You might also consider discussing them with your colleagues.

OBJECTIVES

▶ Discuss issues regarding positive reinforcement

▶ Plan to implement a schoolwide recognition and reward system

▶ Discuss how to increase consistency among the adults at school

▶ Develop a recognition and reward plan

Reflection

What You Always Wanted to Know about Praise and Rewards

1. **Shouldn't children at this age already know what is expected of them and how to behave?**

   Behavior that is acknowledged is more likely to occur again. Behavior that is ignored is less likely to be repeated. No good behavior should be taken for granted, or it may decline—regardless of the student's age.

2. **Praising feels unnatural. Won't kids think that it is phony?**

   If you are not used to praising, it may feel unnatural at first. But the more you praise, the more natural it will feel. If you praise good behavior that truly has happened, then there is nothing phony about it. Students who get praise will tend to praise others too, so praise won't seem phony to them. It may help to think about "noticing" desired behavior instead of "praise" and using the phrase "I noticed . . ." or "I saw . . .".

3. **Isn't praise manipulative and coercive?**

   The purpose of praise is to reinforce and increase positive behavior with the student's knowledge. Praise or noticing desired behavior helps clearly describe expectations so that students can successfully meet them. Helping children succeed is a positive thing to do!

4. **Isn't giving a reward like bribing students to do what you want them to do?**

   A bribe attempts to influence or persuade someone to produce a desired behavior that hasn't yet happened, whereas a reward reinforces a desired behavior that has already happened. A reward is given after the behavior occurs.

5. **Won't students come to depend on tangible rewards? Don't extrinsic rewards decrease intrinsic motivation?**

   Tangible rewards should be accompanied by social rewards. When a message that recognizes a student's efforts as being responsible for success is given with a reward, internal motivation will actually be strengthened.

6. **Shouldn't rewards be saved for special achievements?**

   This gives students the message that everyday behaviors and efforts don't count. Small steps on the way to achievement (such as homework completion) also need to be recognized and rewarded.

7. **Where will I get enough money to supply all these rewards?**

   Tangible rewards do not need to be very expensive. As students learn the desired behavior, the tangible rewards can gradually be faded out. Rewards can be privileges, too, such as being able to go to lunch first or getting extra computer time.

8. **Do students in middle school and high school still need rewards?**

   People of all ages, including adults, need to be recognized and rewarded for their efforts. Students of all ages need recognition, praise, and rewards—particularly during the difficult transition to adolescence.

Adapted by J.C. Rusby from Webster-Stratton, C., & Herbert M. (1994). Troubled Families—Problem Children. New York: John Wiley & Sons.

Students may be motivated by the following consequences for their behavior: (1) adult attention, (2) peer attention, (3) avoidance of an activity or task, and (4) something tangible (O'Neill et al., 1997).

For students seeking attention in particular, an efficient and effective way to get their reinforcement needs met is to misbehave. When misbehavior occurs, the teachers (or peers) may respond to it quickly. For example, if a student has been working quietly, no one may give attention to her. But, if she misbehaves (e.g., whines, screams, throws objects), she will get attention immediately. She gets what she needs (attention), therefore the acting-out behavior is reinforced.

Although some students need a greater amount of attention, we have found that we need to maintain at least a four-to-one ratio of positive to negative interactions with every student. Teachers should also recognize students for ignoring the disruptive behavior of others and for displaying appropriate behavior. Chapter 13 provides instruction on how to learn this important skill.

> **4:1 Rule:** Adults need to engage in four times as many positive interactions as negative interactions with every student.

By focusing on positive behaviors and the positive language of stated rules, teaching expected behaviors, and reinforcing positive behaviors, we increase their likelihood of occurrence. This creates a positive school culture, from planning stage to results.

Implementing a Consistent, Schoolwide Recognition System

A schoolwide reward and recognition system requires consistency, specific features (identified for you here), and the use of a variety of strategies for the greatest effectiveness and inclusiveness.

Adult Consistency in Implementation

The biggest influence on the success of recognition systems is achieving consistency of implementation among the adults in the school. Although at first it seems paradoxical, we have found that the more you pay attention to behaviors (good or bad), the more you will get those behaviors. For example, if students are misbehaving and you constantly reprimand them, they may actually misbehave more. It is better to catch the students being safe, responsible, and respectful. You will see more of the behavior you want.

Features of Effective Recognition Systems

The following list outlines the features of effective schoolwide recognition systems. The reinforcement system should be implemented across the entire school. All students in the school should have access to positive feedback, even those who may challenge the system.

- Give public recognition to model for other students.
- Use recognition and rewards that students want.
- Recognize teachers as well!
- Increase recognition before difficult times.
- Reteach behaviors if things don't go well.

Recognition Should Be Made Publicly Research has shown that public display and delivery of recognition has a powerful modeling effect. When students see their peers getting recognized for good behavior, they will be motivated to display the same behavior. As students get older, public recognition may not work for some students who prefer private feedback about their behavior.

Use Recognition That Is Meaningful to Students *(e.g., social, tangible, or in the form of desired activities)* Good ways to find out what students want include asking them to participate in the development of the recognition program and observing their behavior when recognitions are delivered. If they are not excited or fail to respond to the recognition, then it may be time to choose others. Variety in recognitions also increases their value, as students respond to novelty. For tangible rewards, keep an eye out for current student fads. However, as explained in Figure 15, cost does not equal value—some of the best rewards are cheap, free, or even pay out to the community. Many specific ideas for meaningful recognition and rewards are detailed in the remainder of this chapter, particularly in the section entitled **Activity-Based Reinforcers**.

FIGURE 15   Schoolwide Recognition . . . Keep It Simple, Keep It Cheap

Many schools are tempted to offer relatively expensive tangible rewards, such as food, movie passes, t-shirts, and toys. These can be used but should not be the primary focus of your reward system. Whatever tangible reward you choose will be motivating to some students and not to others. These types of rewards are also significant drains on school resources or require continual begging from local merchants. Minimize the use of tangibles and look for activity reinforcers that are cheap or free and that maximize what students really want: positive adult attention.

The secret to reinforcement is recognition, not the cost of the reinforcer. In one elementary school, the students winning the weekly drawing obtain a primary reinforcer that includes:
- Having their picture taken.
- Printing the picture in a 3"x5" format.
- Posting the picture on a bulletin board in the hallway.
- Periodically taking down the photos and sending them home, where they are often proudly displayed on the family refrigerator.

One of the ways that this school knows that this is a successful reinforcer is that students will nag the office if, for some reason, the drawing is not held on time.

Recognize Teachers as Well Teachers can also benefit from recognition and surprises for their hard work and participation in the program. We have found that students really enjoy it when their teacher gets publicly recognized.

Increase Recognition Before Difficult Times There are predictable times of the year (e.g., before holidays, vacations, or tests) when students are more likely to be disruptive. It is recommended that rule reteaching "boosters" and increased recognition and monitoring be provided during these times.

Reteach Behaviors If Things Don't Go Well Even the best systems will not be perfect. As problem spots are noted, use rule teaching boosters and increased positive reinforcement and monitoring.

Multiple Strategies for Reinforcement

When designing systems of positive reinforcement, it is important to use a variety of strategies. We have found that if only one system is used (such as a good behavior ticket), then only some students will benefit, and others may end up feeling left out because they "never win." Teachers may also find that a single system gets stale as they attempt to consistently deliver the tickets. In the game of reinforcement, variety is the spice of life!

Figure 16 provides an example of a school that uses rich and varied reinforcement strategies. Please review the plan for the fictional Lucky Middle School and ponder the implications for your school.

FIGURE 16 **Provide Positive Feedback—Recognize and Reward Expected Behavior: The Plan for Lucky Middle School**

Reward System	Who Receives the Reward				
	Individual Students	Whole Class	Schoolwide	Parents	Teachers/ Staff
1. Good-news referral (student goes to the office to be recognized)	X			X	X
2. Good-news calls to home	X			X	
3. Teacher-delivered good behavior tokens	X	X			
4. Positive teacher notes in student planner	X			X	
5. Student-delivered praise notes	X				
6. Value coupons obtained from local businesses (e.g., two-for-one movie ticket)	X			X	X
7. Activity coupons (e.g., extra recess, lunch with teacher, etc.)	X	X	X		X
8. Good behavior activities or trips	X	X	X		
9. Media recognition (e.g., loudspeaker, newsletter, newspaper)	X	X	X		X
10. Postcards or self-management checklists sent home (see Chapter 19)	X	X	X	X	X

Activity: Develop Your Reward and Recognition Plan

Now that we have covered the basics of developing recognition systems, you will have an opportunity to develop a system for use in your school or classroom (see Figure 17). A recognition system using tokens (e.g., tickets, buttons) is a simple way of creating a consistent recognition system. When used in combination with reduced attention for minor problems and correcting behavioral errors, this type of system is effective in reducing challenging behavior.

Feel free to use the reproducible sample school tokens at the end of this chapter, or design your own.

FIGURE 17 Checklist of Essential Components of a Schoolwide Recognition System

Give a clear statement of the expected behavior for each item (use the behavior expectations you developed in Chapter 5). Then answer the following questions.

1. Who will be involved (e.g., teachers, staff, administrator, volunteers, others)?

2. How and when will tokens be distributed?

3. Where will the tokens be turned in?

4. What backup incentives will be used (e.g., what will the tokens "buy")?
   - How and where will you obtain backup rewards?

5. Will you develop an economy where different amounts of tickets can be exchanged for rewards?

6. Will you implement a lottery system where winning tickets are drawn for a prize?
   - When and where will drawings for backup incentives occur?
   - Who will conduct the drawings?

7. When and how will you review if the system is working?
   - Count the tickets to see how many are given and by whom (you don't have to do this all the time).
   - Look to see if office referrals are reduced when more tickets are given out.
   - Look for any problems in the system and be willing to change it often.

Golden Tickets: A Token Economy Example

The golden tickets used by a classroom became so popular that the entire school adopted them. In addition to earning golden tickets from their teacher for academic achievement, students could turn in 50 regular "thumbs-up" tickets for a golden ticket. A golden ticket could be used for (1) being first in line or (2) eating on the stage. At the end of the school year, one 5th grade student had saved 28 golden tickets from throughout the year so that she could invite her entire class to have lunch on the stage!

Token Design

Before teaching starts, the staff needs to decide on a token. We have provided many examples of tokens at the end of the chapter. The crucial principle behind the reinforcer is that the token must always be paired with a verbal or nonverbal interaction between teacher and student. The students must be clear on why they have received a token. Tokens should not be carelessly given or deposited.

Disposable Tokens Most schools develop a token that has the following information:

1. Umbrella rules (e.g., be safe, respectful, responsible)

2. Student's name

3. Name of adult who gave the token

4. Date

This type of token may be collected in individual classroom containers. Once or twice a week, the containers are collected and the tickets are drawn for special privileges.

Recyclable Tokens Other schools have recyclable, permanent tokens. These tokens contain only the three umbrella rules and no place to write on them. When a child receives a token, he or she records it on a list with class names. This way, the teacher can check if tokens are being distributed evenly. If, for example, a student doesn't have many checks for receiving a token, then the teacher can ask other adults in the school to catch him or her being good so that the student can earn a token from them.

Credit: Speciaal Basisonderwijs Scholen van Stichting CSO het Gooi. The Netherlands.

Coins Other schools use different color coins. Once coins are received, the student makes a checkmark after his or her name on the class list and deposits the token in a class container. Once a week, the containers from each classroom throughout the school are gathered, and the class with the most tokens wins a class reward. The different color tokens are used in specific settings. The school is to keep data on the numbers of different color tokens that are dispersed. These data are particularly helpful when a problem arises on the playground because the team can check and see if the playground people are handing out sufficient tokens.

"Scoobies" Some schools give scoobies to the students. Scoobies are inexpensive, small colorful cloth stretch bands that are typically used for weaving potholders on a small loom. They can be found in most craft stores. Scoobies are particularly convenient when a teacher is trying to improve positive interactions. For example, teachers can start the day by putting twenty scoobies on their left arm and set a goal to distribute all the scoobies paired with a compliment or positive interaction before lunch time. Students can wear their scoobies until the end of the day and record the number of scoobies earned on a class list sheet. When a certain number of scoobies has been earned, students can enter the weekly schoolwide drawing. Other ideas for scoobies are to have students loop them together. When they have reached from one end of the room to another, they have earned a class activity. Or, the earned scoobies can be put around a bottle; when the bottle is covered, the class earns a special class activity. The scoobies can also be woven into squares for a potholder, cover, or quilt.

Students could also save their individually earned scoobies and trade them in for privileges on the menu. For example, they could go to lunch or recess two minutes early, be first in line, sit in the teacher's chair for a period, have extra computer time, or listen to music for a short time.

Chips Another school gives poker chips. Each teacher has his or her own color, and each classroom has a poster with the students' names and a small cardboard container underneath each name. As students receive their chips, they deposit them in their container. As with the class list, the teacher can quickly see which students have not received a chip and which adult is not giving out chips, as each adult has a different color.

Key Elements: Generosity and Chance

To be effective, the tokens should be passed out generously. They are a representation of the teacher's positive regard for the student and a signal that they have been noticed doing the right things. They should not be reserved and given primarily for doing special things like cleaning up the classroom, but for doing the routine behaviors that make for a successful school: following the rules, staying focused in class, handing in homework, getting to class on time, and so forth.

> Recognition should not be reserved for doing special things, rather for routine positive behaviors that are the foundations of a successful school.

What makes it all work is randomness and the element of chance: you never know when you will get a surprise.

- Getting the ticket itself should be a surprise.
- Randomize how you hand out the tickets.
- Don't always give them at the same time or for the same behavior.
- When passing out tickets in a location like the cafeteria, circulate throughout the room and give a ticket to only one student at every table at a time.
- Give a ticket to about every five to seven kids in line.
- Go back and do it again.
- Keep circulating.
- Make it unpredictable.
- Be generous.
- When giving a ticket, say the student's first name and the behavior that earned the ticket.

Instant Winners

Some children are not as motivated by the drawings as others. This is probably due to their calculation that they have little chance of winning or because the prizes themselves are not very motivating. To increase the probability of winning, several schools have modified their tickets by including an instant winner in each packet of tickets at a rate of one instant winner per 20 tickets. Students with instant-winners may submit their ticket to the office or to their teacher at an appropriate time for an instant prize, usually a special privilege. The instant-winner factor increases the chances of winning sufficiently to engage students who would otherwise not be motivated by the schoolwide or class drawings, yet it maintains the element of chance.

Students Who Don't Turn in Their Tickets

There are some students who don't turn in their tickets. Some staff members see this as another instance of misbehavior and try to figure out ways to encourage students to submit them. We seldom see tickets being thrown away, either in the trash or on the floors of schools. We suspect that something else is going on.

Students without Problem Behavior

It is important to think about the possible motivations for this behavior. It is true that the system will not be motivating for a few students and that they will simply throw the tickets away or even refuse them when offered. If the student is one who consistently follows the rules, then he or she may have decided that the system is not necessary and doesn't apply to him or her. If this is the case, we suggest that you let them be. The purpose of the program is to encourage desired behaviors. Obviously, these children don't need the system.

It also may be helpful to informally ask the student how he or she feels about the tickets. Respect the student's opinion, and ask what would be helpful. The student may offer ideas that you hadn't considered.

Discouraged or Resistant Students with Behavior Problems

The *few* students who seldom follow the rules may have a different motivation. They may have decided that the system or the reinforcement menu is "stupid." This label could, for some, mean that they are discouraged by their lack of success and defend themselves by nonparticipation; for others, it may mean that they don't find the rewards rewarding enough. For the former, investigate ways that they can access the golden ratio of 4:1 positive to negative interactions with teachers. For the latter, interview them to find out what types of things might be more reinforcing and how the menu could be expanded.

Some students, however, may resist the program because they resent the fact that it is an attempt to alter their behavior. They may need an individualized program with more a powerful, predictable, or personalized reinforcer to help them change their behavior.

Saving Tickets

Interestingly, there is a much more common reason for students not turning in their tickets: They really like them and are hoarding them to see how many they can collect. Some students will save hundreds of tickets and even purchase special wallets to carry them around in and keep them safe. Some students like to save their tickets for display, and other students want to take their tickets home.

Others may have calculated that they will have better odds of winning if they turn in a few hundred tickets at one time, or they may just like to save them. Clearly, the tickets are motivating to them. We suggest that you establish the rule that the tickets are the property of the students who receive them and that they may do what they want with them.

Allowing for Choice in Receiving Tickets

Some schools have decided to have a continuum for providing tickets. The continuum extends from giving a ticket with a positive comment to telling the student, *"You are being respectful by walking with your voice off. Would you like a ticket?"* Students who are intrinsically motivated, or for other reasons don't want them, might opt out of getting a ticket.

Saving for a Cause

These examples may explain hoarding, but they also can be intentionally used as part of your school's program to increase the students' interest in obtaining tokens.

Holiday Store In one K–8 school where students like to save their tickets, the team decided to try to have a holiday store managed by 8th graders. Students and staff collected small household items, jewelry, books, games, and toys through donations and garage sales. Before winter break, a store was established in the hallway. Students could come and buy gifts for their family with their tickets. The gifts were wrapped and taken home. This program became highly successful. Many students saved most of their tickets all year so that they could get gifts for their family and friends.

> Students that have more choice in how to use their tokens may be more motivated to earn and receive them.

School Garden Another school started a garden. Students could buy seeds and small plants as well as time to work in their garden spot. Some classrooms had a classroom garden where everyone worked together to take care of the garden. When the vegetables were ready, students picked and cleaned them and made salads. Other students would buy garden items to take home with their tickets.

Volunteering Time In several high schools, students saved their tickets to buy time to volunteer in community settings, such as nursing homes, automotive garages, shops, and hospitals.

Another school used the tickets to buy the opportunity to go to elementary or middle schools to teach recess games, art, music, computer skills, or other pastimes they wanted to share with younger students.

Cafeteria Ideas

The noise level in cafeterias is often a concern for supervisors. Cafeterias typically have terrible acoustics and even if students are using indoor voices, it can sound extremely loud and irritating to supervisors. We have found that it can be helpful to videotape a lunch session in the cafeteria and replay it with the sound off. If you observe students sitting at tables, eating, talking, and being respectful, then turn the sound on and see what a difference that makes. Following are some ideas that have been used to improve cafeteria behaviors and staff ability to identify positive behaviors.

Visual Cues Several schools decided to implement the following in addition to handing out schoolwide tokens for being safe, responsible, and respectful in the cafeteria: Use large visual signs to prompt students. For example, when it's time to dismiss a table, rather than tell the kids, simply put up a table tent saying, "Please line up at the windows" or "Please line up at the back wall."

Alternative Indoor Recess One school with 600 students was able to provide an alternative supervised recess in the library for about 50 students who preferred staying in or for students who had challenging behavior when they were outside for recess. These students were invited to stay in the library for recess. Large purple cards labeled "Library" were created. During lunch, the lunchroom supervisor simply walked around the lunchroom holding up the purple cards. Students who raised their hand would get a purple library pass and would go to the library instead of outside recess. This was also a nonthreatening way to provide an alternative recess for students who had a difficult time handling outside recess (thereby providing a Tier II or higher intensity intervention for recess behavior).

Eat First, Talk After In other cafeterias where children were throwing away large amounts of food, music was played for the first ten minutes of lunchtime. During this time, students were not allowed to talk. As soon as the music stopped, they could visit with each other until the end of the lunch period. These schools were amazed at how much less food was thrown away. Students actually took time to eat instead of talk.

Small-Group Lunches In schools where small groups of students are served or where students eat in the classroom, it is nice when students wait until everyone is seated before beginning to eat. The teacher leads a relaxing activity, such as everyone holding a finger up to his or her mouth, taking a deep breath, and pretending to blow out a candle. This is repeated three times. In other words, students take three deep breaths and slowly release them. This relaxes students before they start to eat. In other classrooms, students sit with their food in front of them and recite a short poem before starting to eat. Others do a short sign-language activity. The goal of all these activities is to relax the students before they start to eat.

Activity-Based Reinforcers

Activity-based reinforcers are special activities or privileges that can be used as rewards. For example, students will often work very hard for the privilege of eating lunch in a special place. This doesn't have to be a special lunch, just a special place, such as the classroom, the stage, or even just a special table.

> The secret is that the reward activity is not something that everyone gets to do all of the time. It is a special and rare treat.

Most students are highly motivated by activity-based reinforcers, like the following.

- Eating lunch in a special place
  - in the classroom
  - on the stage with friends
  - in a café
    » the café can be on the stage, in the library, or in the teachers' lounge
    » the café can simply be a special table decorated with a tablecloth and flowers
- Eating lunch with a preferred adult
- Going to the front of the lunch line
- Having recess in the classroom or library
- Riding in the red wagon (a cart used to carry lunches and library books)
- Using an iPod during independent work

One 4th grade teacher we know is very protective of her lunch break and doesn't want to spend it with kids. This teacher has great success with increasing the rate at which students hand in homework by giving away Golden Tickets to students who have 100% homework completion in a 3-week time block and to instant winners. When the student chooses to present the ticket to the lunchroom supervisor, the students get to do something that is otherwise forbidden . . . cut in line.

Younger children and many older children are highly motivated by such privileges as:
- Being first in line for lunch or recess
- Being the door holder
- Passing out papers or other materials
- Helping the teacher in some way
- Getting extra computer time
- Being the messenger
- Being the new-student helper

Older students may also enjoy:
- Having extra time in the gym
- Taking pictures for publication in a newsletter or for posting on a bulletin board
- Making intercom announcements
- Receiving homework passes
- Using an iPod
- Getting food or beverage treats

It is not coincidental that these privileges are frequently accompanied by just a little positive individual attention. At one school where the students had behaved wonderfully during an all-school assembly, the staff team decided to reward the students by having an all-school 15-minute recess. The entire school got to go outside with the entire staff team. The students loved it. This reward combines many good elements: generosity, elements of chance, and novelty, and it is activity based.

> Adult attention is the most powerful reinforcer there is.

The Power of Choice

The other significant factor in a successful reinforcement plan is the power of choice. We suggest that you take quite a bit of time to develop a schoolwide list of simple, age-appropriate activity reinforcers so that you have a menu from which students can choose. This can be helpful when a student is selected in a schoolwide drawing or for teachers to select from when planning their classroom-based reinforcement practices.

Lists of menu choices can be generated in different ways:
- Each teacher can brainstorm a list with his or her homeroom.
- Students can develop lists at home as a homework activity.
- Someone can compile the classroom lists and develop a schoolwide list.
- School staff can generate a list and let students decide which activities would work.

Be thoughtful about what you put on the list. It needs to be motivating for students, but the adults have to be able to live with it and follow through on allowing the students to carry out their choices. A model list is provided for you here.

Sample Rewards Menu

- Invite a friend from another class into the room for indoor recess.

- Invite a friend for recess in the library.

- Use a beanbag chair for a day.

- Read to someone else (or a younger child) for 20 minutes.

- Add 15 points to your class reward system.

- Keep a stuffed animal on your desk for a day.

- Write in ink for a day.

- Have a special sharing time to teach something to the class.

- Invite your teacher to have lunch in the lunchroom with you.

- Use a rolling chair all day.

- Lead a class game.

- Call home with a positive message.

- Have the teacher phone parents to tell them how wonderful you are.

- Be a class helper in another class for 30 minutes.

- Use a calculator for typical mental math problems.

- Use a computer for typing instead of writing by hand.

- Use an iPod during independent work time.

- Leave class five minutes early.

One of the biggest surprises that teachers often experience is when students choose items from the list that the teachers don't think are motivating. One of the most popular items on the above list is having the teacher phone home to tell a parent "how wonderful you are." It often takes teachers by surprise and is always a very positive relationship builder. The kids love it, and so do the parents. Choice is a very powerful element in a successful plan.

> Students love when their teacher calls home and tells their parents how wonderful they are doing in school.

More Tricks of the Trade

Happy Grams/Telegrams Happy grams are given by students and teachers to each other. A tag board poster is prepared with mailboxes (e.g., library pockets) that have the names of each student and adult who works in the classroom. Depending on the age level of the students, preprinted happy grams (e.g., "I saw you . . . Good for you! Signed . . .") or blank notepaper can be made available in an additional envelope on the poster.

Students are taught to write positive comments to a peer or to an adult and put the happy gram in a pocket. The teacher can review the happy grams before they are retrieved, remove inappropriate comments, and note which students haven't received any. During the course of the week, the teacher can prompt kids to write to those who haven't received any. The teacher can add notes as well. At the end of the week, students can empty their mailbox and read the positive notes and keep them. A student can also use tickets to buy the opportunity to empty the mailboxes and hand-deliver the notes to each student.

Have You Filled a Bucket Today? There is an awesome book *Have You Filled a Bucket Today?* (McCloud & Messing, 2007). Many teachers use this book to promote positive interactions. Using a children's book is also good because it can help support student literacy development as well as encourage good behavior. Using this method, teachers will put buckets on a bulletin board with each student's name on one. Students are encouraged to drop positive notes into the buckets of their peers. Occasionally, the buckets are emptied and the positive comments are shared. Adults can drop positive comments in the buckets as well.

Positive Notes Home Another effective way to inform students and parents that the student had a positive day is to send home a positive note. Below is an example.

Positive Notes

Student's Name: _____ Date: _____

YOU ARE AWESOME!

Today I noticed that you . . .
→ Worked cooperatively with others
→ Followed directions
→ Worked quietly
→ Completed your work
→ Volunteered to help
→ Treated others with respect
→ Other: _____
→ Other: _____

Signed by: _____

Good Job!

Star or Sunshine of the Week A large poster is prepared with a spot for a large picture of one student's face. This spot has several yellow rays coming from it. In large words, write "Sunshine of the Week." Each week, a student is chosen (or buys) the opportunity to be the sunshine. During the week, individual students and teachers write positive comments about why this student is sunshine. At the end of the week, the student takes the poster home to keep. In one school, a parent who was an artist made a sunshine chair for each classroom. The sunshine student got to sit in the chair for the entire week. The photo below shows an example of a sunshine chair.

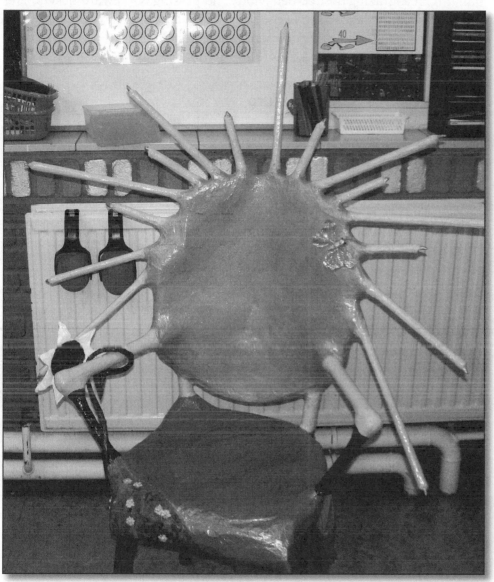

Credit: SBO "de Wijngaard," Huizen, The Netherlands.

Reinforcing Staff Members

The biggest problem with any reinforcement system is sustaining it. One problem is financial resources, but the most difficult problem is maintaining adult commitment. It is so easy to get distracted, forget to reinforce the desired behaviors, and begin to nag and punish once again. To counteract this tendency and to build the reinforcement system into the culture of your school, it is necessary for the administration and the office staff to take an active part. The principal must be observed circulating throughout the building, recognizing desired behaviors, and passing out reward tickets. The principal, with the assistance of the office staff, must also consistently notice the staff members who are implementing the system. Figure 18 shows how staff commitment can affect school culture.

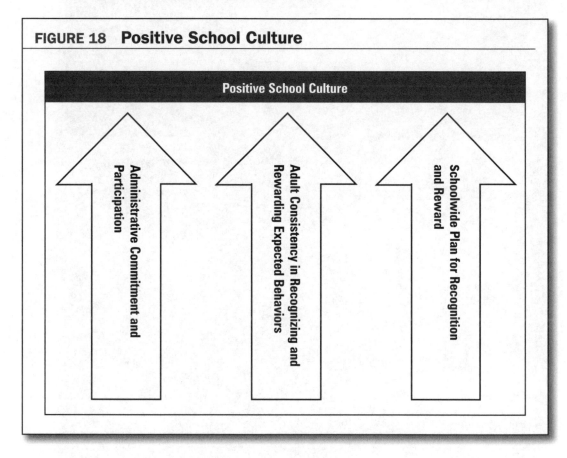

FIGURE 18 Positive School Culture

Piggybacking on Student Tickets There are many ways for the principal to reinforce the ticket system. At several schools, the teacher who initials a ticket drawn in the schoolwide drawing also receives recognition. One school has recently purchased a raffle drum where all the tickets for the last several weeks are stored. During each staff meeting, and occasionally at other times, tickets are drawn from the drum, and small prizes are awarded to the teacher who signed the ticket. These prizes are not expensive. In some schools, teachers win privileges, such as a free recess, going home an hour early, handing their class over to the principal for one hour, or coming to work one hour later on a specific day.

> Administrators must actively take part in the system for it to be sustained and vital to school culture. They must recognize and reward staff for their efforts to recognize and reward students and each other!

Whole-Class Behavior Tickets We know of one school that has three different kinds of reward tickets. In addition to the individual student tickets, there are also larger yellow and purple tickets that are presented to teachers.

Any staff member may present the yellow tickets to a colleague when he or she observes an entire class following the schoolwide rules. Examples include:

- Everyone in the class focusing on their work in the computer lab.
- Everyone in the class participating positively during music class.
- Everyone in the class walking quietly and in line in the hallway.

In one school, an envelope labeled "Class Tickets" and a pen is taped on the wall next to the hallway rules. This way, the tickets are easily available. When a teacher wants to give a ticket to an entire class, he or she simply takes a ticket out of the envelope, signs it, and gives it to the classroom teacher or to a student with a compliment to the entire class.

Teachers will often reward the class with points for their class reinforcement systems, but the teacher is also recognized for doing a good job.

Staff-Specific Behavior Tickets Another idea is for the principal and his or her designees to award purple tickets to teachers and other staff members who are engaging in desired behaviors. This may include being observed passing out reward slips, engaging in teacher leadership activities, and so on. When a teacher collects five purple slips, the steps can be traded in for a latte certificate at the coffee truck that regularly visits the school. Teachers like being recognized for their contributions, and the culture of noticing positive contributions is reinforced. Sometimes, students will ask if they can give a purple ticket to their teacher because of something that the teacher has done. This can be very rewarding.

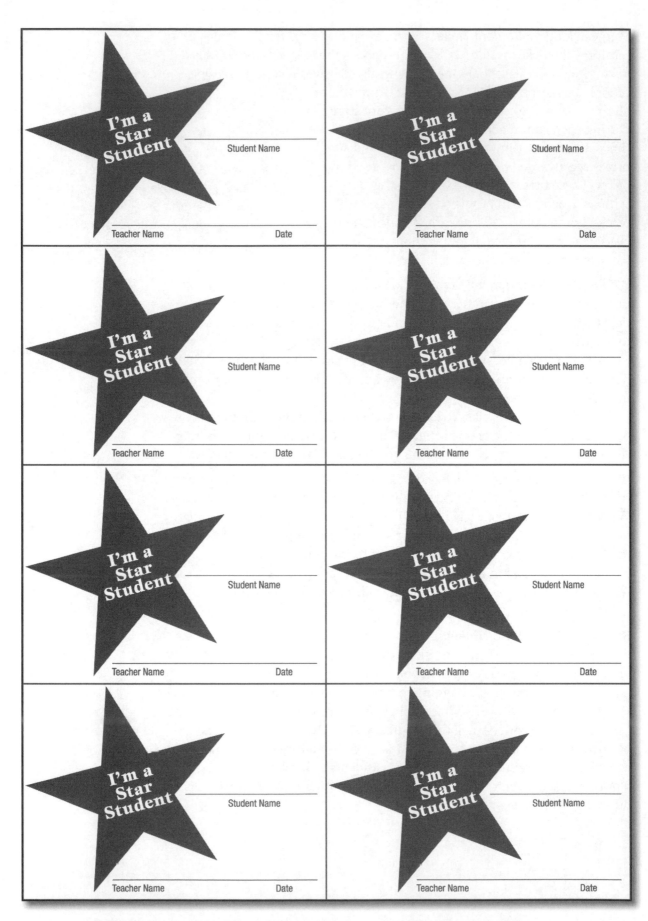

Student Name	Points Earned	Student Name	Points Earned

For Being...

Teacher	Date	Teacher	Date

Student Name	Points Earned	Student Name	Points Earned

For Being...

Teacher	Date	Teacher	Date

Student Name	Points Earned	Student Name	Points Earned

For Being...

Teacher	Date	Teacher	Date

Student Name	Points Earned	Student Name	Points Earned

For Being...

Teacher	Date	Teacher	Date

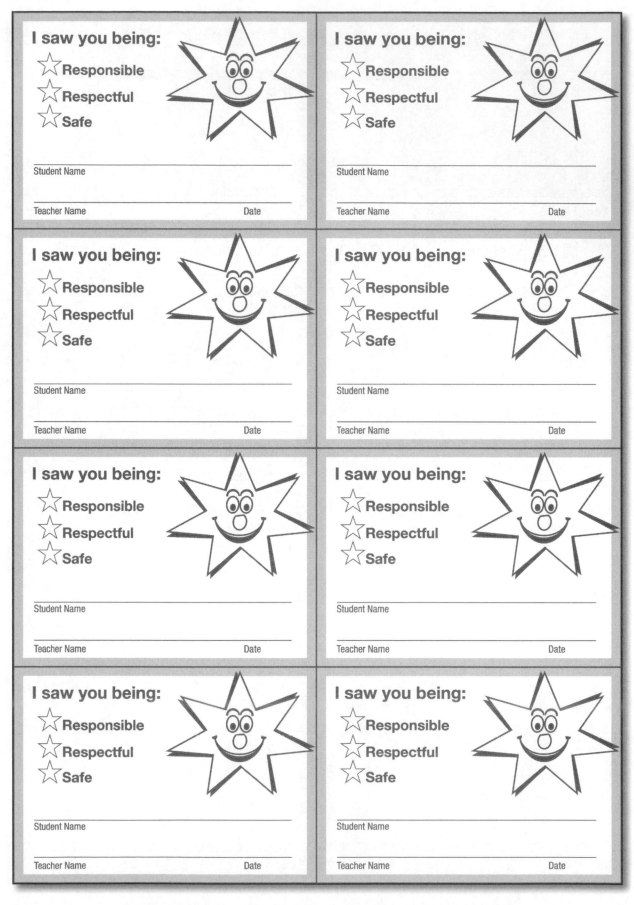

I saw you being:
☆ Responsible
☆ Respectful
☆ Safe

Student Name

Teacher Name   Date

I saw you being:
☆ Responsible
☆ Respectful
☆ Safe

Student Name

Teacher Name   Date

I saw you being:
☆ Responsible
☆ Respectful
☆ Safe

Student Name

Teacher Name   Date

I saw you being:
☆ Responsible
☆ Respectful
☆ Safe

Student Name

Teacher Name   Date

I saw you being:
☆ Responsible
☆ Respectful
☆ Safe

Student Name

Teacher Name   Date

I saw you being:
☆ Responsible
☆ Respectful
☆ Safe

Student Name

Teacher Name   Date

I saw you being:
☆ Responsible
☆ Respectful
☆ Safe

Student Name

Teacher Name   Date

I saw you being:
☆ Responsible
☆ Respectful
☆ Safe

Student Name

Teacher Name   Date

I was seen being...

_____

Student Name
_____

Teacher Name   Date

I was seen being...

_____

Student Name
_____

Teacher Name   Date

I was seen being...

_____

Student Name
_____

Teacher Name   Date

I was seen being...

_____

Student Name
_____

Teacher Name   Date

I was seen being...

_____

Student Name
_____

Teacher Name   Date

I was seen being...

_____

Student Name
_____

Teacher Name   Date

I was seen being...

_____

Student Name
_____

Teacher Name   Date

I was seen being...

_____

Student Name
_____

Teacher Name   Date

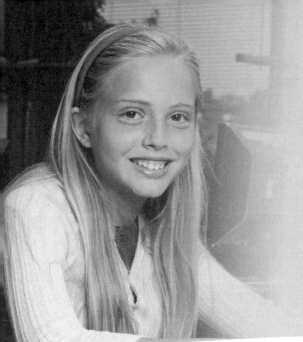

CHAPTER 8

Systematic Supervision of Common Areas

Background: Supervision Versus Effective Supervision

Systematic supervision is a term applied to a method of student behavior (Smith & Sprague, 2004). Systematic supervision methods work well in the following situations:

1. Large areas

2. High census (a lot of students)

3. Lightly staffed (one or two adults for every 80+ students)

4. Unstructured, student-directed activities (such as playgrounds, cafeterias, and hallways)

Systematic supervision techniques also work very well in classrooms and other medium- to small-group activities or areas (Colvin, Sugai, Good, & Lee, 1997; De Pry & Sugai, 2002).

It is important to emphasize that simply maintaining an adult presence in common areas and merely attending to inappropriate behaviors is an insufficient and ineffective behavior practice. Common area supervisors must also:

1. Develop and state the rules.

2. Effectively and efficiently teach the rules.

3. Effectively and efficiently enforce the rules.

4. Provide frequent monitoring and positive feedback to students.

In Chapters 5 and 6, you learned about the importance of developing and communicating a common set of behavioral expectations. This is particularly important in common areas, as they can be some of the most problematic areas in a school (Lewis, Colvin, & Sugai, 2000).

OBJECTIVES

▸ Define systematic supervision

▸ Describe systematic supervision techniques

▸ Develop a systematic supervision plan for one area of your school

▸ Assess common areas for supervision needs

Teaching Common Area Behavior Expectations

Common area expectations are typically taught in context (e.g., hallways, cafeteria, bus, classroom, or playground) at least once toward the beginning of the school year and 10 to 20 times a year in the classroom. It should be noted, however, that common-area behavior may need additional support in terms of teaching and practice in context. That is the main reason for using corrections as the universal consequence for low-level, minor misbehavior. In addition, common-area supervisors may find it useful to develop and teach from a more formal lesson plan in certain situations: when minor problem behavior is common among the student body, when misbehavior rates are high, or before certain times of the year when increased minor misbehaviors are anticipated in a specific common area. Use the **Expected Behavior Lesson Plan** format from Chapter 6 to develop lessons to meet these needs.

Staff members often focus on punishing disruptive behavior in common areas, but as we discussed in Chapter 7, students with behavior problems will not make meaningful educational or behavioral progress unless they are taught more functional skills (i.e., positive behaviors) to use in those areas.

Activity: **Develop Supervision-Friendly Common Area Rules**

Use what you've learned to formalize rules for a common area in your school in a way that will work for the adults supervising.

1. Take out a copy of your school's **Defining Schoolwide Expectations Worksheet** (matrix from Chapter 5) and work with your supervisory team (or other pertinent group).

2. Use the umbrella rules (be safe, be responsible, and be respectful).

3. Refer to (or add to) the list of the common areas to be addressed (e.g., playground, hallways, cafeteria, etc.).

4. Pick one common area for which your team will define the expectations and complete the behavior expectation matrix.

Figure 19 provides an example playground rule matrix (Smith & Sprague, 2004). Use this and your rule matrix to decide if additional detail is needed in your schoolwide plan.

FIGURE 19 **"Playing by the Rules": Playground Rules and Expectations from the Systematic Supervision Program**

Safe	Responsible	Respectful
• Keep hands, feet, body, and objects to yourself. • Stay in the designated area.	• Follow the directions of all adults the first time. • Use equipment properly. • Help others if they are in trouble. • Take proper care of the property of others, the school, and yourself.	• Use good/appropriate language. • Follow game rules. • Be a good sport. • Line up and walk quietly to and from the playground.
Report these things to an adult (supervisor, teacher, principal, or other school staff person). 1. When someone is doing something dangerous that may harm themselves or others (throwing rocks or sticks, smoking, using playground equipment in a dangerous manner, etc.).	2. When someone gets hurt. 3. When someone is being mean to you or to another student (bullying, threatening, or teasing). 4. When someone steals or vandalizes something. 5. When there is a fight. 6. When you see a stranger on or around the playground or school.	7. When you find broken playground equipment. 8. When you see or find something that doesn't belong at school or on the playground (a broken bottle; a knife or other weapon; beer cans; sharp objects, like nails or needles; a cigarette lighter or matches; etc.).

The Skills of Systematic Supervision

There are seven major skills in a comprehensive and systematic supervision approach. We describe each in Table 3 and cover them in more detail.

> Hall duty shouldn't be just standing by your door during transition times. Effective supervision in common areas requires mastery of specific skills and is critical to schoolwide behavior.

TABLE 3 Systematic Supervision Skills

	Feature	Elements/Components
1.	Movement	a. Constant b. Randomized c. Targets known problem areas
2.	Scanning	a. Constant b. Targets both appropriate and inappropriate behaviors c. Targets known problem areas d. Uses both visual and aural cues e. Increases opportunities for positive contact
3.	Positive Contact	a. Friendly, helpful, open demeanor b. Systematic, noncontingent c. High rate of delivery
4.	Positive Reinforcement	a. Immediate b. Contingent on behavior c. Consistent (with behavior and across staff team) d. High rate
5.	Instructional Responses to Problem Behavior	a. Immediate b. Contingent on behavior c. Nonargumentative, noncritical d. Specific to behavior e. Systematic: correct, model, lead, test, and retest f. Consistent (with behavior and across staff team)
6.	Respond to Problem Behavior with Choices and Mild Consequences	a. Neutral, businesslike demeanor b. Give the student a choice and time to respond c. Nonargumentative, noncritical d. Consistent (with behavior and across staff team) e. Fair, nonarbitrary, and preplanned consequences
7.	Team-Driven Supervision Planning	a. Administrative buy-in and support b. Regular weekly meetings c. Intervention and behavior data collection and analysis d. Inter-staff participation and communication e. Part of a schoolwide behavior support program

Movement

Why is movement important? There are many reasons, but the most important are as follows.

- Greater visibility of, and direct observation by, the supervisor across more students, areas, and activities.
- More opportunity for supervisor-student contact, both positive and negative (remember the 4:1 rule).
- More opportunity for positive reinforcement of appropriate behavior.
- Greater likelihood of encountering and correcting covert inappropriate behaviors, such as bullying and harassment.

What constitutes effective movement? Movement should encompass three main practices in order to be effective and efficient: Supervisory movement should be continuous, planned, and deliberate.

First, movement should be continuous. Continuous movement tends to give students the impression that you're everywhere at once. Movement provides the opportunity to have positive contacts

> Movement should be continuous, planned (but unpredictable), and deliberate.

with more students and to stay in close proximity for behavior support.

Second, movement patterns should be somewhat randomized and unpredictable. If possible, supervisor movements should follow no regular or set pattern. Students become used to routines, and inappropriate behavior may be easier to hide when supervisory movement is too predictable. Although it is necessary for movements to have a plan that establishes close proximity to all students, areas, and activities being supervised, the patterns of movement should be varied from period to period and day to day.

Last, movement should be deliberate. This includes deliberate randomness of movement, deliberate continuous movement, and deliberate movement in response to behavior and problems.

Scanning

Common areas such as hallways, cafeterias, playgrounds, and free-time areas are typically high census (having a high students-to-adult ratio), are large and irregular in shape, and are difficult for a supervisor to effectively cover. As we have discussed, high rates of movement can greatly increase supervisor effectiveness in these areas. But what about the more distant, obscure, or hidden areas outside the immediate presence of the supervisor as he or she moves about? The mastery and use of scanning techniques can give the supervisor an effective long-range tool.

Too often we tend to observe only those things close at hand—especially in high-activity, high-census situations. It is natural to focus on activities or individuals that are close by. However, developing the ability

> Scanning increases the range of the supervisor beyond the immediate proximity.

to systematically scan more distant parts of an area and recognize signs that may indicate problem behavior is invaluable to effective common-area supervision. Some of the more useful scanning methods and techniques follow.

Maintain Constant Visual Movement Engage in constant visual movement, whether standing, walking, or talking. Shift your field of view with attention to visual indicators that target behaviors. This type of scanning practice effectively expands the supervisor's area of proximity by making eye contact with students outside the supervisor's immediate location. This practice also increases the opportunity for positive visual contact and reinforcement: Supervisors should smile and wave to students who are engaged in expected, appropriate behaviors outside their immediate vicinity.

See Behavior Train yourself to look at the students' behaviors, not just their games, their clothes, their hair, and so forth. People tend to look at familiar individuals without attention to subtle contextual, physical, or behavior clues that may be signs of distress.

Listen for Problems Train yourself to listen for behavior. Visual cues are not always good or sufficient indicators of what may be happening. There are many aural cues signaling that a target behavior may be taking place at a distance, such as angry or whining and plaintive tones of voice, arguing, panicked voices, and bossy and authoritative voices or commands. Try to keep eyes in one direction and ears in another while scanning.

Get the Big Picture Train yourself to look at the big picture—not just one student or activity, but at as much activity as possible. People who watch students play often find themselves watching the game itself, instead of attending to the exhibited behaviors.

Broaden Awareness Train yourself to focus on as many different areas as you can. Start small and work to increase your field of awareness.

Recognize Problem Behavior Identify and attend to behaviors that are typically associated with problem behaviors, such as games breaking up for no apparent reason; students frowning and gesturing to others, perhaps angrily; students seemingly shrinking back from a peer or peers; quick, violent movements for unapparent reasons; someone running away from a peer or peers outside of any apparent game; scared looks; or someone making a fist or obscene gesture.

Attend to Triggers Train yourself to recognize situations that may precede problem behavior (see **Chapter 15: Responding to Escalating Behavior and Power Struggles**). As mentioned in the previous example, problem behaviors, such as aggression, are typically preceded by arguing, rough play, high states of arousal, or unsportsmanlike conduct and over-competitiveness. Supervisors who recognize these precursor behaviors and take immediate action can often stop the behaviors before they escalate.

Attend to Trouble Spots Train yourself to recognize potential trouble spots and scan them often. For example, tetherball is often a source of arguing, typically leading to verbal and sometimes physical aggression. Supervisors need to move around to all areas but keep an eye on the tetherball game for signs that something is interfering with the game (e.g., the game has stopped and someone is holding the ball and keeping it away from others).

Practice the Two-Minute Rule Maximize both movement and scanning time by minimizing the time spent dealing with problem behaviors. Use the Two-Minute Rule. If you can't solve a problem or correct a behavior in two minutes or less, then refer the problem to the office (depending on severity) or some other prearranged place. If the problem is not severe and processing with the student or students can wait, then defer lengthy intervention until after recess ends and students are back in class or other structured activities. Then, at a later time, the supervisor can finish correcting the student or students in private and without interfering with supervision during recess. When identified, solve or correct problems quickly, fairly, consistently, and as privately as possible and move on. Figure 21 (later in this chapter) provides an example of this Correction Sequence.

Positive Contact

Positive contact between a school's staff members and students should encompass a few specific elements. In general, staff members should project a friendly, helpful, and open demeanor, especially when in close proximity to students who are appropriately engaged and exhibiting expected behavior. Supervisors should cultivate a personal touch when in contact with students. This personal touch should establish the staff member's role as a caring member of the school community, fostering trust and respect with the students. In addition, staff members should pay attention to maintaining their authoritative role in the school community.

Positive contact can include:

- Smiling
- Waving
- Giving high-fives
- Conversing about something of interest to the student
- Greeting
- Remembering birthdays
- Asking about health, family, and so forth.
- Attending extracurricular events (sports, art shows, musical performances, etc.)
- Listening

Positive contact should be systematic. Positive contact establishes the conditions for appropriate behaviors, increasing the likelihood that they will occur while decreasing the incidence of inappropriate behaviors.

Positive contacts are noncontingent, rather than prompted by or based on a specific student behavior—as long as the behavior at the time is not inappropriate. Avoid inadvertently rewarding inappropriate behavior if at all possible.

> Staff should systematically pursue and create opportunities for positive contact with students.

Supervisors should strive to deliver a high rate of positive contact, using the student's first name when delivering it. It is recommended to maintain at least a four-to-one ratio of positive to negative contacts.

Positive contacts can provide opportunities to precorrect students concerning appropriate versus inappropriate behavior. Deliberately providing positive contact with those students who are at risk or high risk in terms of problem behavior may allow the supervisor to precorrect those students before they have a chance to misbehave.

Positive Reinforcement

In contrast to positive contact, positive reinforcement is contingent upon specific student behavior. That is, the student must demonstrate a specific appropriate behavior that has been targeted for reinforcement. Compare the two interactions below.

An example of positive contact is:

> *"Good morning, Jimmy. It's nice to see you!"*

An example of positive reinforcement is:

> *"Jimmy, I saw you helping Susan pick up all the things she spilled out of her backpack. That was very thoughtful. I'm going to give you a positive referral. I want you to know how much I appreciate what you did and how proud I am of you. You should be proud of yourself, too! You showed a lot of character."*

Notice that the staff member in this last example was very specific about the behavior being rewarded. Also note that the reward was paired with positive adult attention as well as a prompt for the student to acknowledge his own behavior.

Certain practices increase the effectiveness of positive reinforcement. First, reinforcement should be delivered immediately, as close to the expected behavior as possible. Any delay in the delivery of a reward lessens the likelihood that the student will associate the reward with the behavior targeted for reinforcement. Time lag between behavior and consequence (no matter whether the behavior was positive or negative) increases the chance that the consequence may be paired in the student's mind with an unrelated behavior. This decreases or eliminates the effectiveness of the consequence, which was to tie it to the specific desired behavior.

Second, positive reinforcement strategies need to be consistent, both in the behaviors reinforced and across staff members. If a student is reinforced for a certain behavior on one occasion but not on the next, either by the same or different staff members, then the student may be confused about exactly why the reinforcement was given. Staff members should be especially careful not to reinforce a behavior one time and inadvertently punish it the next time.

Third, positive reinforcement should follow the four-to-one ratio rule. High rates of positive reinforcement have been shown to be highly effective in increasing the likelihood that students will engage in the target behavior.

The reinforcement system for common areas should be an extension of the schoolwide reinforcement system. *All* children in the school should have access to positive reinforcement, even those who challenge the system. As covered in Chapter 7, a token economy (e.g., Scoobies, Tickets), or perhaps tangibles (e.g., candy, sports cards) coupled with specific adult praise, is a simple way of creating a consistent system of positive reinforcement. When used in combination with planned ignoring (see Chapter 13), tokens have been proven effective in reducing acting-out behavior.

Behavior is lawful; it happens for a reason. Behavior is functional; it serves a purpose. A person is likely to use behaviors that provide access to rewards that, in turn, increase the likelihood of that behavior recurring. To be useful, behaviors should be effective and efficient. This holds true for inappropriate as well as appropriate behavior.

Effective interventions address the function of the problem behavior and make it inefficient and less functional than some form of acceptable replacement behavior.

Rewards should be made public (except for those students who are embarrassed or somehow feel punished by public acknowledgement). Public display and delivery of rewards has a powerful modeling effect, a kind of vicarious reinforcement. When students see their peers get rewarded for good behavior, they are often motivated to display the same behaviors.

Implementing a Reward System in Common Areas

There are six issues to consider when implementing a schoolwide reward system on the playground or in other common areas. By addressing these issues and by planning for them, staff can help assure a successful application of the schoolwide reward and reinforcement system. The six issues are:

1. Attend to the behaviors you want.

2. Pick your battles.

3. Practice consistency.

4. Use rewards that students want.

5. Increase reinforcement before difficult times.

6. Reteach expected behaviors if inappropriate behaviors increase.

Planning should include attention to how rewards will be distributed and how or where backup rewards will be obtained. Systematic planning should also consider the possible barriers or problems in implementing the system in these common areas. In addition, it is always good to have established backup rewards lined up. Like anyone, students may get tired of a single type of reward, especially middle and high school students. Refer back to Chapter 7 for more information on positive reinforcement and to review the plan that you developed.

Instructional Responses to Problem Behavior

The use of corrective responses for inappropriate or low-level problem behavior is an effective and efficient first-step response. Instructional responses should be:

- Immediate
- Contingent on behavior
- Nonpersonal, nonargumentative, and noncritical
- Specific to behavior
- Systematic (correct, model, lead, test, and retest)
- Consistent (with behavior and among staff)

There are several key steps to an effective corrective strategy. First, define what you are requesting. Tell the students exactly what behavior is expected of them. Next, model it. Show the students what it is, what it looks like, and how it's done. Then, lead the students through the behavior sequence. After that, it is critical to have the students practice the behavior, making sure that they correctly practice the skills. It is essential to reward or otherwise acknowledge students for successful practice. If the students still do not "get it" or if they engage in incorrect behavior, then it will be necessary to reteach the skill. Last, it is very important to test the students' mastery of the skill. You can do this by either asking the students to show you the right way to behave in this common area or by watching for students using the skills in natural settings and routines.

> Reward the following:
> - Successful practice—such as at an adult's request during a correction
> - Spontaneous appropriate behavior—look for naturally occurring, expected behaviors

After correction for inappropriate behavior, it is important to look out for and acknowledge the students' use of the appropriate behavior. Supervisors should watch for students doing what is expected. Systematically look for students doing the right things and then reinforce them. Look for progress and attempts by students who are at risk. Some students need more than one correction and practice sequence before they begin to master the skill. For every student, correct errors immediately by reteaching appropriate behaviors with a consistent delivery of consequences.

In addition, it is highly recommended that supervisors communicate with other staff members. Inform other staff members concerning both positive and negative behaviors, behavior patterns, and intervention problems and successes regarding specific behaviors, common areas, and students. A staff that communicates is more consistent and effective in supporting appropriate student behavior and reducing inappropriate behavior.

Responding to Problem Behavior with Choices and Mild Consequences

Before correcting inappropriate behavior, be sure you have the facts straight. The following steps can be used as a general guide to delivering consequences effectively.

1. To the greatest extent possible, take the student(s) aside—never reprimand or potentially embarrass students in front of others if you can avoid it.

2. Review what you saw with the student(s) in a calm, businesslike, impersonal manner. Don't argue and don't be drawn into an argument. Define the problem behavior and establish a clear focus of the appropriate behavior.

3. Ask the student(s) to acknowledge the inappropriate behavior. Ask them to state the appropriate, expected behavior for the situation. If they can't or won't, state the appropriate, expected behavior and ask them to repeat it to you.

4. Give the student(s) choices on how to correct the problem behavior (e.g., "You can show me how to use the swing appropriately, or you will have to stand with me for five minutes.").

5. Tell the student(s) the school-prescribed consequences for the particular behavior (use the least aversive consequence indicated for the behavior). Follow school guidelines concerning repeated or chronic violations.

6. Apply the consequence immediately or as soon as practical.

Figure 20 provides an illustration of this algorithm. More detail is provided on this process in **Chapter 13: Preventive Interactions**.

FIGURE 20 **When a Problem Occurs**	
Supervisor defines problem and gives the student a direction, a correction, and/or a consequence.	
Student is compliant	*Student is noncompliant*
Supervisor acknowledges cooperation (thanks, praise, or reward).	Supervisor redirects and gives student choices for compliance (e.g., restate the expected behavior and do it the right way or you will face a small, negative consequence).

The Two-Minute Rule for Responding to Problem Behavior

Common areas typically have a high level of student engagement. This consists of lightly structured or unstructured student-directed activities, lots of students at any given time, and a high student-to-staff ratio. We call this the "bees in a jar" scenario. Students have been engaged in various school activities, many of them more structured and demanding, so they are typically restless and ready for social and recreational activities. They are like bees in a jar, cooped up in classrooms until we open the lid and let them go outside or to a common area. We tell them to have fun, but we also always say, "Don't do this and don't do that."

Staff persons supervising these areas need to be able to quickly, efficiently, and effectively convert problem behavior. Supervisors may have anywhere from 50–100 students to each adult present during a 15- or 20-minute recess. These numbers imply that supervisors can ill afford to spend 15, 10, or even five minutes trying to correct a problem. When a supervisor is engaged with a student or with a group of students, that supervisor is effectively "out of the picture" in terms of supervising and supporting the remaining students, areas, and activities.

The need for the supervisor to be able to correct a problem and move on has led to the development of the Two-Minute Rule. Simply put, if a supervisor can't successfully correct a problem behavior within one or two minutes, then that problem should be referred to an alternate setting and/or staff member for processing. If a student is compliant when confronted with a correction or consequence, then the process should take no more than a couple of minutes to complete.

If a student presents defiant, disrespectful, or noncompliant behavior in response to a correction or consequence, then the chances of that particular supervisor being able to successfully get the student back on track in a reasonable time without using threats or intimidation (never recommended) are probably slim to none.

By following these simple steps and by prearranging for alternate setting support, common-area supervisors can quickly correct problem behavior or make a determination that the problem needs to be referred to an alternate, more supportive setting. Figure 21 provides a narrated example of this method.

FIGURE 21 Correction Sequence Example

Here's how the Two-Minute Rule Correction Sequence works, with two scenarios: one for cooperative or classic response (stream one), and one for uncooperative student response (stream two).

Time 00:00 minutes

Problem Occurs: The supervisor is in the hallway on her way out to recess when Billy comes blasting by. The school rule is "no running in the hallways." Here's what the supervisor should do.

Time 00:05   **Supervisor's Instructional Response:** She would say something (using a calm, respectful voice) like, "Hold on Billy. You are running. What is the rule about hallways?"

[STREAM ONE]   **Cooperative Response:** Usually, Billy would tell her the rule, but if he either can't or won't, then the supervisor would tell him the expectation and have him repeat it: "Oh yeah! Walk in the hallways." The supervisor would then ask why ("Because it's safe!") or remind him that this is a safety issue, connecting the rule to the big idea or schoolwide rules.

Time 00:30   Then, the supervisor would ask Billy to go back a little distance and demonstrate walking (or some other positive practice). This is a classic instructional consequence sequence. Total time for completion: about one minute or so.

Time 00:30

[STREAM TWO]   **Uncooperative Student Response:** The supervisor stops Billy and asks him what the rule is, to go back and walk, and Billy is passively defiant. He just doesn't cooperate or comply, or perhaps he is overtly disrespectful, saying something like, "Forget it, you jerk!" or "I'm not doing it!" What does the supervisor do then? Well, let's take a look at the behavior. The supervisor is calm, reasonable, and respectful in confronting the problem behavior and interacting with Billy.

Time 01:00   Billy reacts with refusal and noncompliance, ignoring the request or perhaps socially withdrawing. Or, he reacts by being overtly defiant, disrespectful, or confrontational. Either way, it's very clear that the supervisor doesn't have a "running in the hallway" problem. The supervisor is most likely not going to be able to correct the original behavior in two minutes or less, much less satisfactorily deal with the subsequent defiant behavior, without resorting to lengthy and extreme measures, such as arguing, intimidation, or threats of punishment or direct punishment.

Time 01:30   Billy is exhibiting "red flag" behavior that says he needs additional supports—the kind provided by the principal, dean, counselor, school psychologist, or other designated staff resource. Furthermore, this is a problem that should not be dealt with in the hallway or in other common areas where there are other students present, if at all possible. In this case, Billy must be referred to an alternate support setting. Total time for completion: about two minutes, maximum.

Reviewing the Behavior and Subsequent Actions

What Happened? OK! Now think back to the first example of Billy in the breezeway. The supervisor stopped him and he was compliant—doing what the supervisor asked. What should take place now? All too often, that is the end of it as far as adults are concerned. But let's think about what just happened. The supervisor "busted" Billy, and he may be angry or upset and probably embarrassed. Here is what it looks like: Billy is pulled aside and busted for running when the rule is to walk. Now the supervisor asks him to stand there and tell the supervisor the rule and then to go back to show the supervisor how it should be done.

Acknowledge Compliance When students are compliant, supervisors need to acknowledge it! Remember, we are striving for a four-to-one ratio of positive interactions to negative or corrective interactions. This is the perfect time to finish this corrective consequence in a positive, reinforcing manner. After Billy complies, the supervisor should tell him, "Thank you Billy. You showed a lot of character. I appreciate the way you respectfully followed directions. I am proud of you, and you should be proud of yourself. Here's a Bronco Buck for being so respectful!"

Don't Forget the Praise! The supervisor should be sincere. If a behavior is important enough for her to correct, then its flip-side is important enough for her to acknowledge. The acknowledgement should be designed to reward or reinforce student compliance and the positive practice of the expected behavior. Acknowledgement should include praise and perhaps a tangible (like a Bronco Buck or other small token), paired with specific, positive, and sincere adult attention for the appropriate behavior, and then further paired with a prompt to self-reinforce.

Remember the Goal After all, what is our goal in terms of behavior for our students? It is to self-manage their own behavior. Some kids already do this—it will not hurt to acknowledge them as well. The rest of the kids need our help and support to learn how to successfully self-manage their behavior. Any consequence that will successfully and effectively change behavior needs to be based on the positive support and acknowledgement of expected, appropriate behavior.

Team-Driven Supervision Planning

The final feature of systematic supervision is team-based planning. Team-based interventions are considered more stable over time, and team-driven activities are more sustainable and consistent over time. The supervision team serves three important functions:

1. It collects data: It serves as the basis for behavioral data collection and analysis.

2. It responds based on the data: It decides on, develops, and implements intervention plans and activities based on specific behavioral data.

3. It communicates: It disseminates information about behavior and interventions to the rest of the school community.

Like with the schoolwide behavior support team, there are five critical features of an effective supervision team:

1. Administrative buy-in and support.

2. Regular weekly meetings.

3. Intervention and behavior data collection and analysis.

4. Inter-staff participation and communication.

5. Part of a schoolwide behavior support program.

As it is true for maintaining a positive school culture, administrator buy-in and support is the first and most important feature of an effective and sustainable systematic supervision program. Without the support, commitment, and participation of the school administration, the effectiveness and sustainability of a supervision team is seriously compromised, and it is likely to fail. Likewise, the establishment and maintenance of regular weekly meetings is essential to the functions of the supervision team, particularly in terms of data collection, data analysis, and intervention planning, development, and implementation. These are the most important functions of the supervision team. Without effectively performing these activities, subsequent behavior support measures will be, at best, happenstance and, at worst, detrimental.

Another function of the supervision team includes participation and communication between staff members. Effective behavior-support activities are based on schoolwide programs. This implies that all staff participate and effectively communicate with all other members of the school community. Communication between, and the participation of, all school staff will help ensure critical elements of consistency across settings, as staff is so integral to successful behavior support programs. Finally, the supervisor team and its activities should be viewed, valued, and treated as an important part of a schoolwide behavior support effort.

Activity: Supervision Planning

Visualize what supervision will look like at your school. Create a map, brainstorm and discuss areas and problems, and apply the skills you learned in this chapter to plan your supervisory team's response. Make a deliberate plan for success in a common area.

1. Get some poster paper and large magic markers.

2. Draw a map of your school's playground (or other common area, if applicable).

3. Identify problem areas on the map.

4. Draw out planned and purposeful movement patterns.

5. Outline the reinforcement and correction strategies to be used.

6. Discuss how you will train and support supervisors.

Activity: Assessing Common-Area Needs

As was initially discussed in Chapter 4 and covered to a degree in the common areas portion of the *Best Behavior* **Self-Assessment Survey**, it is necessary to focus special attention on common areas.

The **Checklist for Common-Area Supervision** provided is designed to allow deeper analysis of common areas and to support team planning and goal setting around common-area supervision plans. We recommend using the checklist to target specific objectives for improving common-area supervision. For example, if you rate item 4 (rocks and sticks removed from the playground) as a 1 (Not at all), then a plan to remove those hazards should be developed and carried out.

Complete the assessment with your colleagues and then set improvement goals and systematic supervision plans. Use the goals form at the end of Chapter 4, add to your matrix of behavior expectations from your work in Chapter 5, and create lesson plans using your school format developed in Chapter 6.

Checklist for Common-Area Supervision

School _____ Date _____

Circle your response indicating to what extent you think the items or features listed are present in your school common areas using the following 1–4 scale.

1 = Not at all . . . 4 = Extensive

Environmental Items and Features

1. Common areas are easily observable (unobstructed views) from any given position in the area. 1 2 3 4

2. It is easy for supervisors to make close physical contact with students in all common areas 1 2 3 4

3. Playground or recess equipment is safe 1 2 3 4

4. Rocks, sticks, and other potentially dangerous or hazardous objects or materials are removed from the playground and other common areas. 1 2 3 4

5. Access to and from the playground, recess, or free-time areas is easily supervised 1 2 3 4

6. Transition to and from the common area is safe and efficient (quick, orderly, and supervised with established routes and behaviors) 1 2 3 4

7. Procedures and behavioral expectations for all students entering and exiting common areas have been developed, taught to *all*, and practiced 1 2 3 4

8. Formal emergency or crisis procedures for students and staff on playgrounds and in other common areas have been developed and are practiced at least twice a year 1 2 3 4

9. There are adequate staff personnel in common areas (playgrounds, during recess and free time, etc.) to effectively supervise the number of students present. 1 2 3 4

10. Supervisors have a common attention signal or other cue that signals students when it is time to transition, stop activities, and so forth. 1 2 3 4

11. Common-area supervision staff has been trained in systematic supervision techniques and methods this year 1 2 3 4

12. A system of positive reinforcement is in place in all common-area settings. 1 2 3 4

13. Common-area supervision staff has weekly or biweekly team meetings (includes a school administrator) 1 2 3 4

14. A system for addressing minor problem behavior in common areas (during recess, on the playground, etc.) is in place and is practiced by all common-area supervision staff. 1 2 3 4

15. A system for addressing serious or major problem behavior in recess, playground, or other common areas is in place and is practiced by all common-area supervision staff. 1 2 3 4

16. Off-limits areas are clearly identified, taught to students and staff personnel, and known by all. 1 2 3 4

17. Students are restricted from access to unsupervised areas during recess and free time 1 2 3 4

Behavioral Concerns

18. Student-to-student arguing is a problem. 1 2 3 4

19. Students engage in "hands on others" behavior (grabbing, "rodeo hugs," etc.) 1 2 3 4

20. Students engage in play fighting 1 2 3 4

21. Students engage in rough play (pushing, shoving, tackling, etc.) 1 2 3 4

22. Students use disrespectful language with and against their peers 1 2 3 4

23. Students violate or ignore school playground, recess, free time, or other common-area behavioral expectations or rules 1 2 3 4

24. Students ignore playground, recess, free-time, or other common-area game rules. 1 2 3 4

25. Students tease other students 1 2 3 4

26. Students engage in name calling or other personally offensive language with other students. 1 2 3 4

27. Students limit-test with supervisors 1 2 3 4

28. Students are overtly disrespectful and defiant with supervisors. 1 2 3 4

29. Students verbally or physically threaten other students 1 2 3 4

30. Students engage in illegal activities (i.e., alcohol, tobacco, drugs, weapon carrying, etc.) 1 2 3 4

31. Students fight physically with each other. 1 2 3 4

32. Students bully and harass each other. 1 2 3 4

33. Students verbally or physically threaten supervisors 1 2 3 4

34. Supervisors are afraid of, or are intimidated by, some students. 1 2 3 4

35. Certain activities or games are more challenging, in terms of student behavior, than others 1 2 3 4

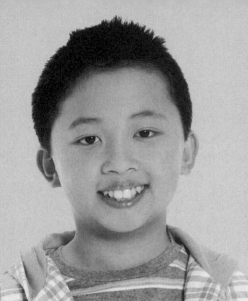

CHAPTER 9

Preventing and Responding to Aggressive Social Behavior, Bullying, and Harassment

Background: The Problem of Bullying and Harassment in School

No matter what their experiences or background with growing up are, most adults can remember at least one or two occasions during childhood where they were picked on, made fun of in front of peers, humiliated in some way, threatened, intimidated, or perhaps even beaten up (Knoff, 2007; Nishioka, Coe, Burke, Hanita, & Sprague, 2011; Swearer & Cary, 2007). Most can clearly recall the student or students who did these things, as well as details and circumstances surrounding the incident(s), even though they may not be able to remember much else from this period in their lives. Not surprisingly, such unpleasant situations are often initiated and sustained by the same student or students who are commonly identified as school bullies.

Gender and Bullying

Nearly everyone who has attended school has had some experience with bullying. In the vast majority of cases, such experience tends to be negative and emotionally searing, whether it plays out directly or indirectly. Perhaps the bullying that former students experienced resulted from other students picking on them or others, calling them names, teasing them, or somehow embarrassing them in public. Maybe the bully took something from them or deliberately broke a prized possession just to be mean, or the bullying student did it simply because he or she knew it could be done.

OBJECTIVES

▶ Describe the background of various forms of aggression, bullying, and harassment in schools, including forms of cyber bullying and misuse of information technology

▶ List the components of an effective response to these aggressive behaviors

▶ Discuss how a schoolwide bullying prevention strategy can integrate with *Best Behavior*

Overt, painful, and intimidating events of this nature are more likely characteristic of boys than girls, and they tend to occur in school settings where there is limited adult supervision and monitoring to prevent them. Girls also engage in bullying and peer harassment at rates that some researchers say approximately equal those of boys (Nishioka, et al., 2011); however, their bullying is typically expressed in more subtle behavioral forms, known as relational (or social) aggression (Lafferty, 2007). It is much more covert in nature and can occur in any setting at basically any time.

Those engaged in relational aggression tend to exclude others from activities; damage reputations through backbiting, lies, and rumors; try to ruin existing friendships through alienation; and engage in social manipulation and discrimination of others for indefensible reasons. Typically, girls do not display as much of the kind of overt, "in-your-face" bullying that is identified as characteristic of boys. It should be noted and stressed however, that both genders engage in both overt (direct, physical) and covert (indirect, social) bullying and harassment behavior. Although in the past it seems that male bullying consisted mostly of overt behaviors and female bullying was largely confined to covert behaviors, today this division along gender lines seems to be blurring in society, and especially in schools. It is obvious from media accounts, school reports, and legal actions that female aggression and violence is occurring on a daily basis. Likewise, any boy in school will tell you that boys regularly engage in social bullying. The fact is that both types of bullying and harassment can be extremely damaging to both the victim and the perpetrators, because long-term social and academic outcomes for bullies are so negative.

> Traditionally boys are implicated in more overt or physical bullying, while girls are implicated in more covert or relational bullying. However, this difference seems to be blurring in modern times.

Cyber Bullying

Cyber bullying, or electronic aggression, has emerged as another form of aggression as students have increased access to computers, cell phones, and other electronic devices (David-Ferndon & Hertz, 2009). This form of bullying refers to aggression that is executed through personal computers or cell phones to send e-mail, instant messages, text messages, or posts on social networks (Wang, Iannotti, & Nansel, 2009). Though research is limited about the extent of this new form of bullying, available studies show that 9–35 % of students report being the target of cyber bullying, and 4–21 % report being aggressors of bullying (David-Ferndon et al., 2009).

Most students report receiving electronic aggression via instant messaging, and about one quarter report being bullied by e-mail messages, in chat rooms, or through posts on websites. Fifth grade students report fewer problems with this type of bullying, and 8th grade students report the highest involvement (Williams & Guerra, 2007). These electronic communications can include teasing, threats, playing mean tricks, and spreading rumors that are intended to harm the emotional well-being, social status, and peer relationships of another student (Agatston, Kowalski, & Limber, 2007).

Cyber bullying presents unique challenges for students as well as for school administrators. Among these is the ability of the aggressor to remain anonymous—a situation that many believe increases the level of cruelty, mean tricks, and power of the student bullies. Another challenge is the capacity of the bully to engage in the aggressive behavior at any time of day. In fact, 70 % of students report that 70 % of the cyber bullying that they encounter—and the extent to which the bully can send or post damaging messages to a wide audience—occurs well beyond the classroom or school hours of operation (David-Ferdon et al., 2009; Agatston et al., 2007).

What Students Believe about Aggression

Beliefs about aggression tend to predict our behavior and influence our motivation to change (Huesmann & Guerra, 1997; Swearer & Cary, 2007). In a large study conducted in the western United States, students in grades 3–8 were asked an extensive set of questions (presented in Figure 22) about their beliefs and experiences regarding bullying and harassment in school (Nishioka, et al., 2011). This study indicates that certain types of aggression, in certain situations, are accepted among the students surveyed. If change is to happen, adults will have to drive it.

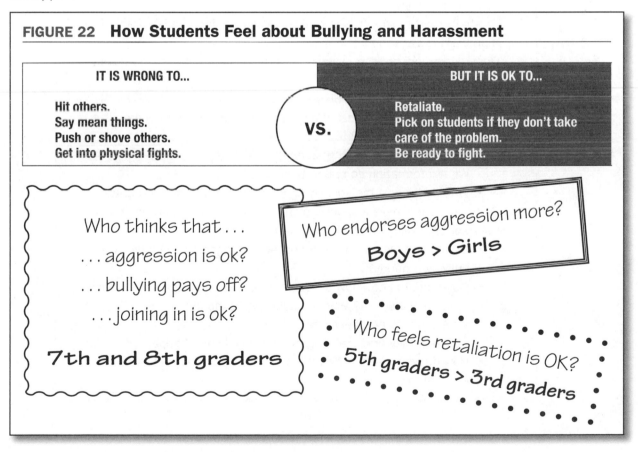

FIGURE 22   How Students Feel about Bullying and Harassment

IT IS WRONG TO...		BUT IT IS OK TO...
Hit others. Say mean things. Push or shove others. Get into physical fights.	**VS.**	Retaliate. Pick on students if they don't take care of the problem. Be ready to fight.

Who thinks that . . .
. . . aggression is ok?
. . . bullying pays off?
. . . joining in is ok?

7th and 8th graders

Who endorses aggression more?
Boys > Girls

Who feels retaliation is OK?
5th graders > 3rd graders

This study and many others clearly shows that aggression is prevalent in all grades. Lower grade levels (elementary and middle) report higher victimization from overt bullying, as aggression increases in grade five and peaks in middle school. Throughout middle and high school, relational aggression is a priority area for intervention. This study also suggests that we consider addressing students' beliefs about social and relational aggression.

Use the reflection below to write down your thoughts and knowledge about aggressive behavior (including overt and covert) and bullying in your school. Even better, sit with a colleague or a group of colleagues and discuss the questions listed below.

Reflection

Socially Aggressive Behavior and Bullying in Schools

1. Does our school have a schoolwide program, such as PBIS, that teaches prosocial skills to *all* students, creating a respectful social climate?

2. Does your school have a policy and curriculum that addresses the specific skills to prevent, report, and respond to cyber bullying, such as discussions about social network use, and safe, legal, and responsible use of technology?

3. To what extent is socially aggressive behavior, bullying, and harassment a problem in our school?

4. Does our school or school district have a specific policy about socially aggressive behavior/bullying?
   - If so, what does the policy require us to do?

5. What is the proper response if a student reports a socially aggressive behavior/bullying incident to me?
   - What should I say to the student?
   - What information do I need to collect?
   - Who do I report the socially aggressive behavior or bullying to?

6. Does our school have a specific plan or program on socially aggressive behavior or bullying prevention and response?
   - Do students know how to report socially aggressive behavior or bullying properly?
   - Do students know how to respond to a socially aggressive behavior or bullying incident? When should they respond?
     - When they are the victim?
     - When they are "standing by" and watching it happen?
   - How do we respond when the socially aggressive person/bully won't stop?

Changing a Destructive Peer Culture

Transforming the culture of bullying and harassment is perhaps our most formidable task in the area of school safety and discipline. This culture may not be of the schools making, but aside from families, schools are perhaps the only social institution capable of addressing it effectively. Addressing this problem is critically important and complex. Figure 23 provides a summary of the best practice recommendations.

FIGURE 23 **What Can We Do about Aggression and Bullying?**

1. Create a school culture that encourages communication.
   - Student-to-student, student-to-adult, and adult-to-student communication.
   - Respectful communication between all members of the school community.
   - Respectful use of electronic devices and all other forms of information and technology.

2. Create a school culture that encourages trust.
   - Promises to follow up are kept.
   - Students are listened to.
   - Students are supported and protected.

3. Understand the school's antibullying policies and procedures.
   - Be able to explain them to students, colleagues, and parents.
   - Follow their proscribed processes.
   - Commit to them as vehicles for positive culture change.

4. Develop and maintain a safe and inviting system for reporting incidents.
   - Encourage reporting by involved parties when they see or experience aggression or bullying, including students, teachers, and parents.
   - Take all reports of aggressive behavior or bullying seriously.
   - Respect confidentiality.
   - Collect evidence.
   - Respond as soon as possible.

Steps to Address the Problem and Develop a Culture of Respect

A schoolwide culture of respect can be developed and maintained through the teaching of positive social skills and systematic rewards for the positive behaviors taught, as well as through a systematic response to negative ones. Effective interventions, therefore, consist of two research-based components:

1. **Social Skills Curriculum** Curricular or instructional programs centered around social skills training and adult response protocols (Atlas & Pepler, 1998; Garrity, Jens, Porter, Sager, & Short-Camilli, 2004; Knoff, 2007; Menard, Grotpeter, Gianola, & O'Neal, 2008; Olweus, 1993)

2. **PBIS** Positive Behavior Intervention and Support programs designed to teach and reinforce positive behavior for the majority of the students and the school community (Agatston, Kowalski, & Limber, 2007; Garbarino, Bradshaw, & Vorrasi, 2002)

Social skills curriculum provides for the consistent and comprehensive teaching, practice, and reteaching of social emotional skills such as:

- Empathy
- Friendship-building and maintenance
- How to recognize and respond to aggressive behavior, bullying, and harassment
- How to report these types of behaviors to adults

When behavior expectations based on or supported by these social and emotional skills are included in the school's *Best Behavior* plan (a PBIS program), they harness the teaching, practice, and reteaching strengths of this program as well.

In general, schools seeking to reduce or eliminate aggression and bullying should follow a series of steps designed to introduce, teach, embed, and infuse a system-wide intervention program. The program must be ongoing and supported at district and school administrative levels. It must also be research based, financially feasible, and acceptable to the various stakeholders involved.

These steps should include the following.

1. Formulation and implementation of a bullying and harassment policy at the campus-specific or district level (Knoff, 2007; Menard, et al., 2008).

2. Assessment of the nature and extent of the problem through surveys and observations.

3. Selection of an appropriate schoolwide response (Garbarino, et al., 2002).

4. Solicitation of family support and involvement.

5. Training all staff, students, and families in behavior expectations and policies.

6. Training all students, teachers, and parents on the role of bystanders in preventing aggression or bullying.

7. Promoting active supervision of students in common areas (see Chapter 8).

8. Assisting students who are repeat victims to be more assertive, gain friendship skills, and avoid dangerous situations by increasing supports and proven interventions (e.g., the tiered intervention model) (McDonald & Stoker, 2008; Menard, et al., 2008; Ross, Horner, & Stiller, 2011).

9. Responding to repeated incidents of aggression or bullying with increasing supports, sanctions, and proven interventions (e.g., the tiered intervention model).

10. Recording all instances of aggressive and bullying behavior, analyzing data for patterns, and incorporating results into ongoing efforts.

We will now add detail to each implementation step listed above.

Antibullying Policy

Increasingly, we see local school districts and states developing and requiring implementation of antibullying and harassment policies and laws. Here is a checklist of items generally required by such laws.

Considerations for Compliance with Antibullying Laws

☐ Do you have a specific policy against social aggression, bullying, and harassment?

☐ Do you have a written code of conduct that publicizes the policy?

☐ Does the policy address all forms of social aggression and bullying (sexual, racial and ethnic, sexual-orientation, and differently abled harassment)? Cyber bullying is a new and unique form of these behaviors and should be addressed specifically in the policy. See **http://cyberbulling.us/** and **http://csriu.org/cyberbulling/docs/cblegislation.pdf** for more information regarding state laws on cyber bullying, which may help inform your policy.

☐ Are there references to social aggression, bullying, and harassment in the following handbooks?
- Student handbook
- Staff handbook
- Parent handbook

☐ Is there a policy on use of personal (phones, tablets) and public devices, such as school computers?

☐ Does the policy contain the following detailed elements: procedures, sanctions, a definition, and a prescribed method for notifying people?

☐ Is there a procedure to inform new employees and students of the policy?

☐ Are there references to social aggression and bullying in the school discipline code?

☐ Are the following parties and places notified of the social aggression, bullying, and harassment policy?
- Student extracurricular activities
- School-associated event sites
- Job-training work sites
- Visiting vendors and salespersons

Assess the Nature and Extent of Your School's Problem

There are a number of methods and tools available to help you gather data to determine the nature and extent of aggression and bullying at your school. These include surveys and observations.

- Prevention and response systems
- Procedures and policies
- Reporting
- Responding to chronic problems
- Collecting student-level data
- Conducting surveys such as the following ones provided
  - Olweus Bullying Questionnaire (Bauer, Lozano, & Rivara, 2007)
  - Vernberg Peer Experiences Questionnaire (Vernberg, Jacobs, & Twemlow, 1999)
  - Local or state-level "Healthy Students" survey

Select a Schoolwide Response

The *Best Behavior* program and other Schoolwide Positive Behavior and Intervention Support programs (SWPBIS) offer methods, strategies, and decision-making frameworks for the systematic prevention of and response to aggression and bullying. These programs are schoolwide, requiring the commitment and involvement of all members of the school culture.

These programs, including *Best Behavior,* identify some standard practices. First, establish a committee to oversee interventions for addressing aggression and bullying. We recommend that the PBIS team take on this responsibility. Second, establish a positive social culture using *Best Behavior* or SWPBIS. This includes teaching schoolwide behavioral expectations (we recommend "Be respectful, be responsible, be safe" as seen in Chapter 5). Teaching is followed by acknowledgement, rewarding appropriate behavior (Chapter 7), and establishing clear consequences for inappropriate behavior (these should be specified in the policy).

Include Families

Solicit family support for the program and family and community involvement. The more adults who are involved and supportive, the greater the impact on students through repeated exposure to the concepts, skills, and policies. Parents can contribute to culture change at the school, and they can be involved in the planning, training, and review of data. All parents should be kept informed of the program developments and results.

Train All Participants

All staff, students, and families must be trained. Training can be differentiated for each group, as each has different needs.

- Conduct committee and staff trainings.
- Hold staff discussion groups.
- Introduce the school rules that encourage prosocial behavior and discourage socially aggressive behavior or bullying.

- Hold a school kick-off event to launch the program for all participants.
- Teach (and reteach) aggression- and bullying-prevention skills.
  - Prosocial skills
  - Strategies for dealing directly with aggression and bullying, such as the "stop," "walk," and "talk" strategies.

Following are some examples of behavior expectations, which schools commonly teach, that relate to aggression and bullying. Refer back to Chapters 5 and 6 for guides on developing behavior expectations and for strategies for teaching them effectively via formal lesson plans. Teachers can also precorrect (provide quick practice of appropriate skills just before going to problem areas, such as the playground or cafeteria) to provide some of the review required throughout the year.

Teach the "Stop" Signal The stop signal is a verbal and nonverbal signal that is standardized schoolwide as one strategy to halt aggression or bullying situations. Lessons should include how to use the stop signal in various situations in which one is the target of aggression or bullying, or in which others are targeted. Bystanders can use this strategy as well. Tie the problem behavior back to the core school rules (e.g., be safe, be respectful, be responsible). The nonverbal signal is commonly a hand held with the palm out, just like police directing traffic.

Choices of verbal signals can include:
- "Stop"
- "Enough"
- "Don't"

The language and signal need to be age appropriate and contextually acceptable.

Teach "Walk Away" Most socially initiated problem behaviors are probably maintained by peer attention. Victim behavior inadvertently maintains taunt, tease, intimidate, and harassment behavior. Walking away ends the bullying interaction and, therefore, any peer attention. In planning for supporting walking away, build social rewards for the victim. See Figure 24 for a sample behavior expectation and lesson plan for the walk-away strategy, based on what we learned in Chapter 6.

Teach "Talk" Even when students use the stop signal and they walk away from the problem, sometimes other students will continue to behave inappropriately toward them. When that happens, the victim should talk to an adult. It is common practice to identify the line between tattling and reporting so that students can differentiate and practice the appropriate behavior.

Here are some guidelines for students on talking versus tattling.
- **Talking** is when you have tried to solve the problem yourself and have used the stop and walk-away steps first.
- **Tattling** is when you do not use the stop and walk-away steps before you talk to an adult.
- **Tattling** is when your goal is to get the other person in trouble.

FIGURE 24 ABC School Antibullying Expectation: "Walk Away" Rule

Step 1: Introduce Rule

A. Outline focus of the lesson: "Today we are going to learn about being safe, respectful, and responsible by walking away from someone who is bullying or aggressive."

B. Check for student understanding: "What are we going to learn about?"

Step 2: Demonstrate Rule and Practice

- Model (or provide a story) positive and negative examples of an adult or child being in a situation that might or might not require the walk-away behavior.

- Have students label the situation as safe or unsafe, respectful or not respectful, responsible or not responsible.

- Discuss relative merits of walk away and other related school behavior choices, such as "stop" or "tell an adult," for each role play.

- Note that, in student role plays, students should never be the aggressor or the bully, nor should they practice nonexample behaviors. The adults can model these instead.

Examples	Nonexamples
Role Plays—Some Examples to Use • Your friend starts making fun of what you are wearing today. One of his siblings joins in. • You have used the "stop" signal, but another student keeps grabbing for your ball. • During a recess game, people get quite heated and someone gets in your face and yells.	**Role Plays—Some Examples to Use** • At recess, a student in your class is talking about what she did on vacation, and you are more interested in what's happening on the football field. • Someone is saying mean things to another student and you are uncomfortable. • You are in a group discussion, and one of your group members doesn't agree with your idea and says so in a polite way. Nevertheless, you are highly annoyed.

Step 3: Provide Monitoring and Feedback

Discuss the role play.

- Ask students to indicate or show more examples of how and when to use the walk-away behavior strategy in response to aggression or bullying.

- Encourage and support appropriate discussion and responses. Minimize attention to inappropriate responses.

- When you see a student using the walkaway strategy appropriately, provide specific and immediate praise to the student. Use positive rewards/tokens.

- When you see a student who does not use the behavior as needed, or who uses it when it is inappropriate, state the rule and redirect. Ask the student to state the expected behavior, watch the student, and give feedback. Escalate to interventions (Tier II or Tier III) if the student repeatedly is the victim of or has difficulty dealing with aggression or bullying.

Teach How to Respond to "Stop" What should you do when you are asked to stop by someone else? Eventually, all students will be told to stop. When this happens, they should do the following things, even when they don't agree with the stop signal:

- Stop what they are doing.
- Take a deep breath.
- Go about their day (no big deal).

Active Supervision of Common Areas

Common student areas, as discussed in Chapter 8, are frequent problem areas for all types of negative behaviors, including aggression and bullying. As discussed in that chapter, review these areas and refine your school's supervision system to effectively maintain a safe environment. Focus on common-area settings, such as the cafeteria, gym, playground, hallways, bus area, bathrooms, and media center or library.

Intervention for Bullies For students who are repeatedly engaged in aggressive or bullying behaviors, your school's tiered intervention plan should identify the needs for increased levels of intervention. The following are common program components to support these students.

- Conduct individualized assessment.
- Involve the parents of the perpetrator and victim.
- Teach appropriate social skills.
- Hold individual (and separate) conferences with the person who was the bully and with the person who was the victim.
- For students with high rates of physical and verbal aggression, consider precorrection and on-site practice.

Intervention for Victims For students who are repeatedly the target of aggressive and bullying behaviors, your school's tiered intervention program should also provide support. Assist them in learning positive social and friendship skills and avoiding dangerous situations.

The following are common program components to support these students.

- Teach specific social skills in assertiveness, friendship, and avoiding dangerous situations.
- Involve the parents.
- Separate frequent victims from the negative peer group.
- Embed students in constructive peer groups.

Important Role for Bystanders Provide specific instruction on the role of bystanders in preventing socially aggressive behavior or bullying. Bystanders make up the majority in schools and thus have the power of numbers and of providing positive peer role models for those engaged in both the bully and victim roles.

Record and Review Data

All instances of aggressive and bullying behavior must be recorded. Develop and use a data-collection system for monitoring your school's program and for making decisions. There are a number of potential data sources, including surveys, observation, and data gathered from discipline referrals. Referral forms can be altered so that sufficient detail is collected on aggression and bullying to be informative for decision making (see Chapter 10). The regular review of data will allow for the identification of patterns or problem areas and for building on successes.

Summary

Just as *Best Behavior* (a PBIS program) can be used to systematically support a wide variety of positive behaviors, so too can it be used in preventing and responding to aggression and bullying. All expected behaviors can be supported by the PBIS model. Integrate your expected behaviors with preventing aggression and bullying. Use those new insights, and work them into the tasks you completed in the previous chapters of *Best Behavior*, such as your school matrix, your lesson plans, and your schedule of lessons.

Here is a list of the big ideas from this chapter:

- Create school cultures where bullying is ineffective and inefficient—PBIS.
- Focus on prevention first.
- Choose evidenced-based interventions and implement them with fidelity.
- Give special emphasis in your policy and protocols to cyber bullying and inappropriate use of technology.
- Always take a student's report seriously and follow up!

Activity: **Planning to Implement Your Antibullying Program**

Turn back to your reflection earlier in this chapter to help you identify areas of need among the action steps provided here. In the notes column on the following chart (Figure 25), you might list current status, available data, resources (policies, tools, or area experts), completion deadlines, responsible parties, and general ideas for implementation.

FIGURE 25 Planning Your Antibullying Program

Action Step	Notes about Your Plan
Formulate and implement a bullying and harassment policy at the campus-specific or district-based level. Provide specific rules and procedures for preventing and responding to cyber bullying and inappropriate use of technology.	
Assess the nature and extent of the problem through surveys and observations.	
Select an appropriate, schoolwide response, such as *Best Behavior.*	
Solicit family support and participation.	
Train all staff, students, and families.	
Promote active supervision of students in common areas (see Chapter 8).	
Respond to chronic aggression and bullying with increasing supports, sanctions, and proven interventions.	
Assist students who are chronically targeted as victims to be more assertive, gain friendship skills, and avoid dangerous situations.	
Provide specific instruction on the role of bystanders in preventing socially aggressive behavior or bullying.	
Record all instances of socially aggressive and bullying behavior and watching for patterns so that programmatic changes can be made.	

CHAPTER 10

Using Data to Diagnose Schoolwide, Classroom, and Individual Student Systems

Background: Data Use in Schools

Schools that are safe, effective, and violence free are not accidents. They are environments where considerable effort has been made to build and maintain supportive and positive school cultures. Part of that effort consists of monitoring and evaluating the types of behaviors students exhibit.

Data-Collection Methods

Office discipline referrals are used by schools as one method for managing and monitoring disruptive behavior. In other schools, teachers handle minor offences without sending the student to the office with a referral. The teacher may remove the student from the group or send the student to another classroom or to a reflection area. Students may also lose a privilege for displaying inappropriate behavior. It is important that these incidences are recorded so that the staff can analyze the data and help get the student on the right track as soon as possible. For this reason, many schools use Behavioral Incidence Reports for the types of infractions that do not end up as office referrals (Irvin, Tobin, Sprague, Sugai, & Vincent, 2004; Smith & Sprague, 2004).

What the Data Tell Us

Referrals and incidence reports are more than indexes of student behavior; they are indexes of the consistency and quality of the school discipline system. The major advantage of discipline referrals is that they are already collected in most schools and provide a source of information to document

> **OBJECTIVES**
>
> ▶ Describe features of an effective office discipline referral tracking system
>
> ▶ Review and revise your system for using and tracking office discipline referrals
>
> ▶ Discuss increasing the consistency of discipline referral procedures
>
> ▶ Identify program needs based on referral data patterns

whether interventions result in positive change (Skiba, 2002; Spaulding et al., 2010; Tobin, Sugai, & Colvin, in press).

We must be cautious when using discipline referrals as sources of information and decision making about behaviors. Each school defines and applies referral procedures differently (Irvin et al., 2006). Just because a school has a high rate of referrals does not necessarily mean that the students are less well behaved than the students at other schools with fewer referrals. The same student may evoke different responses from teachers in different schools, and different relationships between teachers and administrators will affect the use of discipline referrals across schools. This reminds us again of the importance of consistency within your school. Despite these cautions, office referral data are useful in identifying discipline patterns of students, the effects of schoolwide and classroom interventions (Sprague, Cook, Wright, & Sadler, 2008), and staff training needs (Tobin, et al., in press).

> We can use discipline referrals to identify problem areas in the school, determine if interventions are working, and identify students needing extra supports.

Many of us are accustomed to looking at data on individual student performance. It is also useful to look at data on the performance of the whole school or on a particular classroom regarding discipline referral patterns.

Many schools use referral data and/or behavior incidence reports for decision making. They also use regular cycles of data collection and reporting, such as daily recording of each referral, monthly feedback to staff members, and annual updating of the system and revising as needed. If the data are consistent and useful, people will use them! We must also ensure that the process is efficient (low effort, time, and cost).

The process for using referral data is not complex. However, for the data to be comprehensive and valid, it is important that all staff agree to use the referral forms or data-gathering methods in the same way. Please refer to the sample referral forms at the end of this chapter and examine their features.

Please take a moment to reflect upon your school's use of discipline referrals.

Reflection

My School's Discipline-Referral Data

1. How are discipline-referral data used in my school?

2. What are some concerns about using discipline referrals to make school discipline decisions?

3. What are some practices that make the use of discipline referrals effective?

4. How often do I get information about discipline-referral patterns from my administrator?

5. What needs to be improved in our office discipline-referral system?

Data-Driven Benefits

With a system of behavior management, we would expect to see better behavior over time. However, the work around data gathering, tallying, and analysis takes effort. Is it worth it?

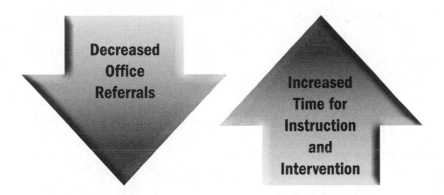

Let's look at the fruits of the effort applied to referral data (a common data source) in order to reduce referrals. One of the clearest benefits of reduced office referrals is increased time for student learning. Administrators also tell us that they have more time to spend with the neediest students in the school when they are not dealing with excessive amounts of minor inappropriate behaviors. Figure 26 provides a simple illustration of this pattern and concrete gains for this school.

FIGURE 26 What Is the Benefit of Reduced Referrals?

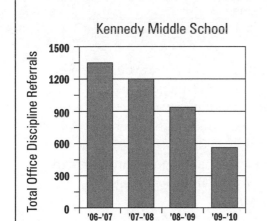

What does a reduction of 850 office referrals and 25 suspensions mean?

Kennedy Middle School

- Savings in administrative time
- ODR = 15 minutes
- Suspension = 45 minutes
- 13,875 minutes
- 231 hours
- 29 8-hour work days

- Savings in student instructional time
- ODR = 45 minutes
- Suspension = 2165 minutes
- 413,650 minutes
- 7281 hours
- 121, 68-hour school days

What to Look At: The Key Indicators

We look at key indicators to examine discipline referral patterns. Each indicator requires that the office referral form (or other data-gathering system) actually collects the relevant data. Therefore, we have identified basic elements that must be included on a school's referral form, as indicated below.

Required Referral Form Elements

- Date and time
- Student name
- Student grade
- Cause of the referral (the behavior)
- Possible motivation for the referral (e.g., attention, escape/avoidance)
- Location of the referral
- Referring staff member
- Reteaching opportunity, consequence, or other follow-up for the student

Each of the key indicators, which are summary statistics, is easy to derive and tells a lot about what is happening in the school. The following list provides a summary of each indicator.

Key Indicators

- Total number of office discipline referrals
- Referrals per enrolled student
- Average referrals per school day per month
- Location of referrals (e.g., common areas or classrooms)
- Percentage of students with 0–1 referrals
- Percentage of students with 2–5 referrals
- Percentage of students with 6 or more referrals
- Number of suspensions and expulsions

Making Data-Based Decisions

We will now begin to look at how these data can really guide our discipline program decision making by finding successes and trouble spots.

Each key indicator can be tracked to monitor change, and schools will relate their findings to known changes in their building, populations, events, or other context elements. Also, each school may find particular indicators to be especially relevant. However, we have found that the following rules are helpful for using the key indicators to identify improvement areas.

Rules for Improvement Opportunities

- **Schoolwide improvement** is needed when the total referrals per year per student are high or when the number of referrals per school day per month is high.
- **Common-area improvement** is needed when there is a specific area in the school with more referrals.

- **Classroom-management improvement** is needed when there are:
  - More referrals coming from all classrooms.
  - Specific classrooms with more referrals.
- **Individual student support and intervention** is needed when:
  - The proportion of students with two to five referrals is high.
  - There are students who have received more than six referrals.
  - There are many suspensions and expulsions.

Figure 27 graphically relates the indicators to the areas of the program in need of change.

FIGURE 27 Relating Key Indicators to Specific Improvement Opportunities

	Total number of office discipline referrals	Referrals per enrolled student	Average referrals per school day per month	Location of referrals (e.g., common areas or classrooms)	Percentage of students with 0–2 referrals	Percentage of students with 2–5 referrals	Percentage of students with 6 or more referrals	Suspensions and expulsions	
Schoolwide improvement		X	X						Note: Either one may indicate need.
Common-area improvement				X					Note: Common areas in general, or one in particular, may be indicated.
Classroom-management improvement				X					Note: Either one may indicate need.
Individual student support and intervention						X	X	X	Note: If the 2–5 column is high, the suspension/expulsion is high, or there are any students in the >6 column, then change is needed.

Activity: Which System Needs Improvement?

Now that you have reviewed the decision rules, it is time to practice. The next worksheet provides a format for applying the decision rules. Please review the "Rules for Improvement Opportunities" and then read the table of sample key indicators. Indicate on the worksheet which school needs improvement in each area and why.

After you have completed this activity, you will want to work with your PBIS team to create decision rules that make sense for you and set a schedule for regularly reviewing and reporting the data to all staff members.

Analyzing Office Discipline Referrals
(Which System Needs Improvement?)

Activity Chart

School	Grades	# of Referrals	Referrals per Student	Referrals per Day per Month	% from Classroom	% from Common Area	% with Two to Five Referrals	% Students with Six or More Referrals
A	K–5	250	.90	1.5	25	20	32	4
B	K–6	331	.50	1.9	28	50	12	1.5
C	6–8	3520	3.0	20.6	30	25	65	1
D	9–12	1300	.90	7.6	50	15	20	8

Activity Worksheet

1. Schoolwide system improvement is needed when the average number of referrals per day is high (>2/day elementary, >6/day middle, >12/day high school). **Which school(s) in the chart has this need and why?**

   _____

   _____

   _____

2. Common-area improvement is indicated when 30% or more of all referrals come from a specific setting. **Which school(s) in the chart has this need and why?**

   _____

   _____

   _____

3. Classroom-management improvement is indicated when 40% or more referrals come from all classrooms or there are specific classrooms with more referrals. **Which school(s) in the chart has this need and why?**

   _____

   _____

   _____

4. Individual student improvement is needed when (a) the proportion of students with 2 to 5 referrals is high, (b) there are students who have received >6 referrals, and (c) there is a high frequency of suspensions and expulsions. **Which school(s) in the chart has this need and why?**

   _____

   _____

   _____

Activity Answer Key

1. **C.** This school needs schoolwide improvement because it has a high number of overall referrals and referrals per day.

2. **B.** This school needs common-area improvement because 50% of all referrals originate from those areas.

3. **D.** This school needs classroom-management improvement because 50% of all referrals originate from classrooms.

4. **C and/or D.** School C has a high proportion of students with 2–5 referrals, and School D has a high proportion of students with 6 referrals or more.

Designing Your Data-Collection System

Although your school may already have referral or incidence forms in place, it will be well worth your time to carefully consider your data-collection system, both in the big picture and in the details. Reconsider your responses to the reflection earlier in this chapter as you design, redesign, or improve your system.

Perhaps more than anything else, PBIS provides a data-based decision-making framework. The decisions to be made under PBIS are based on data rather than on a staff member or parent's opinion, a student's reputation, or what a staff member wants to do with a student (e.g., removal from the classroom). This integrity is the backbone of PBIS. However, the adage "garbage in, garbage out" applies to the data-collection procedures used in PBIS-based systems as well. Thus, for a PBIS approach to function properly, you will need to identify user-friendly and technically sound data-collection procedures.

> "Garbage-in, garbage-out" applies to PBIS systems too: make sure your system is well thought-out and implemented with fidelity.

One of the first steps to undertake when starting a PBIS approach for behavior, then, is to select the data-collection procedures that will serve as the basis for making data-based decisions. Data must not only be collected on the student's response to the positive behavior supports, but also on how well the behavior supports are being implemented. Collectively, the regular use of data in these areas will allow you and your colleagues to make educationally valid and legally defensible decisions when selecting, maintaining, modifying, or dropping behavior support procedures.

System Fidelity

Does your system actually function as it was intended? Are the procedures being followed as written and trained across staff members and across time? These are the questions that address system fidelity.

Intervention fidelity, sometimes referred to as *treatment fidelity* or *procedural reliability* in the applied behavior analysis literature, refers to the extent to which an intervention plan or PBIS system is implemented with integrity as planned. Research has demonstrated that poor intervention fidelity often undermines the effectiveness of interventions. As a result, when the data indicate that a particular system of supports results in poor outcomes, one cannot leap to conclusions—particularly about specific students. The first question that the school team must address before any other conclusion can be reached is, "Was the intervention implemented with integrity?" Data must be collected on fidelity, as well as on student outcomes. Without the collection of intervention fidelity data, it is impossible for the school team to determine whether the lack of response on the part of the student was due to poor implementation of an otherwise effective system, or whether there was resistance on the part of the student to a high quality intervention implemented with fidelity.

Two dimensions are important when examining the extent to which an intervention is implemented as planned. These two dimensions are consistency and accuracy.

- **Consistency:** Refers to whether the intervention is routinely implemented day to day.
- **Accuracy:** Refers to whether the intervention is implemented correctly on a daily basis.

For example, if a teacher does well at implementing the intervention Monday through Wednesday but does poorly later in the week, then there is a problem with consistency. On the other hand, if the teacher regularly fails to implement particular components of the intervention every day of the week, then there is a problem with accuracy.

There are several different methods for collecting data on system fidelity:
- Direct observation
- Checklists
- Self-report
- Permanent product (e.g., examining products, such as your rule matrix, lesson plans, or office referral form for quality and completeness)

Chapter 4 provides the *Best Behavior* Self-Assessment tool, a very useful checklist for assessing intervention fidelity across all of the PBIS systems we describe. We recommend using this assessment at least annually to gather information about what is in place and what needs improvement. These data can be compared over time to patterns of change in office referrals, suspensions, and expulsions, and they can help you detect areas in need of improvement, including system fidelity and specific expectations or interventions.

Staff Training to Support Consistency in Data

We have mentioned that consistency is needed to obtain comprehensive data (i.e., nothing left out) and to have useful data. If everyone fills out the form under different situations, at different thresholds, or interprets how to complete the form differently, then the data gathered will be of dubious or limited use. How do we reduce these inconsistencies so that our well-conceived forms are put to good use, efforts to complete them pay off, and the data can be used to drive improvement?

Consistency in data, via the referral form, can become part of the staff education and the staff-expected behaviors. To achieve consistency among the staff team, consider the following.

1. When is it appropriate to complete the form?

2. Which form is appropriate (if there is more than one)? Consider the threshold for behavior incident versus referral.

3. Are teachers aware of the differences between all the listed behaviors on the form(s)?

4. Are there areas that need to be clarified or that cause confusion?

5. Do specific data need to be hand entered where multiple categories have a single check box? (For example, do we need to write in "social exclusion" or "racial harassment" if the "bullying or harassment" box is checked?)

6. What constitutes minor versus major infractions?

7. Where do completed forms go?

8. Can you present examples of correctly completed forms for common scenarios?

9. Can you present nonexamples of incorrectly completed forms?

10. Are staff aware of how forms affect later decision making?

Your findings can be rolled into changes to the forms to facilitate use and into behavior expectations for staff on how to complete the forms so that they can be used in staff training.

Sample Forms for Capturing Behavioral Data

Following are a variety of forms that may be used by your school to capture data about behavior. Some follow a referral format and others a behavior incident format. Compare your school form to the list of referral form elements provided earlier in this chapter to make sure you have them covered. Also, consider any changes that might help with consistency for staff completion of the form or whether the form captures the data most relevant to your school, as revealed by your work in this chapter.

Behavior Referral Form

Student Name: _____

Teacher: _____ Referring Staff: _____

Grade: K 1 2 3 4 5 6   Date: _____   Time: _____

Location	Problem Behavior	Possible Motivation	Administrative Action
__ Arrival/dismissal area	__ Damage to property	__ Peer attention	For Office Use Only:
__ Bus loading area	__ Defiance/disrespect	__ Adult attention	__ Review of school rules
__ Cafeteria/quad	__ Disruption	__ Obtain items/	__ Loss of privilege
__ Classroom	__ Inappropriate language	activities	__ Recess/lunch detention
__ Library/pod area	__ Physical aggression	__ Avoid peer(s)	from _____
__ Office	__ Tease, threaten,	__ Avoid adult(s)	to _____
__ On bus	harass, bully	__ Avoid task/activity	__ Time-out in office
__ Passing areas	__ Cyber bully	__ Don't know	from _____
__ Playground	__ Other (specify)	__ Other (specify)	to _____
__ Restrooms			__ Suspension for ____ day(s)
__ Special event/assembly	_____	_____	__ Other (specify) _____
__ Other (specify)			__ Parent Contact Y N
_____			

Others involved in incident:

___ None   ___ Peer(s)   ___ Staff   ___ Teacher   ___ Substitute   ___ Other   ___ Unknown

If peers were involved, list them: _____

_____

Classroom management steps taken today to address behavior:

___ None   ___ Warned, rules reviewed   ___ Loss of recess/privilege   ___ Time-out   ___ Phone call

___ Other (specify) _____

Last documented contact with parent/guardian:

___ Conference at school   ___ Phone call   Date of contact: _____

Other Comments:

_____

_____

_____

_____

_____   _____

Administrator Signature   Date

_____   _____

Parent/Guardian Signature   Date

Office Referral Form

Name: _____

Date: _____ Time: _____

Teacher: _____

Grade: K 1 2 3 4 5 6 7 8

Referring Staff: _____

Location (circle one):

Playground   Library

Cafeteria   Bathroom

Hallway   Arrival/Dismissal Area

Classroom   Other _____

Minor Problem Behavior	Major Problem Behavior	Possible Motivation
__ Inappropriate language	__ Abusive language	__ Obtain peer attention
__ Physical contact	__ Fighting/physical aggression	__ Obtain adult attention
__ Defiance	__ Overt defiance	__ Obtain items/activities
__ Disruption	__ Harassment/bullying	__ Avoid peer(s)
__ Dress code	__ Dress code	__ Avoid adult
__ Property misuse	__ Tardy	__ Avoid task or activity
__ Tardy	__ Inappropriate display of affection	__ Don't know
__ Electronic violation	__ Electronic violation	__ Other _____
__ Other _____	__ Lying/cheating	
	__ Skipping class	
	__ Bullying	
	__ Other _____	

Administrative Decision

__ Loss of privilege

__ Time in office

__ Conference with student

__ Parent contact

__ Individualized instruction

__ In-school suspension (_____ hours/days)

__ Out-of-school suspension (_____ days)

__ Other _____

Others involved in incident:

___ None   ___ Peer(s)   ___ Staff   ___ Teacher   ___ Substitute   ___ Other   ___ Unknown

Other Comments:

_____

___ I need to talk to the student's teacher.   ___ I need to talk to the administrator.

_____   _____
Parent/Guardian Signature   Date

All minors are filed with classroom teacher. Three minors equal a major.

All majors require administrator consequence, parent contact, and signature.

Student Citation Form

Student Name: _____ Grade: _____ Time: _____ Date: _____

Referring Person: _____

Teacher: _____

This student has had problems:	Specific problems include:
__ Being SAFE	__ Aggressive play
__ Being RESPECTFUL	__ Vandalism
__ Being RESPONSIBLE	__ Unsafe play
	__ Defiance/disruption
	__ Bullying
	__ Harassment
	__ Inappropriate language
	__ Fighting
	__ Cruel teasing
	__ Obscenity

Other:

_____

_____

_____

_____

_____

_____

_____   _____
Parent/Guardian Signature   Date

Notice to Parents of Disciplinary Action

Student Name: _____ Grade: _____

Referring Person: _____ Date: _____ Time: _____

Day: M T W T F

Location

__ Classroom	__ Commons: Cafe. __ Rec. __	__ On Bus/Van
__ School Store	__ Computer Center	__ Bike Rack
__ Hallway	__ Library	__ Assembly/Activity
__ Front Desk	__ Parking Lot/Driveway	__ Service Learning

Problem Behaviors

__ Abusive, Inappropriate Language, Gesture	__ Harassment, Teasing, Taunting, Bullying, Name Calling	__ Theft/Stealing
__ Fighting or Physical Aggression	__ Disruption _____	__ Lying/Cheating
__ Defiance _____	__ Tardy	__ Vandalism
__ Disrespect _____	__ Skipping Class/Out of Area	__ Property Damage
		__ False Alarm

Possible Motivation / Others Involved

Possible Motivation		Others Involved	
__ Obtain Peer Attention	__ Avoid Peers	__ None	__ Substitute
__ Obtain Adult Attention	__ Avoid Adults	__ Peers	__ Unknown
__ Obtain Items/Activities	__ Don't Know	__ Staff	__ Other _____
		__ Teacher	

Administrative Decision

__ Time in Office	__ Recess Detention/Structure or Alternative Recess	__ Out-of-School Suspension
__ Loss of Privilege	__ Individualized Instruction	__ Other _____
__ Conference With Student	__ In-School Suspension	__ Referral to SST
__ Parent Contact		__ Written Acknowledgment/ Apology

Comments:

_____

_____

_____

Date Parent/Guardian Contacted: _____ School Official Signature: _____

Parent/Guardian Follow Up:

Thank you for your support in encouraging positive behavior at school! Please talk to your child about his or her behavior in this incident.

If you have any questions, please contact us at _____.

Minor Behavior Incident

Presented to: _____ Room: _____

Location	Behavior Incident (circle one)
___ Classroom	• Be there and be prepared
___ Cafeteria	
___ Hallway	• Live Responsibly
___ Bus	___ Uphold Integrity.
___ Other _____	___ Earn and give respect.

Steps	Specific Behavior
1. Name behavior and expectation.	_____
2. State rule and expected behavior.	_____
3. Give positive verbal and social acknowledgment.	_____
4. Give slip to student.	_____
5. File.	_____
	Consequence
	• Parent/Guardian Contact
	• Detention
	• Other _____

Given by: _____ Date: _____ Time: _____

SECTION 2

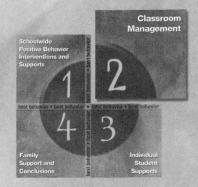

Classroom Management

CHAPTER 11

Classroom Organization: The Foundation of Classroom Management

Background: Integrating Schoolwide and Classroom Expectations

The focus up to this point has been on developing universal, schoolwide strategies, such as setting and teaching schoolwide rules, positive feedback systems for rule following, systematic supervision, and monitoring behavior through referral or incidence report patterns. The universal behavior support system that the school develops provides the basis for your classroom-management system, providing the umbrella rules (e.g., be safe, be respectful, and be responsible) and common expectations for *all* students anywhere in the school, including your classroom. It creates consistent procedures and language for all staff when prompting, reinforcing, or correcting students. These schoolwide systems support a positive and consistent school culture. Without the universal, schoolwide system in place, classroom management strategies will be less effective. In order to support the schoolwide system, and also reap its benefits in the classroom, the classroom-management system should be consistent with it.

> The classroom-management system must be consistent with the schoolwide system in order to support it and also reap its benefits.

OBJECTIVES

▸ Relate the classroom-management system to the schoolwide one

▸ Describe the effective organization of a classroom's physical and behavioral environment

▸ Evaluate your classroom environment using the classroom organization checklist

▸ Set goals for improving your classroom environment

Most teachers, however, will want and need to develop specific expectations and routines in their classroom for behaviors not covered by the schoolwide program. We suggest that these expectations and routines be similar from classroom to classroom throughout the school in order to avoid confusion and improve behavior. This could be achieved by the PBIS team or grade-level teams, depending upon how your school is organized. For example, if your school adopts "be safe, be respectful, and be responsible," then those umbrella expectations should be seen in every classroom and common area. What those behaviors look like may be different depending on the individual teacher. We will learn more about this in Chapter 12.

The expectations you develop, teach, and recognize should be taught in the same manner as the schoolwide expectations and use the same language (e.g., be safe, respectful, and responsible). It is expected, however, that you will develop specific language in your classroom to match your expectations for basic routines like turning in homework, staying on task, or asking for help. You will see how this is addressed later in this chapter.

Any reward and recognition system you create for your classroom should work on the same principles as the schoolwide system and be consistent with it (frequently, the same token system can be used). Make sure that all universal practices are in place with regard to the reward system: Teach and positively reinforce clear expectations, minimize attention for minor inappropriate behaviors, and provide clear consequences for unacceptable behavior (see Chapter 7).

Organizing the Classroom Environment

Teachers need strategies for teaching appropriate behavior and managing problem behaviors in the classroom. This work should begin before the start of the school year. Teachers must establish a structured classroom environment that encourages safe, responsible, and respectful behavior and that fosters learning. Effective classroom managers know what they want to see in their classroom throughout the day (entering, leaving, transitioning, and completing independent work) and what they want to hear from their students (noise level, being respectful, asking for help) (Darch, Kame'enui, & Crichlow, 2003; Emmer, Evertson, & Worsham, 2000; Marzano, Pickering, & Pollock, 2001).

Effective classroom managers also do not assume that students instinctively know what is expected. They explicitly teach and provide positive and constructive feedback until the behavior becomes an automatic part of the daily classroom routine. The teaching is ongoing and cannot be done in one or two teaching sessions.

The Physical Environment

An effective and efficient classroom-management system begins with organizing the physical environment. Before the school year begins, you need to plan the physical arrangement of the classroom.

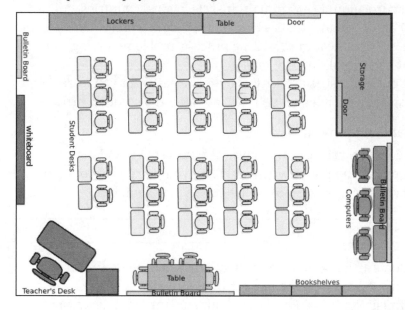

Careful physical organization makes it easier for kids to meet your expectations.

- Set the seating arrangement:
  - Make sure all students can see and hear instruction.
  - Place high-need and low-performing students where you have easy access to them for reinforcement and feedback.
- Decide where you want to place the teacher desk and who has access to it. Consider eliminating a single teacher desk and instead placing instructional materials near the teaching stations (e.g., use rolling cart, small bookshelf, or drawers).
- Organize space:
  - Provide areas for different types of activity (e.g., quiet area, class meeting area, group work area).
  - Make sure areas with opposite needs aren't right beside each other (e.g., don't put a quiet area or time-out area near the group work area).
- Organize all furniture or structures so that you can:
  - Visually monitor students at all times (no groups or students behind bookcases or dividers).
  - Circulate easily throughout the classroom to gain physical access to all students (sufficient space between desks).
- Organize tools and materials:
  - Those frequently in use and freely available to students must be easy to get to.
  - Those for which access is limited should be kept separate and, if possible, behind doors.
  - Students need personal storage space (e.g., in desk, cubbies, bins).

Plan for uncluttered bulletin board areas. Too much visual stimulation will be distracting, and too little may feel cold and uninviting. Use semipermanent display areas to save time and to keep the visual environment uncluttered. These may include thematic displays related to the grade-level curriculum (e.g., animals, insects, plants, countries, cultures, transportation) and permanent areas to display student work, schedules, and expectations (e.g., paper headings, writing process, problem-solving steps, as well as relevant behavioral expectations).

After these physical issues are settled, it will be easier for you to deal with the many demands and challenges you will face after the students arrive.

The Behavioral Environment

When you have a clear picture of the physical aspects of your classroom, think a few moments about what you would like your ideal classroom to look like in action. Then, take a look at the following example.

EXAMPLE

Imagine students arriving in the morning, quietly sitting down, starting a warm-up activity, and working respectfully until all the students have arrived and you give a transition signal. Your students change groups efficiently and respectfully. When they arrive at their next subject area, they are equipped with appropriate books, paper, and pencils and are ready to follow directions. While you instruct, everyone can see you and everyone listens respectfully. During independent work time, your students know how to work quietly, access help, and obtain materials. You circulate among the students and provide them with positive feedback and corrective feedback. At lunchtime, your students get ready efficiently, orderly, and respectfully.

You are going to teach your students how to live up to your expectations by defining them clearly. We will examine developing and teaching classroom expectations in Chapter 12, but first we recommend that you think about and complete the following **Classroom Organization Checklist**. Write answers in the space provided. For those items you feel are complete or in place, just put a check in the box to the right. When you are finished, decide which areas need improvement.

Classroom Organization Checklist

1. Teacher's Tools and Space

- Where are your teaching materials kept (teacher manuals, writing tools, etc.)?_____
  _____ ○

- When or how are students allowed to use your space (e.g., desk, chair, teaching materials)?
  _____
  _____ ○

- How will you monitor the entire class when you are at your teaching stations (e.g., direct instruction, group
  instruction)?_____
  _____ ○

- When can students come up to you when you are at your desk? Do you have a special
  space where they wait until you can speak with them?_____
  _____ ○

- What are procedures regarding the phone in your classroom?_____
  _____ ○

- What other expectations do you have regarding your workspace?_____
  _____ ○

2. Material Storage

- Where are frequently used supplies stored?_____
  _____ ()

- Where are textbooks stored? Are the ones you use daily easily accessible?_____
  _____ ○

- What do students do when they need supplies while working on independent work
  (e.g., are there abundant supplies stored near to where the students are working)?_____
  _____ ○

- Where do you store seasonal or infrequently used materials?_____
  _____ ○

3. Start-of-Class Procedures

- What are students expected to do when they enter the room? List in order (e.g., attendance, lunch
  choice, hand-ins, class job, seatwork)._____
  _____ ○

• How can students talk to each other at this time? What is the noise-level expectation?

_____

_____ ◯

• What is the initial seatwork (warm-up, read quietly, "question of the day")?_____

_____ ◯

• What is the procedure for dealing with lunch count?_____

_____ ◯

• What is the procedure for dealing with attendance?_____

_____ ◯

• What is the procedure for handing in parent notes?_____

_____ ◯

• When do students need to be in their seats?_____

_____ ◯

• What problems associated with daily start-up do you experience?_____

_____ ◯

• What are some solutions to these problems?_____

_____ ◯

4. General Classroom Procedures

Complete?

• How do students get your help and attention when you are teaching or working (e.g., raise hand, put "I need help" signal on desk)?_____

_____ ◯

• Where can students work (desks, standing stations, floors) during different routine times?

_____

_____ ◯

• What can students do if they finish independent work early (e.g., read a book)?_____

_____ ◯

• When can students sharpen pencils?_____

_____ ◯

• What do students do when their pencil breaks or another writing tool is needed
(e.g., have a can full of already sharpened pencils)?_____

_____ ◯

• What are bathroom procedures (designated times, passes, sign-out/sign-in)?_____

_____ ◯

- What are your expectations about water, food, gum, and so forth?_____ ○

- What procedures need to be followed to go to the office, nurse, counselor, and so forth?_____ _____ ○

- What is the procedure for delivering messages from the office to students?_____ _____ ○

- What procedures need to be followed with regards to iPods, cell phones, and/or other electronic equipment?_____ _____ ○

- When do students complete classroom jobs?_____ _____ ○

- What problems associated with classroom procedures do you experience?_____ _____ ○

- What are some solutions to these problems?_____ _____ ○

6. Independent Work Procedures   Complete?

- What are students expected to do during independent seatwork?_____ _____ ○

- Under what conditions can students leave their seats?_____ _____ ()

- When or how can students talk to each other (e.g., socially, ask each other for help)?_____ _____ ○

- If talking is allowed, what voice level is expected?_____ _____ ○

- When can students interact with the teacher (e.g., while teacher is teaching a small group, circulating, working at his or her desk)?_____ _____ ○

- How do students signal for assistance (e.g., raise hand, card on desk, approach teacher)? _____ _____ ○

- What do students do when the assignment is finished (e.g., buffer activity, read a book, write in a journal, stay in seat)?_____ _____ ○

- What problems associated with independent work do you experience?_____
_____ ○

- What are some solutions to these problems?_____
_____ ○

7. Transitions   Complete?

- Where is the daily schedule posted?_____
_____ ○

- How are students cued or signaled to a move to new activity?_____
_____ ○

- What are the steps for the students to move from one activity to another (e.g., clear desk or workspace, collect materials, walk)?_____
_____ ○

- How do students move from one classroom to another (line in hall, along certain wall, through outside door)?_____
_____ ○

- Where will students line up for transitions? Is this space appropriate (large enough, not obstructing halls or other areas)?_____
_____ ○

- What problems associated with transitions do you experience?_____
_____ ○

- What are some solutions to these problems?_____
_____ ○

8. Dismissal Procedures   Complete?

- How are students dismissed to go to break, lunch, or other activities?_____
_____ ○

- What procedures are in place for end-of-school dismissal (e.g., handshake, high-five, walk to exit with class, wait for pick-up)?_____
_____ ○

- What are special procedures for Friday dismissal (Friday folders, communications, and work home)?____
_____ ○

- What problems associated with dismissal do you experience?_____
_____ ○

- What are some solutions to these problems?_____
_____ ◯

9. Homework Policy

- What is your homework policy (e.g., due on a daily basis, weekly packets, turned in)?_____
_____ ◯

- How do you provide feedback on homework (e.g., correct in class, hand back next day)?
_____
_____ ◯

- Where do students write down the assignment to be completed (e.g., planner, assignment sheet, or
notebook)?_____
_____ ◯

- Where do students record that their homework assignments are complete (e.g., homework assignment
envelopes, agenda planners, or notebooks)?_____
_____ ◯

- How do you communicate to parents about homework expectations and specific assignments
(e.g., online, newsletter)?_____
_____ ◯

- Where and when do students turn in completed homework assignments?_____
_____ ◯

- What is your recordkeeping system for assignments (we suggest an electronic grade book program)?___
_____ ◯

- What happens when students don't turn in completed work?_____
_____ ◯

- What is your reinforcement system for completed homework (e.g., points, grades, free homework pass)?
_____
_____ ◯

- What are procedures for chronic homework problems?_____
_____ ◯

- What problems associated with homework do you experience?_____
_____ ◯

- What are some solutions to these problems?_____
_____ ◯

10. Common Classroom Problem Procedures

Complete?

- What happens when a student talks out in class?_____
  _____ ○

- What happens when a student gets out of seat without permission?_____
  _____ ○

- How should students deal with interpersonal conflict?_____
  _____ ○

- What other common problems do you experience?_____
  _____ ○

- What are some solutions to these problems?_____
  _____ ○

11. Computer Procedures

Complete?

- When and for how long can students use the computer?_____
  _____ ○

- How do you handle fair-access issues (sign-in sheet, rotations)?_____
  _____ ○

- What are your expectations about water, food, gum, and so forth, related to computers?_____
  _____ ○

- What problems associated with computer use do you experience?_____
  _____ ○

- What are some solutions to these problems?_____
  _____ ○

12. Quiet Time/Reflection Areas

Complete?

- What is your procedure for a student who works better in a quiet, less distracting area?
  _____
  _____ ○

- What environment have you provided for quiet reading (e.g., bean bag chair, rocking chair)?
  _____
  _____ ○

- What is your procedure for a student who has lost the privilege to be part of the class for a short period
  of time? Is there a quiet place in the room, or can students go to another teacher's classroom when they
  have lost the privilege to be in your room?_____
  _____ ○

- What type of work is provided for students who have to be in an in-school suspension (e.g., work should not require adult assistance)?_____
_____ ○

- How and when will you teach your students about the quiet-time procedures?_____
_____ ○

- What problems associated with quiet time do you experience?_____
_____ ○

- What are some solutions to these problems?_____
_____ ○

13. Parent Contact Policies   Complete?

- How do you deliver general news or information and return student work (class newsletter, info fliers, Friday folder, website)?_____
_____ ○

- What is your plan for contacting parents?_____
_____ ○

- How frequently do you contact parents when things are going well (e.g., e-mail, phone call, note)?_____
_____ ○

- What do you do when things are not going well?_____
_____ ○

- What problems associated with parents do you experience?_____
_____ ○

- What are some solutions to these problems?_____
_____ ○

Classroom Improvement

Before you select areas in your classroom that need fine tuning, please examine the **Sample Classroom Improvement Form** in Figure 28. Then, complete the blank **Classroom Improvement Form** to initiate the improvement for your classroom.

FIGURE 28   Classroom Improvement Form (Sample)

Procedures	Particulars
Pick one area that needs improvement in your classroom.	It bothers me when students yell when they need my attention or when they come up to me and interrupt while I am helping other students.
What do you want to see instead?	I would like my students to notice when I am available for attention and raise their hands quietly.

Say: "During my Monday class meeting, I will explain that I've seen some behavior that doesn't fit the schoolwide rule "be respectful." I will explain how interrupting and yelling are not respectful of others. I will then show an example and a nonexample."

Give examples.	Say: "When you need attention, look and see if I am talking to another student. When I am finished talking, raise your hand quietly and wait for me to call on you. Like this." Demonstrate.
Demonstrate nonexamples.	Wave your hand and yell: "Teacher, teacher!" Say: "Is that the right way to get my attention?" or "Walk up to me and say: 'I don't know how to do this.' That is not the right way. Let me show you the right way one more time."

Classroom Improvement Form

Procedures	Particulars
Pick one area that needs improvement in your classroom.	
What do you want to see instead?	
How will you teach your students the new expectation?	
Give examples.	
Demonstrate nonexamples.	

CHAPTER 12

Designing and Teaching Classroom Behavioral Expectations

Background: Building from Positive Expectations

If you do not know exactly what you expect to see and hear in the classroom, then neither will your students. If you don't communicate your expectations, in detail, then your students will not know what behaviors to enact, or when. For example, students should know when they can talk quietly and when they need to be silent. They must understand exactly how to be respectful to others and what that looks like under a variety of circumstances.

Teach only behavior expectations you can support; for example, if you are going to use a colored star to indicate "stay in seat," then you have to commit to always using this star when you want students to stay in their seats. Further, have, teach, and expect only behaviors that you are willing to enforce. If the teacher expects no talking while a student raises his or her hand, then anything less is not acceptable. Otherwise, students will learn that expectations are flexible and can be broken—and that every expectation you have is compromised.

The emphasis when developing effective classroom expectations is on clarity, consistency, and precision (Emmer, Evertson, & Worsham, 2000; Marzano, Pickering, & Pollock, 2001). In this chapter, you will become clear on your own expectations so that you can develop them into effective lesson plans, enforce them, and make changes as needed.

As with schoolwide expectations, classroom expectations should be short, simple, and positive so students can remember them. Clear expectations are one of the building blocks for your classroom management

OBJECTIVES

▶ Describe how establishing and teaching classroom behavioral expectations contributes to effective classroom management

▶ Develop positive classroom rules and expectations that are aligned with the schoolwide expectations

▶ Set a plan to directly teach and review classroom expectations

plan, so be sure to devote as much time and energy as possible to forming an effective, comprehensive list. If you have a clear idea of what your expectations are in your classroom, and you consistently enforce those expectations, then many problem behaviors will disappear or be prevented.

Expectations and procedures might vary from teacher to teacher, but effective teachers have very clear expectations. It is very difficult to run an effective classroom if there are no clear expectations about walking around in the room, interrupting the teacher, or working productively. In addition, inefficient procedures and a lack of automatic classroom routines can waste enormous amounts of time and take away from valuable instructional time (Hofmeister & Lubke, 1990; Kame'enui, Carnine, Dixon, Simmons, & Coyne, 2002; Latham, 1992).

Classroom expectations begin as your vision and plan and end as an ongoing and flexible tool for classroom management. Figure 29 illustrates how your work so far, and how your work in this chapter, will support your vision of your classroom.

> "High achievement
> always takes place
> in the framework of
> high expectation."
>
> –Charles F. Kettering

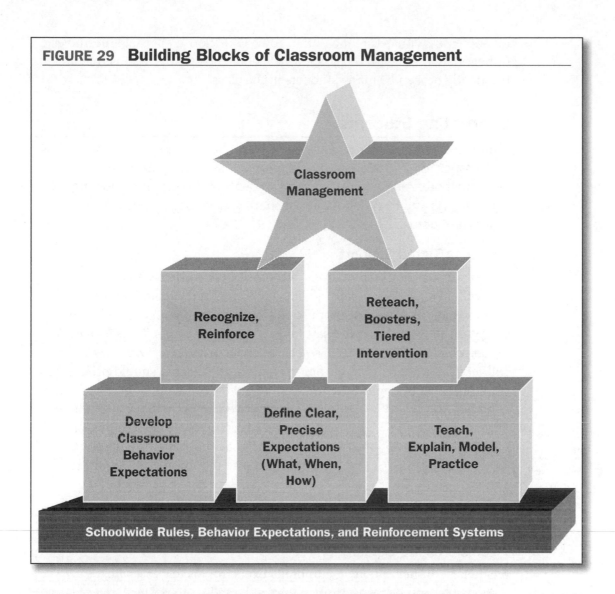

FIGURE 29 Building Blocks of Classroom Management

Classroom Management

Recognize, Reinforce

Reteach, Boosters, Tiered Intervention

Develop Classroom Behavior Expectations

Define Clear, Precise Expectations (What, When, How)

Teach, Explain, Model, Practice

Schoolwide Rules, Behavior Expectations, and Reinforcement Systems

To begin, you should describe and teach the expectations during the first few days of school. You need to provide your students with a rationale for each rule and discuss how following them can help with following all of the school rules (e.g., be safe, be responsible, and be respectful).

Next, when you provide descriptive noticing or specific feedback on following the expectations, students learn what it means to be safe, responsible, and respectful. Examples include: *"Nico, I noticed that you brought your notebook and pencil to group. That's responsible." "You were sitting quietly while I was talking. That's respectful." "You remembered to walk down the hallway. That's being safe."* Remember to include the student's first name when you provide your comments.

Last, you can remind students of the expectations and appropriate behavior throughout the year by providing booster activities, such as reteaching a lesson, practicing expected behaviors, displaying new posters of the expectations, or changing incentives for following the expectations. For example, you might initiate "Responsibility Week" and reward students for successes with extra lunch time. You could choose alternate incentives or negotiate them with the students. Practice those expectations that are frequently broken by many students in the class.

Supporting Students

Students should be supported in many ways. Besides the solid expectations and lessons for *all* students, you will provide tiered support for students needing more. Also, you can support students and yourself by posting expectations and by collaborating or sharing classroom expectations with other classrooms.

Providing Tiered Support

Tiered support, at different levels of intensity, may be needed for *some* or a *few* students. When several students have a difficult time following expectations, a class-wide motivational system can be very effective (see Chapter 13). A teacher could say, for example, *"Sometimes it's really hard to remember all the expectations in school. You are working on it, and I am sure you will get it."* If a student has chronic problems, the teacher should privately ask the student what might be done to change the situation and perhaps agree on a positive plan to help the student be more successful. Extra challenging or chronic behavior problems will require more intense planning and support to achieve success (see Chapter 16 for techniques to "think functionally" about challenging behavior).

> Individual students who are having a hard time following classroom expectations need to be encouraged to keep trying.

Visuals: Posting Expectations

It is helpful if the schoolwide umbrella expectations (e.g., be safe, be responsible, and be respectful) are defined, made into posters, and placed at eye level in the classroom. A posted set of classroom behavior expectations provides a message that certain behaviors are very important to you. Students can also put a copy of the expectations in their notebooks or tape it onto their desks. One copy may be sent home to be returned with a parent or guardian's signature, to promote awareness and support from families as well.

Developing Your Classroom Expectations

The expectations you choose should reflect how you want your students to behave at all times. If your schoolwide umbrella expectations are "be safe, be responsible, and be respectful," then define what that looks like in your classroom and explicitly teach it. When you define expectations, it is helpful to ask the following two questions.

1. What do I want to see?

2. What do I want to hear?

The following reflection provides a place to write down your thoughts and vision.

Reflection

Visualizing Success

Close your eyes and visualize your perfect classroom on a perfect day. What do you want to see and hear?

Now open your eyes and write the five most important things you saw and heard.

1. _____

2. _____

3. _____

4. _____

5. _____

Defining What You Want to See and Hear

In this section, you will come up with your clear and precise expectations to bridge the gap between the students' natural behaviors and your vision. You will use a matrix to identify and define your expectation for your classroom, as we did schoolwide in Chapter 5.

Be careful not to fall into the trap of saying, *"My students will never be able to do what I would like to see or hear,"* or *"My students come from such diverse backgrounds; they can't show the kind of respect I want."* If your expectations are very clear and are taught well, then most students will do what you expect of them.

It is especially important to have very high expectations for students from inconsistent, unpredictable home environments. They will rise to the occasion. It helps them feel safe, and it gives them a sense of belonging when they know exactly what to do or how to act. It makes their school lives predictable. Predictability helps them make good choices because they know exactly what will happen if they do or don't follow directions (Katz, 1997; Nelson, 1996).

For the *few* students who will consistently provide a challenge to your classroom management, you will need to design additional supports for their success. We describe some of these in **Section 3: Individual Student Supports**.

General Guidelines for Generating Expectations

As you identify your expectations and detail the exact behaviors you expect, remember the following.

- State the expectations in a positive way—what behaviors do you want to see?
- Make examples simple and precise.
- Display expectations publicly and at students' eye level.
- Establish and teach classroom expectations immediately—on the first day!
- Teach, reinforce, and review expectations often throughout the year.

Activity: Develop Your Matrix of Expectations

The **Classroom Expectations Matrix** provided here is intended to help you define your expectations. It provides examples of common classroom behavior expectations using the schoolwide rules of be safe, be respectful, and be responsible. Use the blank form to develop your own classroom behavior expectations matrix based on your school's rules and your vision for your classroom.

1. Refer to the **Classroom Organization Checklist** you created in Chapter 11 and write out exactly what you want your students to do for each expectation.

2. Decide whether the expectation fits best under the column Safe, Respectful, or Responsible (or the categories that fit your school's umbrella rules).

3. Refer to your **Classroom Improvement Form** to make sure that the area you chose as needing improvement is covered by your expectations.

4. Examine your school's **Schoolwide Expectations Worksheet** developed in Chapter 5 for ideas and to ensure consistency with the schoolwide rules and expectations.

5. Add expectations, change the columns to match your school's umbrella rules, or add to or change the expected behaviors listed, as needed.

Classroom Expectations Matrix (Sample)

Expectations for:	Safe	Respectful	Responsible
Teacher's Desk	Use only with teacher permission.	Wait for teacher to let you know when to come up to desk.	Put things back after use.
Materials	Hold scissors and sharp objects appropriately. Use walking feet.	Share materials with others.	Put materials back after use.
Entry and Exit	Use walking feet.	Keep personal space and quite voices.	Pickup your belongings.
Free Time	Use walking feet.	Share with others.	Put items away when you are finished.
Asking for Help	Raise your hand quietly.	Notice when the teacher has time to help.	Keep working on something you can do until the teacher can help you.
Quiet Time	Walk to the quiet-time area.	Keep your voice off.	Do what the teacher asks you to do.
Seat Work	Stay in your seat.	Keep your voice off.	Work quietly.
Drinks	Use water fountain or bottle.	Wait until others have had a turn at fountain.	Keep water in fountain or bottle.
Bathroom	Flush toilet, wash hands.	Knock on stall door.	Put towels in garbage. Return to class when you're done.
Additional Categories			

Classroom Expectations Matrix

Expectations for:	Expectation 1: _____	Expectation 2: _____	Expectation 3: _____

Teaching What You Want to See and Hear

Now that you have defined your expectations clearly and precisely and have covered all the segments of your school day, you need to develop lesson plans to effectively teach them. This activity will support you in doing that.

Teaching classroom expectations is the same as teaching schoolwide expectations. One difference is that schoolwide expectations are the same for all students in the building, whereas classroom expectations may vary from classroom to classroom. Expectations should be periodically reviewed, especially during more difficult times (e.g., before or after school breaks and holidays). Instead of allowing things to get out of hand, review the expectations and heavily reinforce those students who follow the expectations.

Activity: Develop Your Classroom Expectations Lesson Plans

The following lesson plans use the same lesson format that was used for schoolwide lessons in Chapter 6.

In the following examples, we have set up a teaching plan using a feedback technique that involves red and green cards. When teaching the behavior expectation, have your students practice giving you feedback as you model behaviors (expected and nonexamples) in the same way that you will be giving them feedback during regular instruction on their behavior (Knoff & Batsche, 1995; Walker et al., 2005). As you read these, consider what method you would use to signal to your students to continue with expected behavior ("go") or discontinue a behavior ("stop"). For example, with older students you might use a "thumbs-up" and "thumbs-down" signal. It's up to you, as long as it's clear to your students.

Materials A large green and red card can be used to teach and reinforce the skills. By using the green and red cards, students will become familiar with your nonverbal signal that provides feedback on their behavior. This type of signal will also allow you to continue the lesson and still provide nonverbal feedback to students. Students are taught that the green side of the card means "Go! Keep doing what you are doing" and that the red side means "Stop. Think about what you're doing and go back to doing the right thing."

Role Plays During the following role plays, use a set of small green and red cards. Each student can have a green card in the right hand and a red card in the left hand. Tell the students that they are going to be teachers and show you the green card when you're doing the right thing and show you the red card when you're not doing the right thing. Tell them to hold up one of the cards and keep the other card behind their back. Notice that reinforcement is built into the adult and student role plays, so the students are immediately rewarded for positive participation, correct identification of expected behavior, and their own practice of it.

Lesson Format The language of the lesson can be adjusted to the appropriate age level. It is important that a rationale is given for the expectation, so the teaching sequence should start with a positive example, be followed by a few negative examples, and always end with a positive example. It is highly advised that students demonstrate and practice only positive examples and that the teacher demonstrates the negative examples. See the lesson plans provided, which detail expectations for behavior. You can fill in the blank spots with your responses to the questions and then fill in the blank lesson plan form with details specific to your classroom.

Classroom Expected Behavior Lesson Plan

Topic/Rule: Keep Hands and Feet to Yourself

What do we expect students to do?

1. Use "gentle contact."

2.

3.

How will we teach the expected behavior?

Explain why following the rule is important.
"It's important to keep our hands and feet to ourselves so that they don't invade another person's space. We keep our feet on the floor so that we don't kick and our hands by our side so we don't hit."

List examples and nonexamples of the expected behaviors (two to three each).

a. **Positive examples:**

- Ask another adult to help you.

- Say: **"We are going to pretend that all of you are teachers and that I am a student. We are going to be playing. You have to watch and see if I do it the right way."**

[Play nicely.]

- Ask: **"Did I keep my hands and feet to myself?"**

- Ask students to hold up a green or red card. When they all have the card on green, tell them: **"Wow. Look at those green cards!"** Ask for feedback and tell the students: **"You are such fabulous teachers! You knew that I was being safe by keeping my hands and feet to myself. Let's try that again."**

b. **Nonexamples:**

- Ask another adult to help you. This time, while playing, push each other.

- Stop and ask: **"Was that an OK thing to do?"** "Nooo! Show me the red card." "Let me try that again."

[Play nicely for a while, then hit and kick the other person.]

- Stop and ask: **"Was that an OK thing to do?"** "Nooo! Show me the red card."

- When they all have the card on red ask them: **"Did I keep my hands and feet to myself?"**

- Ask for feedback and tell the students: **"You are such fabulous teachers! You knew that I was not being safe or respectful. Let me try that again."**

[Use another negative example.]

- Have them hold up the red card and ask for feedback. Say: **"Boy, I'm sure not keeping my hands and feet to myself. Let me try that again."**

Provide opportunities to practice and build fluency.

1.

2.

3.

4.

Classroom Expected Behavior Lesson Plan

Topic/Rule: Use Personal Space Properly

What do we expect students to do?

- Keep personal space when lining up (e.g., bubble space, eagle wings).

How will we teach the expected behavior?

Explain why following the rule is important.
"If we are too close, people can get 'flat tires,' trip, or get pushed. All of these are not OK. So, to be safe, we keep our personal space. The walls need to be kept clean, and any artwork needs to be protected as well. To be respectful, we make sure there is space between us and the wall. To be responsible, you will be in your spot, between your lines, with space on all sides of you."

List examples and nonexamples of the expected behaviors (two to three each).

a.   **Positive examples:**

- Say: **"I will pretend to be a student. All of you are pretend teachers. I'm going to do something, and you get ready to tell me if I did the right thing."**

- Choose one student (who is being respectful) and say: **"I need you to be my helper. We both will be students, and we're going to line up."**

[Put the student in front of you. Make a circle (like a bubble) with your arms over your head and stretch your arms out in front.]

- Say: **"I don't want to touch** (name of student helper), **the person in front of me. I need to have personal space."**

- Stretch your arms out to the sides and say: **"I need enough space so what I don't touch any walls."**

- Ask the group: **"Did I line up the right way?"** Have them hold up the green card. **"Yes, I did it the right way!"** **"What did I do?"**

[Now ask several other students to put their cards down and line up with you. Make sure they stretch out their arms to create personal space.]

- Ask the group: **"Did we do it the right way?"** **"Yes, we did it the right way!"** **"What did we do?"** Get feedback, have them hold up the green card, and say: **"You are such awesome teachers!"**

b.   **Nonexamples:**

- Say: **"Now let's see if I can do it the right way again."**

[Push one of the students in front of you, turn around, and put your arm around the neck of the student behind you (exaggerate your movement).]

- Have students hold up the red card and ask: **"Did I do it the right way?"** **"No! I was not being safe and respectful."** **"What do I need to do to line up the right way?"**

- Elicit responses and tell the students: **"You are such awesome teachers!"** *"Let's try that again."*

[Go to a different part of the room and line up the wrong way.]

Provide opportunities to practice and build fluency.

[After students have demonstrated the right way, practice several times during the day for fun.]

- When they do line up for real, heavily reinforce the behavior, and say something like: **"All of you did a great job lining up safely and respectfully! You never know when you'll get a surprise. You have just earned extra recess"** (or another special activity, game).

Procedures if one or more students don't do it the right way.

- Do not single the student out. Simply turn the card to red and say: **"I need to see everyone do it the right way. We need to practice some more. I'm going to pick on students who did it just right."**

[Choose a few students who can model it the right way.]

- Turn the card to green and say: **"That is green-card behavior! You really know how to be respectful and safe. You know how to have personal space!"** **"You never know when you'll get a surprise, if you show me that you can line up with personal space."**

[Practice until they all do it the right way. Provide positive feedback to the students who are doing it correctly.]

- Make comments like: **"Andy, look at how carefully you checked to see that you didn't touch the person in front of you!"** **"Tara, you moved away so that you wouldn't touch the wall. That's being respectful."**

[Stay close to the students who are having trouble. The minute they do it right, give them positive feedback.]

Classroom Expected Behavior Lesson Plan

Topic/Rule: Use Indoor Voices

What do we expect students to do?

- Use calm and quiet voices when inside.

How will we teach the expected behavior?

Explain why following the rule is important.
"Quiet never hurts someone's ears, and it respects their learning time. So, this is one way to be respectful. Also, when you are quiet, you can hear adult instructions, like in a fire drill. So, being calm and quiet is one way to be safe also. You can be responsible by keeping your voice quiet and by giving a gentle reminder using our nonverbal signal: 'Shh' (silent, just finger to lips)."

List examples and nonexamples of the expected behaviors (two to three each).

a.   **Positive examples:**

- Say: **"We are going to pretend that all of you are teachers and that I am the student. I am going to talk to you, and you have to tell me if I'm doing it the right way. When I do it the right way, show me the green card. If I don't do it the right way, show me the red card."**

[Talk to the students in a voice that you want to hear.]

- Ask: **"Did I use a quiet voice?"**

- Have them hold up the green card, ask for feedback, and tell them: **"You are such fabulous teachers! You know exactly when I use the right voice." "Let's try that again."**

b.   **Nonexamples:**

[This time, be loud and obnoxious.]

- Ask: **"Did I use a quiet voice?"**

- Have students hold up the red card, ask for feedback, and tell them: **"You are such fabulous teachers! You know exactly what kind of voice I need to use." "Let's try that again."**

- Use a loud voice several times and have them hold up the red card. Ask for feedback and then say: **"I had better try that again. Listen and see if I use a quiet voice this time."**

c.   **Positive examples:**

- This time, use the right tone of voice.

- Have them hold up the green card, ask for feedback, and ask which students can show how to use a quiet voice.

- Pick some students to use quiet voices.

- Have them hold up the green card and ask for feedback from the "pretend" teachers.

Provide opportunities to practice and build fluency.

1. **Indoor practice:**

   - Say: **"Now I want to see if ALL of you can use a quiet voice."**

   [Collect the green and red cards. Ask them to talk to each other in quiet voices.]

   - Provide feedback and tell the kids: **"Sometimes we might forget to use quiet voices. If that happens, I will ring the bell** (or use other audible signal). **Do you remember what you need to do when I ring the bell and say, 'May I have your attention please?'"**

   - Wait for answers. Say: **"That's right. You stop talking, freeze like a popsicle, and look at me."**

2. **Outdoor practice:**

   - Ring bell and say: **"May I have your attention please?"**

   [Immediately provide positive feedback to students who follow directions.]

   - When everyone is silently looking at you, show the green card and say: **"Please line up at the door quietly and with personal space."**

   [Immediately provide positive feedback to students who follow directions.]

   - When all students have lined up, say: **"May I have your attention please?"**

   [Immediately provide positive feedback to students who follow directions. Show the green card.]

   - Say: **"You have just earned extra playtime outside because you are being safe and respectful. Do we have to use quiet voices when we're outside? Nooo. Do we scream wildly when we're outside? Nooo. Can we be loud when we're outside? Yes! Let's go outside and see if we can use the right voices when we're outside."**

   [Monitor the students outside for about five minutes. Ring the bell. Teach them to give attention to you even outside.]

   - Say: **"May I have your attention please?"**

   - When everyone is silently looking at you, show the green card and say: **"Please line up at the door quietly and with personal space."**

   [Immediately provide positive feedback to students who follow directions.]

   - When all students have lined up, show the green card and say: **"May I have your attention please?"**

   [Immediately provide positive feedback to students who follow directions.]

   - Say: **"I just want to tell you what a great job you did using the right voices outside. No one screamed or made disrespectful sounds. You are being very respectful with your peers outside, and you are using green-card behavior. I need a helper. Who would like to be a helper?"**

   [Preferably, pick a student who displays challenging behaviors but is doing the right thing now.]

   - Say: **"You are standing here so respectfully. Can you pick two other students who are lined up the right way? Now, I want each of you to pick another person who is doing the right thing and stand over here** (create a new line-up). **Now, I want all of you to pick another person who is lined up the right way."**

   - Do this until all the students are in the new line. Then say: **"Guess what? You never know when you'll get a surprise. All of you are doing such a respectful job that you can go and stay out for a few more minutes."**

Classroom Expected Behavior Lesson Plan

Topic/Rule: Raise Hand to Talk during Instruction

What do we expect students to do?

- Raise your hand to talk during instruction.

How will we teach the expected behavior?

Explain why following the rule is important.
"When the teacher is talking, it is important to raise your hand without talking when you want to say something. Raising hands provides a calm, respectful environment for interacting during instruction."

List examples and nonexamples of the expected behaviors (two to three each).

a.   **Positive examples:**

- Give all the students a green and red card and say: **"We are going to pretend that all of you are teachers and I am a student. I am going to pick one of you to be the 'talking' teacher. Everyone else is a teacher helper, and you will watch to see if I do it the right way and show either the green or red card."**

[Choose a student who is being respectful. Give that student a book. Let the student sit in the teacher's chair.]

- Say: **"You are the teacher, and I want you to ask me (and the pretend class) what the book is going to be about."**
- Prompt the student to say: **"What is this book about?"**

[Raise your hand quietly.]

- Ask: **"Did I raise my hand quietly?"**
- Have students hold up the green card, ask for feedback, and tell them: **"You are such fabulous teachers! You knew that I raised my hand quietly. Let's try that again."**

b.   **Nonexamples:**

[This time, talk loudly while raising your hand.]

- Ask: **"Did I raise my hand quietly?"**
- Have them hold up the red card, ask for feedback, and tell the students: **"You are such great teachers! You know exactly that I didn't do it the right way. You showed me the red card." "Let's try that again."**

[Use a waving hand and talk outs several times and ask for feedback.]

- Have them hold up the red card and then say: **"I'd better try that again. Watch and listen and see if I raise my hand quietly this time."**

c.   **Positive examples:**

[Choose another student to be the teacher.]

- Prompt the student to ask: **"What day is it today?"**

[Raise your hand quietly.]

- Have them hold up the green card, ask for feedback, and tell them: **"You are such fantastic teachers! You knew that I raised my hand quietly. You showed me the green card." "Let's try that again."**

[Choose another student to be the teacher.]

- Give the student a prompt (e.g., shape, color, number). Tell the student to ask: **"What shape (color, number) is this?"**

[Raise your hand quietly.]

- Have the student turn the card to green, ask for feedback, and tell them: **"You are such smart teachers! You knew that I raised my hand quietly. I didn't talk out."**

Provide opportunities to practice and build fluency.

1. Precorrect students a few times per week to follow the rule and raise their hand to talk during instruction. Ask students to show you the right way, and repeat the instruction before starting your lesson.

2. Recognize those students who do raise their hand during instruction.

3. Ignore students who talk out, and call on a student who is raising his or her hand.

Classroom Expected Behavior Lesson Plan

Topic/Rule: _____

What do we expect students to do?

1.

2.

3.

How will we teach the expected behavior?

Explain why following the rule is important.

List examples and nonexamples of the expected behaviors (two to three each).

a.   **Positive examples:**

b.   **Nonexamples:**

Provide opportunities to practice and build fluency.

1.

2.

3.

4.

Plan for a Dynamic System

As they say, change is the only constant. Students, class dynamics, maturity, contexts, and issues for specific students and your classroom will change throughout the year (and year to year). You will plan for success despite these changes by scheduling to maintain your system through reteaching, reviewing and evaluating it, and changing it to meet shifting needs.

Change to Meet Changing Needs

Expectations that aren't working should be discarded or changed. For example, to avoid excessive movement during independent work time, one of your expectations may be that students will get a number when they need assistance. But, the result is that students get up many times during a period to pick a number. The system you developed is not working and should be changed. Potential indicators that your expectations might not be working for your classroom include excessive time spent reteaching, having trouble handing out rewards, parent or student complaints, or if you are getting irritated about your results.

These aren't certain indicators that the rule needs to change, but they are indicators you should give consideration to next steps. Some expectations will not work as planned, and some will work better for some kids than others. Efforts to change expectations (or motivators, or adding more recognition, etc.) pay off for all when the classroom runs smoothly.

> "For having lived long, I have experienced many instances of being obliged, by better information or fuller consideration, to change opinions, even on important subjects, which I once thought right but found to be otherwise."
>
> Benjamin Franklin

Teaching and Reteaching Expected Behaviors

Teaching and reteaching isn't done when there is a problem: It is done as a matter of course. Plan for initial teaching and reteaching throughout the year. You might check the schoolwide plan (created in Chapter 6) to find lessons that naturally go together. You might also consider natural times for reteaching, such as after a break, before times of excitement (holidays, school events, assemblies), before changes in classroom routines (eating outside in spring), or during transitions between curricular units. Remember, these lessons do not have to be long, just concise, with all of the components of the lesson, such as the following.

- Take students to the specific setting (e.g., hallway, cafeteria).
- Model and role play the expectations.
- First, show students how to do it.
- Next, show them how not to do it.
- Don't have students model inappropriate behaviors.
- Have students practice how to do it correctly.

Provide "Booster Shot" Lessons

Inoculation isn't permanent. Accept this, and plan to administer booster shots to maintain your classroom's health. Here are some guidelines for boosters:

- Provide a booster if a previously taught rule is consistently being violated.
- Implement a motivational system for doing it the right way.
- Consistently monitor students and provide them with positive feedback.
- Do not fall into the criticism trap; notice students who are doing the right thing instead.

Summary

After making (and while maintaining expectations), remember the following.

- Review expectations regularly and edit them; don't wait for a crisis.
- Monitor and reinforce when a rule is followed.
- Apply expectations consistently to every student.
- If a rule doesn't address a problem, discard it.

Last but not least: Teacher behavior needs to change before student behavior will change.

Preventive Interactions

Background: How Do You Prepare for Challenging Behavior?

When the physical aspects of your classroom have been examined and when the behavioral expectations are clear, you need to be prepared for the small percentage of students who will still experience difficulties meeting classroom expectations and need more teaching. Let's begin with a reflection on how you would respond to a few common classroom-management challenges.

Reflection

Classroom-Management Challenges

How would you deal with each of the following situations?

Scenario 1: When you need to give directions, many students continue to work on their task and don't hear what you are saying.

Scenario 2: One of your students often wanders around the room, bothering other students. You have asked her to sit down and mind her own business. She often ignores your requests, and her peers are annoyed by her behavior.

Scenario 3: Jose has become very upset and is bothering other students during seat work.

OBJECTIVES

▸ Discuss methods to secure students' attention

▸ Describe the use of direct speech (alpha commands) when interacting with students

▸ Present a Predictable Response Sequence to students who are noncompliant

▸ Describe how to prevent power struggles

Do you find that you have specific, detailed, and automatic responses for these situations? Spending some time developing specific plans will help them come quickly to mind when these challenging situations arise. In this chapter, we will suggest specific tools for you to use that will consistently support you and your students in minimizing the impact of negative behaviors on your classroom.

Using an Attention Signal

Teachers need to have a way to get students' attention, such as a verbal signal, a bell, a xylophone, chimes, a clapping rhythm, or lights. For several reasons, we recommend that you use a consistent technique for getting students' attention before giving directions or making announcements. Used consistently, an attention signal can help:

- Reduce the need for repetition.
- Teach students to listen respectfully to others.
- Prevent problem behaviors.

Teaching the Attention Signal

Through the consistent use of an attention signal, students develop an automated response and are taught the expectation that when someone talks, respect is shown by stopping activities, being quiet, focusing on the speaker, and listening. After you select an attention signal, add it to your **Classroom Behavior Expectations Matrix** from Chapter 12, and develop your lesson plan using the school lesson plan format from Chapter 6. Figure 30 shows a sample of how this lesson might look.

FIGURE 30   **Expected Behavior Lesson Plan for Attention Signal Response (Sample)**

> **Rule: Stop and give attention to teacher when you hear the signal**

What do we expect students to do?

1. Stop work.

2. Put eyes and ears on teacher.

3. Wait for a release signal.

How will we teach the expected behavior?

- Explain, model, and practice. Use stopwatch.

Explain why following the rule is important.

- You are remembering to be respectful when you listen to people who are talking.
- You are also remembering to be responsible about your learning, which includes listening to instructions from the teacher so that you can do your best work.
- Responding to this signal can also help you be safe if I have important safety information for you, such as during a fire drill.

List examples and nonexamples of the expected behaviors (two to three each).
Have another adult collaborator help or assign a student to help (one who has been recently behaving, especially if this is challenging for him or her).

a. **Positive examples:**
Use the audible signals to get student attention.

- Say: **"May I have your attention please?"**
- Say: **"Quiet, please"** while using the audible signal.
- Clap your hands in a pattern and have the children repeat the pattern.

1. **Scenario 1:** Stop what you are doing and look at the teacher without talking.

2. **Scenario 2:** Walk through the room and stop immediately while looking at the teacher.

Ask students for feedback after each example scenario. Ask: **"Did I do it the right way? Why or why not?"**

b. **Nonexamples:**
Use the audible signals to get student attention.

- Say: **"May I have your attention please?"**
- Say: **"Quiet, please"** while using the audible signal.
- Clap your hands in a pattern and have the children repeat the pattern.

1. **Scenario 1:** Continue to work or talk.

2. **Scenario 2:** Stop for a moment, then continue to work.

Ask students for feedback after each example scenario. Ask: **"Did I do it the right way? Why or why not?"**

Provide opportunities to practice positive behaviors and build fluency:

1. Ask students to continue working at their seats, and then give the signal.

2. Try the signal the next time they line up.

3. Try the signal when there is a louder, group-based activity going on.

4. When practicing or using the skill, immediately recognize students who are doing it correctly. For example:

- Say: **"When I asked for your attention, you followed directions right away. That's showing respect."**

5. Practice with a stopwatch until all students give attention within 30 seconds.

6. Give a group reward when they meet the 30-second goal.

Automating the Response to the Attention Signal

Following the general guidelines (by now, likely familiar) of teaching, reteaching, and providing booster lessons (along with recognition and reinforcement), students will generally accomplish skill automaticity.

When students' attention is requested, teachers might encounter a few students who will stop what they are doing for a moment but will then engage in activities other than listening respectfully. If this is the case, the entire class needs to be explicitly retaught the specific behavior expectation from the lesson and provided with more modeling and practice: *"When I give an audible signal and say, 'May I have your attention, please?' stop what you are doing, put your eyes on me, and listen until I tell you to go back to work again."* This skill can be taught in a positive way using a motivational system such as the **Concentration/Focus Power Game** (see Chapter 14).

> When the attention-signal strategy has become an automatic part of classroom procedures, it can be effectively used as a preventive interaction.

Such refinement of behavior expectations and lesson plans and reteaching should be repeated until students automatically use the skill. Stopping activities and listening quietly when someone talks is a respectful social skill for people of all ages.

The Attention Signal as a Preventive Tool

The attention signal, once automatic for your classroom, provides a way to focus attention and redirect attention. This is frequently how it is used for instruction in content areas, but it is equally useful for behavioral learning opportunities. The attention signal used in this way functions as a tool for intervention for some students, or a Tier II response.

For example, imagine that during independent seatwork several students are bothering others and keeping them off task. If the inappropriate behavior continues, peers may become aggravated, the situation could escalate, and valuable work time will be lost. Instead of drawing attention to the inappropriate behavior, the teacher can give the usual audible signal and say: *"May I have your attention, please?"* After all students are quiet, the teacher can notice individual students who are following expectations and then say: *"Thank you for giving me your attention right away. Are there any questions about the assignments? I will come around and see how everyone is doing. I need you to work quietly and respectfully in your groups. You may go back to work now."* The teacher should not reprimand and single out the small group, thereby avoiding giving the negative behavior any reinforcement. The entire class is asked to listen and is reinforced for doing so. This strategy focuses on positive behavior, provides the problem students with a moment to calm down, and reassures the rest of the class that the teacher will come and monitor.

If some students are not following directions despite your teaching clear expectations, you may need to increase support to include intervention for a *few* students, or a Tier III response.

1. Minimize attention for the behavior. When it happens the first time, focus on students who are doing it right.

2. If it happens several times, talk to the student alone during a quiet, positive time and say something like: *"It seems to be difficult for you to stop what you are doing and listen to me quietly when I give the attention signal. Is there anything I can do to help you follow directions right away?"* (Listen to response)."*Today I will watch and see how you do. I will appreciate your help."* Follow up if the student cooperates.

3. If a student continues to have problems, speak to the student alone away from peers, and set up a time to role play one on one when you and the student can be alone. It may be necessary to set up an individual incentive for the student.

Activity: **Think, Pair, Share about Your Attention Signals**

Pair up with a colleague and share your experience with attention signals:
- What types of attention signal(s) you use.
- In which situations they work best (and worst).
- How you teach it to students.
- How you solve any problems you have with it.

Using Alpha Commands to Reduce Noncompliance

Noncompliance is simply defined as not following a direction within a reasonable amount of time. Most arguing, tantrums, fighting, and rule breaking are secondary to avoiding requests or required tasks. Following directions is essential for success in school and in society. This basic skill is often overlooked by educators and can be a key issue for many students with behavior problems.

How to Deliver Alpha Commands

Again, we find that teacher behavior must change for student behavior to change. Whether or not a child complies with an adult directive has as much to do with how the command is framed and delivered as it does with the consequences (or lack of them) that follow the delivery (Walker & Walker, 1991).

When students are misbehaving, teachers must give clear and concise directions on what the students need to be doing (positive phrasing), not what they should not be doing (negative phrasing). Clear and positive directions are called alpha commands. An example of an alpha command is *"Pick up your chair, sit down, and draw a picture of your favorite animal,"* instead of *"How many times have I told you not to get up out of your seat? Don't you know how to act in this class? I'm getting tired of telling you what to do a hundred times. Now, get to work."* The latter is an example of a beta command. This beta command does not give the student specific information on what needs to be done. It also conveys signs of frustration from the teacher. Figure 31 outlines the differences between the two command types.

FIGURE 31 Alpha and Beta Commands

Alpha Commands	Beta Commands
• Minimal number of words.	• Wordy.
• Clear, concrete, and specific.	• Vague, may contain multiple steps or directions.
• Reasonable amount of time for behavior to occur.	• No clear time frame.
• No emotional content or tone.	• Often convey feelings of frustration or anger.

As you can see, beta commands may draw more energy away from the task you want someone to complete and more towards emotions about the task, the interaction, or the relationship. Direct, specific, and nonemotional commands are more likely to result in compliance with the requested behavior.

Now that you have reviewed the definitions and importance of using clear speech, set a time to complete the following activity to practice using alpha and beta commands. Work with a colleague so that you can each play the role of teacher and student.

Activity: Alpha and Beta Role Play

- Invite another person to practice with you. One person, Person A, role plays being a teacher; the other person, Person B, role plays being a student.
- Person A uses an alpha command; Person B follows the directions.
- Person A uses a beta command for the same situation; Person B follows the directions.
- Discuss the difference between the first and the second command.

Person A—Pretends to be a teacher	Person B—Pretends to be a student
The teacher wants the student to sit down. First give an alpha command.	Student is walking around the room.
Example: *"John, you need to sit down."*	Student sits down.
Next, give a beta command for the same task.	Student is walking around the room.
Example: *"How many times have I told you that you need to be in your chair when you are doing your assignment? Everyone in the class remembers that expectation except you. I don't like to remind you time and time again what you need to be doing. You need to remember to work quietly while you are in your seat."*	Student keeps walking around the room. At first he or she ignores the teacher and only eventually sits down.

Discuss the differences that you observed in teacher and student behavior.

- Which one got quicker compliance?
- Which one resulted in more student frustration?
- Which one might have been more embarrassing for the student, because the class was watching?
- Which student got more teacher attention for the misbehavior?
- Which interaction might have more easily escalated into a power struggle?

Take a few minutes to think about commands you are likely to give during the day or past situations with students that provided management challenges. Rephrase as needed, and write some alpha commands you might find useful in these situations if they occur in the future.

Predictable Response Sequence

Having a well-thought-out and consistent procedure for all adults in the school to use when dealing with challenging student behaviors is the first step to getting a student back on the right track in a respectful and calm way. The procedure below is a specific, predictable sequence of responses to inappropriate student behavior.

Scenario: The student is not following directions after the teacher gave clear instructions and verbally acknowledged other students for doing the right thing.

1. Calmly tell the student what he or she should be doing. Use the behavior expectations language you developed in Chapters 6 and 12.

2. Walk away calmly. Stay in the vicinity of the student and unobtrusively notice what happens.

3. If student makes an attempt to follow directions within 10 seconds, then tell student: *"You're making a good choice."*

4. If student is still noncompliant after 10 seconds, repeat your alpha command calmly and walk away.

5. If student makes an attempt to follow directions within the next 10 seconds, tell student: *"You're making a good choice."*

6. If student is still noncompliant after 10 more seconds, calmly say: *"You need to . . . or . . . ."* State a preplanned consequence (e.g., lose preferred activity, go to time-out, or stay after school). Walk away.

7. If student engages in dangerous behavior (e.g., throwing, hitting, kicking), see **Chapter 15: Responding to Escalating Behavior and Power Struggles**.

In the above procedure, the teacher privately directs the student using an alpha command and then walks away, giving the student time to comply. If a student complies, the good choice must be reinforced immediately. Also notice that the teacher attempted two verbal corrections before applying a preplanned consequence for noncompliance. Figure 32 illustrates this sequence.

Planful Ignoring
- Minimizes attention to negative behavior.
- Gives a student time to change behavior.

FIGURE 32 Predictable Response Sequence

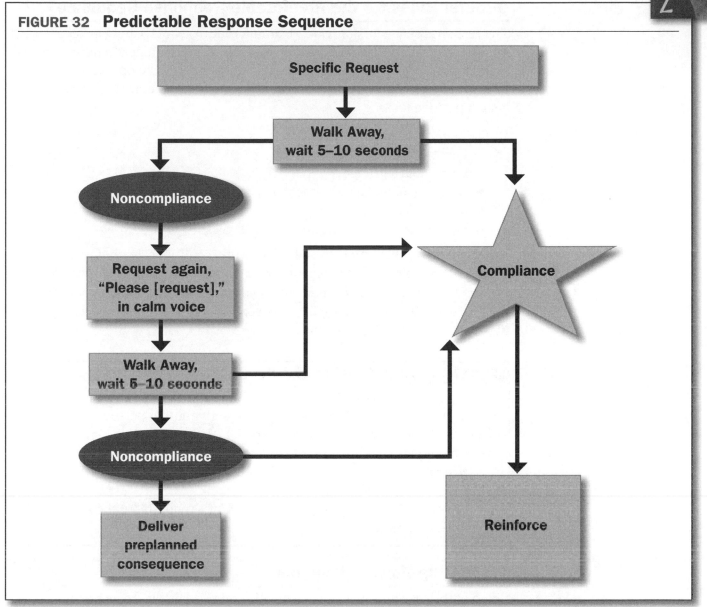

Here is another example to illustrate this procedure.

1. Say: *"Please finish the problems on page 5."*

2. Walk away to give the student a few seconds to comply.

3. Provide descriptive noticing to other students doing the right thing.

3. Deliver a brief warning that alerts the student to choose between displaying the expected behavior and earning positive consequences or failing to comply and experiencing a penalty or loss of privilege. For example: *"You've been asked to complete problems on page 5. If you choose to do that, you can go out to recess with the class. If you choose not to work now, you will need to stay in for recess later."*

4. If the student still doesn't comply, matter-of-factly deliver the penalty or loss of privilege.

General Rules for the Predictable Response Sequence

The response sequences provide a calming routine, which can help keep emotions in check. They also provide time for response, repeat reminders, and preplanned consequences, with the student having the option of returning to compliance and immediate positive reinforcement. This helps keep a positive focus.

While helping a student get back on track:
- Don't argue with the student.
- Don't hold a grudge.
- Don't try to make the student feel badly or guilty for previous poor choices.
- Do acknowledge the desired behavior as soon as it occurs.

When the student attempts to go back to work, continuously reinforce by saying statements like, *"You made an excellent choice to continue your work"* or *"You made a mature choice to sit down and open your book."* Remember that the student is being taught to follow directions and be successful, and every little step toward that goal counts.

Activity: **Role Playing the Predictable Response Sequence**

Practice the predictable response sequence with another person. One person is the teacher, and the other person is the student. You may use the same requests as in the examples above or create your own.
- **Scenario 1:** The teacher gives the student a request. The student complies at the second request.
- **Scenario 2:** The teacher gives the student a request, but the student doesn't comply.

Preventing Power Struggles

Some of the situations you may deal with, even when you are using the predictable response sequence, have the potential to develop into power struggles. Power struggles are probably the most common antecedents to aggression and noncompliance. For example, a teacher may simply give a direction to the entire class, such as: *"Please open your book to page 5."* One student may say: *"You can't tell me what to do!"* Now, the teacher has several choices:

Choice # 1: Ignore the student.

Choice # 2: Tell the student that he or she needs to open the book to page 5.

Choice # 3: Tell the student that this is inappropriate/disrespectful behavior and that he or she needs to leave the room.

Choice # 4: Reinforce other students for following directions.

What would you do? We suggest the following: After you've given a direction to the entire class and a student makes a defiant comment, simply use either one of the following words: **Regardless** or **Nevertheless**.

Teacher:	*"Please open your book to page 5."*
Student:	*"I'm not going to open this stupid book!"*
Teacher:	(Pause briefly to check your own feelings before responding to the student.)
Teacher:	*"**Regardless**, open your book to page 5."*
Student:	*"You can't make me!"*
Teacher:	(While looking at other students and not giving eye contact to the target student): *"**Nevertheless**, open your book to page 5."*
Student:	*"My mother is going to sue you!"*
Teacher:	(Walk calmly among other students and give them positive feedback such as): *"I noticed you have your book open to page 5." "Thank you for opening your book to page 5 right away."*
	Then, tell the target student, *"**Regardless**, open your book to page 5."*

The teacher continues to provide positive feedback to students who are following directions and planfully ignores the target student (unless he or she hurts himself or others). If he or she doesn't open the book, completely ignore that behavior and continue the flow of instruction. Remember that the goal is to minimize attention to negative behavior. Another goal might be to defuse the situation so that a resolution can be reached. The teacher can always return to the student and address the situation at a later time; choose one that will work best for both the teacher and the student. At this moment, the student is not receptive and further attempts to intervene will result in escalating behavior.

> Warning: Do not take these negative comments personally! They have nothing to do with you. There is something else going on; this is not about you. Do not engage in a power struggle!

Recognize the Return to Expected Behavior

As soon as the student follows directions, calmly go over and say: *"You made a good choice, can I help you?"* By saying the words: *"Can I help you?"* the target student knows that he or she is back in your graces and life can go on. Do not hold a grudge! If the encounter needs a consequence, then simply tell the student at the end of class: *"You made a very good choice to follow directions. What you did earlier was not respectful. You need to . . .* (Assign a meaningful consequence, such as writing a reflection paper or form before going out for a break or recess, eating lunch in the classroom without peers, or staying in class a few minutes before getting to going out).

If the student complies, you can problem solve/discuss possible reasons for the inappropriate behavior and how to avoid it the next time. Keep data. If this type of problem occurs more than three times, it may be reinforcing to the student, and you will need to find out the function of the problem behavior and design a positive behavior intervention plan.

Minimize Negative Behaviors

If the student does not comply, the teacher can choose the best moment to deliver preplanned consequences. This moment can be chosen to introduce the least disruption to instruction and the least reward to negative behavior, and it can be a teachable moment, if possible, for the student, whom we want to help develop the skill of following reasonable direction.

Summary

In this chapter, we have discussed a number of specific preventive interactions that the teacher can employ to achieve better results in the classroom management of difficult situations. These are increased-intensity interventions that will be needed by *some* students, or Tier II interventions.

- **Attention Signal:** clear, consistent signal for getting your class' attention.
- **Alpha Commands:** specific, clear instructions, delivered without emotion.
- **Predictable Response Sequence:** planful responses to inappropriate behaviors that include ignoring requests and rewards for positive responses.
- **Avoiding Power Struggles:** using the predictable response sequence along with "regardless" and "nevertheless" in a plan to avoid escalation.

These strategies will allow you to maintain control of your classroom environment and the pace of instruction, and they will minimize disruption. In future chapters, more sophisticated planning strategies for meeting the needs of students with chronic misbehaviors will be discussed.

CHAPTER 14

Using Positive and Corrective Consequences to Change Behavior

Background: Providing Differential Feedback

Students will learn to comply with classroom expectations and routines only through direct teaching and differential feedback regarding the acceptability of their behavior. Differential feedback is when you judiciously use positive and corrective consequences to make clear to the student the boundaries of acceptable and unacceptable behavior. For example, as a corrective consequence, you may spend time clarifying quiet voices by having students demonstrate the right way to talk quietly, which you then recognize with a positive consequence (such as descriptive noticing). In this chapter, we will describe how to give differential feedback to students to change their behavior and conform to classroom behavioral expectations. This includes delivering positive consequences for expected behavior and corrective consequences for misbehavior.

Reflection

Think, Pair, and Share

- What corrective consequences have you tried in your classroom?
- When you have seen other staff members correcting behavior in a way that annoys you, what problems do you see with their approach?
- In your experience, how effective are corrective consequences?
- How quickly do corrective consequences work?
- What are things to avoid when giving corrective consequences?

OBJECTIVES

▶ Understand the difference between descriptive noticing and positive praise

▶ Identify positive consequences to use in your classroom

▶ Identify corrective consequences to use in your classroom

▶ Design and integrate motivational systems, such as the Red/Green Card Game, to reinforce behavior expectations

▶ Teach students how to stay on task during class disruptions using the Concentration/Focus Power Game

Positive Feedback

In our practice, we have noted that a number of people resist the use of positive reinforcement. The reason for this is that people identify positive reinforcement with material objects being provided to reinforce behavior. Occasionally with high-needs children, the use of material objects is useful; however, positive reinforcement doesn't need to be tangible. In fact, we have observed that a verbal form of positive reinforcement, which we now call "descriptive noticing," is by far the easiest to implement and the most powerful tool for adults to use to support the development of academic and prosocial behavior.

> Descriptive noticing is by far the easiest and most powerful tool for changing student behavior.

Descriptive Noticing Versus Positive Praise

Descriptive noticing is simply when the adult notices and describes the desired behavior to the student exhibiting it. Preferably, the noticed behavior is an academic behavior involving the student demonstrating an effort to learn or a prosocial behavior demonstrating improvement. Descriptive noticing is not the same as praise.

Traditional praise is characterized by significant emphasis on the feelings of the adult and minimal emphasis on the actual behavior of the child. Also, it often establishes perfection as the standard. The classic example is, "Good job, Billy. I am so happy you got all the problems right." Notice a heavy emphasis on the teacher's feelings (happy) and the outcome (correct). There is no recognition of effort on the part of the child, and acknowledgement is given only for a perfect outcome. Abundant praise of academic performance occasionally results in a decrease in effort because the child is worried about being able to meet teacher expectations and replicate his or her performance. In addition, other children who have difficulty with academic or socials skills don't perceive that it is possible for them to achieve the perfect standard, and they may give up preemptively (Dweck, 1975).

> ### It's Not about You
> The teacher must maintain a neutral emotional affect.

However, noticing student efforts and noticing the application of a specific skill appears to dramatically increase the likelihood of continued effort and application of the skill. The other benefits of descriptive noticing are that it is extremely cheap, easy to do, and can be abundantly applied in any situation without cost.

When using descriptive noticing, the teacher should use the student's first name, maintain a neutral emotional affect, and accurately describe the behavior of the student. The focus of the attention is on the student's behavior. Here are examples of positive praise versus descriptive noticing.

Positive Praise	Descriptive Noticing
Social Behavior Example	
"It makes me so happy when everyone walks in the hall." Notice how, in this example, the emphasis is on the teacher's feelings and minimal description is given of the students' desired behavior.	*"Ben, Janet, and Tayshon, I noticed that you are walking with your hands by your side and your voice off. We are going to arrive at the library on time."* In this example, the teacher uses first names, has a neutral tone, expresses no particular emotion, and there is a clear description of what walking in the hall should look like.
Academic Behavior Example	
"Good job, Sasha; I am so happy you got all the answers right." In this example, the focus is on the teacher's feelings. There is no accurate description of what skill the student applied, and the teacher establishes perfection as the standard that will secure her positive attention.	*"Tran, I noticed you are focused on working on your problems. You have correctly used the carrying strategy in problems 2, 3, and 5."* In this example, there is neutral emotion, accurate description of the application of effort and of skill, and a lack of establishing perfection as the standard.

It is extremely important that teachers maintain a positive or subdued positive affect. Some students feel responsible for "making the teacher feel happy." These students can be distressed when the teacher expresses disappointment and may be reluctant to attempt difficult tasks for fear of failure. Other students may actually feel powerful when they are able to upset the teacher, and the teacher's expressed negative feelings may reinforce their behavior. The following reflection can be utilized as a self-check for your use of classroom praise and descriptive noticing.

Reflection

How Do I Deliver Verbal Positive Feedback?

- Do I use a neutral tone, so as not to keep the focus on the student's feelings and to imply that the child is responsible for my feelings?
- Do I specifically describe the behavior and/or skill that the child has demonstrated to keep the focus on the effort made?

Reinforcement: Positives and a Negative

Researchers have found that positive reinforcement is a very powerful tool for behavior change (Maag, 2001; Mayer & Sulzer-Azaroff, 1991). In fact, ground-breaking research is demonstrating that a minimum ratio of about 4:1 positive to negative interactions is a basic formula for developing successful relationships (Bradshaw, O'Brennan, & McNeely, 2008; Lambert, Bradshaw, Cammack, & Ialongo, 2011).

The 4:1 Rule for Successful Relationships

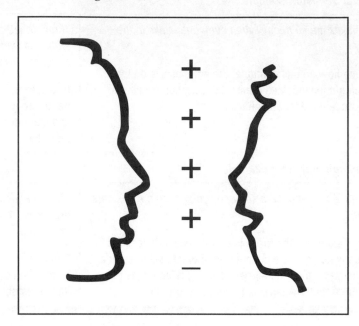

Positive consequences can be verbal (descriptive noticing, as described above) or nonverbal statements, privileges, rewards, and incentives. Positive written or verbal feedback, acknowledgment, and encouragement are among the most readily available, easiest, and most natural forms of reinforcement. The following box lists examples of positive consequences.

Sample Menu of Positive Consequences

Nonverbal	Privileges	Rewards	Incentives
Smile	Seating choice	Stickers	Grades
Wink	Sitting in teacher's	Other tangibles	Token tickets
Pat on shoulder	chair	Edibles	Field trips
Nod	Being first in line		Special events
Note	Leaving class early		
	Free time		
	Trip to office		
	Help teacher		
	Use an iPod		
	Computer time		
	Additional recess		

The only way to tell if a consequence is positive is if the behavior increases in the future. Positive consequences always increase the likelihood of the desired behavior occurring. Corrective consequences, in contrast, decrease the likelihood of the undesirable behavior occurring. Observing student behavior provides information about whether a consequence is positive or corrective. If adults apply consequences believed to be corrective, but the student's inappropriate behavior does not change, then the consequence may be reinforcing for the student and is, therefore, not effective.

What may seem to be a corrective consequence may, in fact, be a positive reinforcement, depending upon the student. Consider the following example of a 5th grade girl, Mieke. She performed at grade level and enjoyed being in the classroom. Each morning during the class' independent math assignment, however, Mieke did not stay on task. She did not complete her assignments and had to stay in for recess to finish her work.

When her behavior did not change after two weeks, the teacher talked with Mieke and asked what was going on. Mieke told the teacher that she did not like to go out to recess because some kids were bullying her. The teacher made an agreement that Mieke could stay in for recess if she got her math assignment completed. The teacher also made plans to deal with the bullying problem during recess.

Public praise or even descriptive noticing are typical reinforcers that may be meant as positive but may in fact be corrective for some students. The developmental and comfort level of students must always be considered when delivering reinforcement. Although public verbal reinforcers at the elementary level may increase positive behavior for students, they may be punishers that decrease the desired behavior for secondary-level students. Hence, it is extremely important for educators to understand the developmental level and the individual preferences of their students.

> **The Students Decide!**
>
> **Q:** Is it a positive consequence?
>
> **A:** Only if the students will do the behavior you want to get.

Reinforcement Schedule Throughout the School Year

The school year should begin with clear, high behavioral expectations combined with frequent feedback and rewards for meeting those expectations. As the year progresses, the frequency of external (extrinsic) rewards, such as tickets or other tangibles, can decrease while the more natural (intrinsic) forms of reinforcement continue, such as academic and social success, and the teacher's attention. This gradual change happens when the teacher observes students monitoring their behavior, as they become intrinsically motivated for doing the right thing. The speed and degree of this change varies by age, different classrooms of students, and also by individual students. Figure 33 shows this change over time.

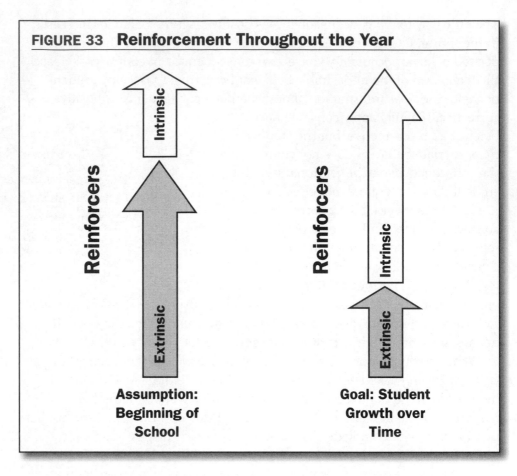

FIGURE 33   Reinforcement Throughout the Year

In advance, the teacher should create a list of possible classroom activity reinforcers that are inexpensive and quick to implement and that fit the teacher's style. These may include extra recess, popcorn party, pajama party, hat day, or crazy-hair day. The key is that the teacher can live with the activity reinforcers. Having a menu of options for the class to choose from provides the students with an element of control that makes the activity more reinforcing.

At the beginning of the year, behavioral goals for the class should be reinforced frequently, depending on the performance level of the class, to shape the behaviors. As performance increases, the time between reward activities lengthens. A reinforcement system can be thinned to span a longer period of time. For example, at the beginning of the year, the class may earn a special activity each day for following directions the first time given. Then, a special activity may be earned twice a week, then once a week, and when students have mastered the skill, a new skill can be chosen and taught with a similar reinforcement schedule.

Nevertheless, the teacher must intermittently provide specific verbal positive feedback until required skills are fluent. After a few weeks, the teacher may say, *"I just want to tell you how respectful this class is. Nearly every time I ask you to do something, you follow directions right away. It is great to be working with a neat class like this one."* Throughout the year, goals must be

clearly communicated to the students, and teachers must continue to provide students with positive feedback when they meet expectations. This system can turn classroom behavior management into a positive experience for everyone.

Reflection

Think, Pair, and Share

Find a colleague and discuss what types of positive consequences you use in your classroom.
- What works for you and your colleague?
- Which of these is easy and cheap to implement?
- Which of these is most effective?

Make a menu of reinforcers that you plan to implement.

Corrective Consequences

It is important to remember that systems based primarily on punishment result in unexpected consequences, such as increased anger, vandalism, truancy, and dropping out (Mayer & Sulzer-Azaroff, 1991; Nafpaktitis, Mayer, & Butterworth, 1985). Researchers have found that the most effective feedback systems include both positive reinforcers for desired behavior and small corrective consequences for undesired behavior.

A classroom system should include a continuum of rewards and consequences, from more natural and easily implemented forms, such as descriptive noticing and corrective feedback, to more comprehensive and intensive forms that require more planning, such as token economies and level systems. An example or corrective feedback follows. If a student is running, the teacher might say, *"Stop. How are we supposed to move in the classroom?"* Response: *"We walk."* Teacher: *"That's right, we walk. Show me."* (See Chapter 12 for teaching behavioral expectations for the classroom.) The following chart provides examples of corrective consequences.

Examples of Corrective Consequences	
• Gentle verbal correction	• Isolation within the classroom
• Loss of points or privileges	• Loss of privilege
• Discussions	• Minimize attention
• Completion of self-report behavior form	• Partner classroom
• Removal into the hall or other time-out area	• Reteach
• Removal to the office	• Reprieve (e.g., take envelope to office)
• Parent contact	• Extra work
	• Planned ignoring

Planned Ignoring

One consequence that is often effective for attention-getting behavior is planned ignoring. Planned ignoring is an active strategy to teach a student to behave in a more mature and responsible manner to earn attention. An effective teacher will never tolerate inappropriate behavior; planned ignoring is an intentional strategy used as a consequence for misbehavior. It lets the student know that some behaviors are not worthy of a response.

> **Planned Ignoring** is intentionally withholding attention (a reward) for misbehavior.

A gentle reprimand, such as *"That's not OK. You need to sit down and open your book to page 5,"* may precede ignoring so that the student will know that the teacher is not condoning inappropriate behavior by ignoring it. The teacher should not only tell the student what not to do, but should also give specific instructions on what is expected at that moment so that the student has a chance to comply.

If classroom expectations are very clear and have been taught, yet a student is still acting inappropriately to obtain teacher attention (e.g., talking out in class, getting up out of seat), then the teacher may choose to ignore the behavior and provide positive feedback to students who are following directions. For example: *"John, I see that you have your book open to page 5. Sally, you have started on the problems on page 5."* As soon as the target student complies, provide reinforcing feedback: *"You made a good choice opening your book to page 5."* (Keep in mind from the section on reinforcement that positive reinforcers vary by person.)

The teacher also needs to be proactive and catch the student doing the right thing at other times, before inappropriate behavior occurs. Students with problem behavior often require more frequent positive reinforcement for desired behaviors than other students in order to maintain these behaviors.

A teacher can never ignore behavior that involves hurting other students or him or herself, or when more than one student is involved in the inappropriate behavior. Rather than escalating the situation by trying to figure out what is going on, provide short, clear directions for what the students should do. For example: *"John, go to your desk and work on the puzzle. Tom, get the poetry book from my desk, go to your table, and look at the book for a few minutes."* In the moment, it is more critical to stop the behaviors than to figure them out or solve them.

Classroom Motivational Systems

Successful motivational systems are built on effective positive consequences for desired behavior. To imitate real-life situations, schools must provide recognition or incentives for desired behavior and small corrective consequences for undesired behavior.

Careful planning is required to choose rewards that actually do increase positive behavior and decrease problem behavior for the particular classroom or students in question. Both positive and corrective consequences must also be ones that teachers will use consistently. The most effective systems use positive consequences liberally and corrective consequences sparingly. In effective classroom-management systems, a teacher should use a combination of group contingencies and individual contingencies. After teaching students classroom expectations and the behaviors needed to meet those expectations, the teacher must design a system to provide feedback to students regarding their success or failure at meeting those expectations. You must be very clear about which situations you can resolve in your classroom and which behaviors need to be referred to the administrator. Teaching appropriate behavior in the classroom through incentives and consequences takes time and effort, but the benefits to the students can often be greater than more severe punishments, such as suspension or expulsion.

Following are a couple of activities you can use—one to motivate your class to practice expected behaviors of your choice and one specifically for helping your class learn to ignore disruptive misbehaviors by their peers.

The Green/Red Card Game

Here is an example of a classroom motivational technique: the Green/ Red Card Game, created for a CLASS program. This game has been very effective with students of all ages, as well as with adults. An administrator in Manitoba, Canada, used the Green/Red Card Game to keep staff from having side conversations during staff meetings. He stated this rule: *"If there are no side conversations during the meeting, then the card will stay on green and you will get to leave at 3:45, 15 minutes before our official dismissal time. I will turn the card to red if I hear side conversations, and we will have to stay until 4:00."* The game can be adjusted to the motivational and developmentally appropriate needs of your students and to reward the behavior of your choice.

Here are several rationales for the Green/Red Card Game:

- Students need to know whether or not they are meeting expectations.
- An external system like this helps students develop an internal self-management system (models monitoring).
- It promotes teamwork and shared responsibility for the success of all team members.

How to Create a Green/Red Card Game Use the following steps to create the game.

1. Make an 8" x 11" card (laminating optional) green on one side and red on the other.

2. Place the card so that the class can see it (e.g., on a string hanging from the chalkboard, on an easel, or magnetized to a whiteboard).

3. Draw two boxes to mark points where students can see them (e.g., on chalkboard, chart paper). Title the boxes "Green" and "Red."

4. Have an intermittent audible signal, such as a computer prompter program, and a timer or stopwatch.

5. Have a class goal chart prepared to track progress on the points earned (see next section).

6. Tell students the following:

    "When the whole class is showing expected behavior and respect, the card will be on green. If someone is not following directions, I will turn the card to red. As soon as everyone is following directions, the card will go back to green."

    "Once in a while, the beeper will sound, and you will get a point. If the beeper sounds when the card is on green, you will get a point on the green side. If the beeper sounds when the card is on red, you will get a point on the red side."

    "If at the end of the period you have more points on green, you will get to move up one space on the chart. When we get to the top, there will be a surprise for the class."

While using this technique, reinforce students for following directions, being responsible, and showing respect. This game has also been very effective in teaching self-monitoring to individual older students.

Tracking Game Scores Class performance may be graphed after each period on a chart placed in a prominent location in the classroom. Tally the green marks, and fill in the spaces on a class goal chart or other object. Charts could be in any form to match classroom curriculum or interests, including thematic designs such as rockets, thermometers, countries, words, parts of the brain, names of bones, muscles, animals, plants, insects, plant names in Latin, and so forth. Use the reproducibles provided with this chapter (target and map) or create your own. Some teachers have taken pictures of the entire class and cut the picture into puzzle pieces. Each time a goal is reached, a piece is added until the whole picture is complete.

Teacher Reinforcement Ratio Data This type of system provides excellent data on a teacher's positive versus negative interactions. Students should have a minimum of four points on the green side for every point on the red side. Below are examples of scores that work and scores that need careful analysis.

A. 25 Green – 2 Red   **D.** 25 Green – 23 Red

B. 10 Green – 0 Red   **E.** 10 Green – 5 Red

C. 75 Green – 4 Red   **F.** 75 Green – 50 Red

In all of the examples above, the students "win" the game. However, examples D, E, and F do not meet the minimum ratio of 4:1 positive-to-negative criterion. In this case, the teacher must refer to the five universal principles of PBIS (Chapter 1) and figure out which of the following problems may be occurring:

1. The teacher's expectations are not clear. In other words, students don't know exactly what to do to keep the card on green.

2. The teacher's expectations are not appropriate as written. In other words, the students can't succeed in them (consider developmental level and other characteristics of the class and whether behaviors could be used to meet the school rules).

3. The teacher has fallen into the "criticism trap" and is not ignoring minor misbehaviors.

4. The teacher is not catching students doing the right thing often enough.

5. The teacher has not correctly identified what things work as positive reinforcers for these students.

Activity: Create a Classroom Motivational Goal

Complete the following activity as a start to creating a motivational system by planning and developing materials and rewards for a first classroom goal.

- Decide which behavior you want to teach or strengthen (e.g., working quietly, asking for help appropriately, transitions).
- Choose or create a visual or theme to record progress.
- Design a poster to record progress (or enlarge a reproducible one).
- Choose and identify a number of spaces or areas to be filled for the class to earn the reward.
- Choose a class reward that will be reinforcing for *all* students (select from the reinforcement menu you created or the one that is provided in this chapter).

Concentration/Focus Power Game

This strategy is an inoculation against the spread of disruptive behavior. It helps students stay on task while there are disruptions in the classroom. In this game, you challenge students to be able to sustain work for an increasing period of time and ignore you while you are trying to interrupt them. The game is ideal for elementary and middle school students. At the high school level, ignoring should be explained and modeled in a similar way, but students who successfully ignore distractions in class should be immediately rewarded. Students need to practice ignoring distractions under controlled situations so that when a similar, real-life situation arises with their peers, they go on "autopilot" and know exactly what to do. They will also know through experience with the game that they will be rewarded for exhibiting focus during such times. This increases their motivation to ignore inappropriate behavior when it occurs. This practice also supports the ignoring strategy present in so many antibullying curriculums; therefore, this learning is transferrable to other real-world situations in which the students may find themselves.

Basic Steps of the Concentration/Focus Power Game Follow these guidelines to implement the game in your classroom.

- Make a chart to record the time.
- Set a goal (number of minutes).
- Tell students you want to teach them to concentrate and focus in spite of minor distractions.
- Tell them the rules of the game. Say: *"I will try to distract you, but you can't look up, smile, or talk until I say 'stop.'"*
- You should be the only person trying to distract students. (Do not let a student be the assigned distractor! Remember that students should practice only positive behaviors.)
- Use a stopwatch to keep track of the time and to look official.
- Model with examples and nonexamples.
- Practice for a short period in the beginning (to assure success).
- Focus only on students who are doing well.
- If a few students are not concentrating, do not draw attention to them, simply say: *"Stop. Some of you did a great job. We'll try again some other time."*

Mark the time on the chart. When students do well after a few trials, tell them that there may be occasions when someone doesn't make a good choice and tries to interrupt others' work. You will then ask them to play the Concentration/Focus Power Game, keeping in mind that they will never know when they will get a reward. For example, if the group has done a great job concentrating and not getting distracted, you may say: *"That was great. Let's go outside and take 10 minutes of extra break time* (or listen to music for 10 minutes while working)." At other times, you may simply thank the students for doing a great job. Students should not expect a reward each time they play the Concentration/Focus Power Game. Progress monitoring, such as on the chart you have created, has been shown to be an effective motivational tool. A visual picture of progress can be a reward in itself. Students can earn a class reward when they have reached a predetermined goal.

Play the game when all students are doing well. Make sure the teacher is the only person who plays the distractor during teacher-initiated game sessions. Don't give the message that you play the game only when someone is misbehaving (or you may get unintended results, like intentional distractors playing the game so that the class can earn points).

Conclusion

A lot of ideas and strategies have been presented in this chapter. Please take a few minutes to reflect on the following questions to consolidate your thoughts.

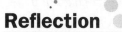

Reflection

Changing Group and Individual Behavior

- What would you do if two or three students in a class of 30 constantly disrupted the class?
- What are some strategies you would use to keep all students on task during independent work?
- Review the first reflection of this chapter; how might your responses be different now?

We're on Target!

Reaching our goal, state by state!

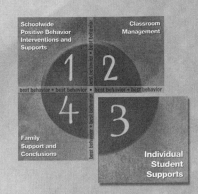

SECTION 3

Individual Student Supports

CHAPTER 15

Responding to Escalating Behavior and Power Struggles

Background: The Challenge of Escalating Behavior

Escalating behavior and verbal harassment exhibited by students seriously undermines proper functioning of a school and classroom. Behaviors such as aggression, severe disruption, and acting-out can cause major problems for adults and students, in terms of personal safety and stress, as well significantly disrupt the teaching and learning processes in school. There is no question that teachers need to develop and implement safe and effective plans for managing escalating behavior.

In this chapter, we will identify common assumptions that lead teachers into power struggles and offer procedures to avoid escalation cycles and de-escalate behaviors. If the escalating behaviors persist despite these measures, then the function of the behavior must be examined and a positive behavior support plan to reduce escalating behaviors must be developed and implemented. In this chapter and in Chapter 16, we will provide you with tools to accomplish these outcomes.

The behavior support techniques that work with students who are developing typically (as is presented elsewhere in this book, for *all* students) may not be sufficient for students who exhibit more severe behavior problems, especially those who are prone to escalation and engaging in power struggles. Such students have likely developed this escalating sequence of behaviors at home or elsewhere. The student's response may have initially resulted from fear or confusion; however, some students learn to use these behaviors to escape an unpleasant situation, such as difficult academic work, being "called out" for off-task

OBJECTIVES

▶ Identify common assumptions that get teachers into power struggles with students

▶ Identify the phases of behavioral escalation

▶ Learn procedures to prevent and respond to escalating behavior

▶ Learn procedures to de-escalate behaviors and restore the classroom or school environment

behavior, or peer teasing and taunting. As such, the child is both a victim and an architect of this failed pattern of interacting with others (Patterson, 1982).

It is important to address the behavior without causing the behavior to escalate. This can be quite a balancing act. Students who act out repeatedly may not have learned strategies for assessing and addressing the problem or for identifying sources of the problem, generating options, evaluating their options, negotiating with others, and acting on their plans. Such strategies need to be systematically and directly taught.

Like everyone else, students with severe problem behavior need to be successful and gain a sense of competence. They will be responsive if appropriate goals can be established that they are likely to meet. In general, these students do not experience academic or social success in school, but often their behavior can be brought under control if a teacher can interrupt the behavior chain that leads to escalation early in the cycle. This does not mean that we have to appease or tolerate; it means effectively responding to students so they learn to manage their own behavior. To begin, reflect on the following scenario and how you would handle it.

Reflection

Personalizing Your Learning From *Best Behavior*

Louis is in a regular classroom and is not eligible for special education services. He is a disruptive student and has a long history of arguing with teachers, shouting out, throwing books on to the floor, and tearing papers angrily. He rarely stays on task when given assignments. At the moment, Louis is arguing with you. How will you handle this situation?

Problematic Adult Assumptions

Often, adults respond to escalating behavior sequences in a manner that makes the problem worse. The table below illustrates some potentially harmful or counterproductive responses. Some of us may be operating from the following assumptions. Each of these assumptions can drive behaviors that we may regret later.

How Certain Adult Assumptions Can Lead to Problematic Teacher Responses	
Problematic Assumption	**Potentially Harmful Teacher Responses**
I can't let a student get away with this. What will the other students think?	Insist or raise ante (escalate) in order to look tough. Publicly berate the student.
I need to establish authority.	Take an aggressive body posture or tone; use power imbalance (bully).
I need to settle down agitated students.	Fuss, soothe, and give attention to the negative behavior (unintentionally reinforce the behavior).
I need to be in control.	Physically block, touch, or otherwise intimidate a student.

At the end of this chapter, we will revisit these assumptions and find ones that better suit our needs and promote more successful outcomes for the students in our classrooms.

Phases of Behavioral Escalation

Rapidly escalating behavior is a common pattern for children and youths with chronic problem behavior. Becoming familiar with the phases of the acting-out cycle can help you to understand the processes and common indicators characterizing behavior at each phase. Geoff Colvin (1993, 1999) and Hill Walker and colleagues (Walker, Ramsey, & Gresham, 2004; Walker & Sylwester, 1998) have illustrated a seven-phase cycle describing the constellation of behaviors that make up escalating behavior sequences. The phases of the escalation cycle are differentiated based on the intensity and order of appearance of the behaviors. Figure 34 provides a graphic illustration of the phases and their sequence. We will review each of the phases in detail.

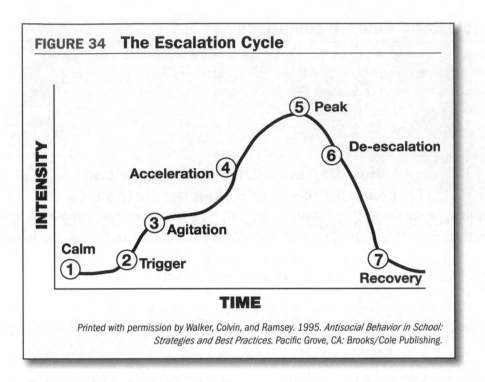

FIGURE 34 **The Escalation Cycle**

Printed with permission by Walker, Colvin, and Ramsey. 1995. *Antisocial Behavior in School: Strategies and Best Practices.* Pacific Grove, CA: Brooks/Cole Publishing.

Phase 1: Calm

During this phase, the student demonstrates appropriate behavior and is generally cooperative and responsive to teacher directions. The student may engage and participate in classroom activities for an extended period of time, follow rules and expectations, be responsive to feedback, and occasionally initiate appropriate behavior toward others.

The student is often ignored during this phase because the adults are taking advantage of this respite from acting out. Instead of ignoring, this is a good time to establish behavior goals and provide consistent positive feedback for appropriate behavior.

Phase 2: Trigger

Triggers are activities, events, or behaviors that set off the escalating phases of the acting-out behavior cycle. Some triggers may be present continuously but have an effect only in conjunction with some other specific event or action.

School-based triggers include conflicts resulting from ineffective communication or miscommunication with others in school. Students exhibiting acting-out behavior often misperceive the actions of others and think they are being treated negatively or unfairly when they are not. Other school-based triggers are listed in the box provided.

Nonschool-based triggers are events, conditions, or situations that may underlie escalation cycles, including home and social conditions. These factors may play a role in making it more difficult for a student to make appropriate choices, including at school, and among his or her peers. Examples of nonschool-based triggers are also listed. Classroom teachers

School-Based Triggers	Nonschool-Based Triggers
• Miscommunications	• Poverty
• Misperception of others' actions	• Unemployment of caregivers
• Changes in routine	• Abuse or neglect
• Peer provocation	• Poor adult modeling of appropriate behavior
• Ineffective problem-solving ability	• Negative neighborhood influences
• Ill-timed teacher corrections	• Sleep deprivation
• Teacher requests or demands	• Inadequate diet
• Interruptions	• Medical conditions
• Transitions	• Developmental delays

have limited influence over the external factors (Walker et al., 1995), so it is important to keep a focus on the here and now. This is covered in the section on teacher responses. When the student has not been taught how to respond effectively to the trigger, he or she may become more agitated (Phase 3), and the behavior may escalate rapidly (Phase 4).

Phase 3: Agitation

Students who do not effectively manage Phase 2 triggers are likely to exhibit agitated behavior. This phase is characterized by emotional responses: anger, withdrawal, worry, anxiety, or frustration. Students' eyes may dart about from here to there, with little focus, and it becomes difficult for them to continue conversations. Agitated students often increase their hand movements—drumming their fingers, tapping their pencils, opening and closing their books, or mumbling under their breath. They may move in and out of groups, vacillate between off-task and on-task behavior, and have difficulty attending to academic tasks (Colvin, 1999). Some students want to be left alone at this point, becoming quiet or withdrawing from group activities.

Phase 4: Acceleration

Students in this phase exhibit escalated behaviors that are likely to dominate the teacher's attention or even cause alarm. They question, argue, and engage in confrontational interactions; they are defiant of teacher demands and expectations and often engage in off-task behavior. Many students provoke others and may use offensive language or destroy property during this phase. Or, they may demonstrate compliance with specific requests but still behave inappropriately. Colvin (1999) calls this "limit-testing." A student may work on an assigned task but also act out, or comply with a demand but only partially, or comply at a lower-than-expected level.

For example, the teacher may ask the student to complete the entire math section, but the student does only half of it. The student starts whining and wants to escape from classroom activities. When the teacher asks for the completed assignment, the student makes threats. Such threats may pose a danger and should not be ignored.

Phase 5: Peak

The peak phase is the most dangerous and disruptive to the class. In this phase, students with acting-out behavior may well be a threat to themselves or others. They may engage in serious destruction of property, physical assault, or self-directed negative behavior, such as physically hurting themselves, hyperventilation, or severe tantrums. Behavior during this phase is out of control. Any discussion with the student during this time is unproductive. When a student is at the peak of escalation, it should be treated as an emergency. We will outline appropriate procedures later in this chapter.

> **Peak Phase is Dangerous**
> - During the peak phase, safety is the teacher's focus.
> - Discussion with the student will be unproductive, at best.

During the escalation and peak phases, the teacher must secure the safety of all students, even if it means having all students except the student with escalating behavior leave the classroom quickly (a "room clear").

Phase 6: De-Escalation

This phase is characterized by student disengagement and reduced acting-out behavior, or de-escalation. Students show confusion by wandering around, staring at the floor, fidgeting, or just sitting or standing. Some students may want to apologize for their behavior; others want to withdraw or even sleep after the incident. Some deny their behavior or blame others for the incident.

Phase 7: Recovery

Recovery is the final phase of Colvin's behavior cycle, during which the student returns to a normal, calm state. In the beginning of this phase, the student is likely exhausted emotionally and physically and slowly regains control. Gradually, the disengaged student begins to respond to teacher instruction, often preferring mechanical or routine tasks that are easy to perform. They generally want to avoid discussing the incident and are not ready for difficult tasks requiring teacher assistance or having to cooperate with peers.

Students engaging in acting-out behavior do not progress through every phase of the acting-out cycle at the same rate. Nevertheless, school staff should be able to identify behavioral signs of each phase and be prepared to intervene as appropriately as possible to minimize the risk that a student will reach peak phase and its potential dangers. Next, we will provide strategies for intervening at each phase of the acting-out cycle.

Basic Approaches to Preventing Escalating Behavior

Specific strategies and interventions have been developed to manage each of the seven phases of Colvin's acting-out cycle. Managing a student's acting-out behavior during the earlier phases of the cycle may prevent the occurrence of more serious and destructive behaviors in the later phases. The emphasis during the first phase (calm) is on teaching acceptable behavior and providing the student with lots of positive feedback. If the problem behavior has been reoccurring, the teacher must find out what triggers the behavior and provide the student with strategies to deal with the trigger. Sometimes, it is very difficult to find the trigger. Classroom interactions may need to be videotaped for several days and analyzed. A staff member other than the teacher may need to conduct an Antecedent, Behavior, Consequence (ABC) observation. Consider the following real example.

Becoming Calm and Successful: Interrupting the Cycle of Escalation

Tes, a 10-year-old girl, was, along with her younger sister, removed from her parents' care at age 5 after both girls had experienced severe neglect and sexual abuse. After living in several foster homes, the girls were adopted by two different families. Tes was placed in a special education classroom at age 8. Her academic skills were low, and she displayed frequent incidents of violent and destructive behavior in an inconsistent manner. It seemed like her outbursts would come "out of the blue." Some days, she would be totally appropriate and at other times, while performing similar tasks, she would suddenly throw her books, tear papers, swear loudly, and throw her chair and desk. After examining hours of classroom tapes, the only trigger the staff could identify was that when Tes slid down in her chair, she would escalate quickly to a major blow-up that was unsafe for her and for the entire class.

The teacher made a large sign, "I am calm and good at what I do," and posted it in the front of the room. During a calm phase, she asked Tes to read the sign and told her, "I want to help you to make good choices when you are having a difficult time in class. Sometimes, I may ask you to read the sign. You can read the sign as often as you need to calm yourself down." Tes smiled and agreed to try.

"I am calm and good at what I do."

The next time she slouched in her chair, the teacher asked her to read the sign. She threw her book and yelled, "I'm calm and good at what I do!" She proceeded to yell the phrase while demolishing her papers with a pencil. The teacher carefully herded the other students in the group to another part of the classroom and ignored Tes' challenge. Soon, Tes was copying the phrase and wrote: "I am calm and good at what I do."

When she had de-escalated, her teacher told her: "You did an excellent job of calming yourself down. How about if, next time, I ask you to go to your desk and calm yourself down?" Tes agreed. During the next few weeks, she had several opportunities to practice her new skill, and each time she became calmer more quickly. After about one month, she was able to attend classes in the regular classroom, where the teachers posted the same sign and gave her a cue to look at the sign when she triggered.

Slouching in the chair was probably not the real trigger, but it was the only behavior that signaled a full-blown escalation. Even though her teacher worked closely with the adoptive mother, she didn't learn until several years later that, all along, Tes had been stealing food and hiding it. In retrospect, the trigger may have been inadequate nutrition. Her adoptive mother punished her by allowing her to eat only certain amounts and types of food at certain times of the day, which may not have been enough for this extremely fast-growing child. Hunger may have irritated her. The teacher didn't have control over the home situation but still had to teach Tes to deal with the (unknown) triggers nonviolently and in a socially accepted way. The strategy worked well for her. Tes has been in a successful marriage for several years, has one son, and is "Calm and happy and good at what she does!"

As this example illustrates, it is most important to identify a trigger, even if it is not the initial one, and interrupt the escalation cycle of a student who demonstrates extreme behaviors. If no trigger can be identified, then the teacher must be aware of the student's behaviors in the agitation and escalation phases, identify when this is happening, and try to divert the behavior from escalating through behavior management and teaching. A teacher can quickly escalate the behavior by engaging in a power struggle, getting in the student's face, scolding the student in front of peers, or touching the student. These tactics must be avoided at all times (see the **Problematic Adult Assumptions Chart** on p. 223). The teacher must give clear and short directions on what the student needs to do. (See the **Predictable Response Sequence** in Chapter 13. Use a neutral, businesslike tone, and remain respectful with the student.)

Considerations Behind the Basic Approaches to De-Escalation

In the remainder of this chapter, we present procedures to prevent and manage escalating behavior. Listed here are several considerations that should be kept in mind.

- **Consideration 1: Escalating behavior is a phase in a chain of problem behavior.** Typically, escalating behavior does not occur in isolation ("All of a sudden, we have a serious incident on our hands."). Rather, there is an identifiable behavior chain in which escalating behavior is one part of the chain, and, most importantly, it occurs later in the chain.

- **Consideration 2: Intervening early in the behavioral chain can disrupt the whole chain.** Given that escalating behavior occurs later in the behavioral chain, strategies can be used to target behaviors early in the chain. In this way, the chain is altered and subsequent behaviors in the chain are prevented from occurring.

- **Consideration 3: The surest method for preventing escalating behavior is to provide a strong focus on school success.** When students succeed at school academically, socially, or through successful participation in school activities (such as drama, music, clubs, and sports), there is much less chance they will engage in the behavioral chain leading to escalating behavior. Having and valuing a wide variety of student groups (as is promoted in antibullying and many prosocial curriculums) can contribute to having a school context in which everyone can succeed.

- **Consideration 4: Escalating-behavior management plans need to be part of a proactive, schoolwide discipline plan.** It has been well established that school faculties that systematically work hard together to establish a strong, positive school climate have less serious problem behavior. In these schools, staff members use a continuum of procedures to directly teach and maintain expected behavior and to address and correct problem behavior. Escalating-behavior management becomes part of the continuum for addressing problem behavior.

The Comprehensive Intervention Plan: Stages and Strategies

Managing escalating behavior involves four stages of teacher intervention. Each stage requires specific strategies that relate to the goal of that particular stage. A comprehensive intervention plan allows teachers to identify the stage of intervention needed and apply the appropriate strategies.

Four Stages of Intervention

These stages of intervention parallel the phases of escalation. The stages align with the seven phases of escalation, though obviously not one-to-one.

1. Prevention

2. Interruption

3. Response

4. Follow-Up

Stage 1: Prevention Initially, the student may be productively or satisfactorily engaged in the class or school activities. In this stage, strategies are designed to maintain the student and essentially *prevent* escalating behavior.

Stage 2: Interruption If events or triggers unsettle the student, giving rise to the beginnings of problem behavior, then strategies are designed to *interrupt* the behavior pattern, in other words, to catch the problems early and redirect the student to engage in the present class activities.

Stage 3: Response The third intervention stage involves what we typically refer to as *response*. This is when the behavioral chain is going to run its course and the student exhibits serious behavior escalation. The intent of these strategies is safety—to minimize the likelihood of anyone getting hurt and to minimize the level of disruption to the class or school activity.

Stage 4: Follow-Up The final component addresses the period following an incident or following the prevention of an incident. At this point, the emphasis is on *follow-up*, in which staff persons meet with the student to debrief the situation and develop, or modify, supports accordingly. It is extremely important at this stage that the student (and the adult) is calm and positively engaged in a directed activity. The student should understand that adult attention is given when behavior is appropriate.

Table 4 provides a summary of the escalation cycle, including behavioral indicators, the best-practice responses for each phase, identification of the intervention stage, and specific strategies to be used.

TABLE 4   Phases, Behaviors, and Interventions of the Escalation Cycle

Phase	Behavioral Indicator	Intervention Stage	Strategy
Calm	• Able to follow directions • Less likely to react to provoking situations • Responsive to praise and other forms of reinforcement • Able to make mistakes and receive correction • Interested in showing work and telling about accomplishments	Prevention	• Conduct functional assessment • Identify alternative behaviors to teach • Teach alternative behaviors • Utilize preventive techniques, such as high rates of positive reinforcement, prompting expected behaviors, rule reminders, and proximity
Trigger	• Provocation from another person • Interruption of routine or reward • Problem-solving situations • Continued errors • Having to face consequences for behavior	Prevention	• Identify the antecedent/trigger • Modify the influence of the antecedent • Teach or practice a problem-solving routine • Prompt alternative or replacement behaviors (e.g., ask for help, a break, or walk away) • Remind use of alternative behaviors
Agitation	• Increased body, eye, hand movement • Cryptic speech/no speech	Interruption	• Provide quiet and alone time • Make easier work available • Provide concrete task or response options
Acceleration	• Engagement behaviors (questioning, arguing, provoking) to get predictable response • Threats, intimidation, defiance • Leaves situation • Physical aggression • Self-abuse • Property destruction	Response	• Intervene early • Rehearse expected behaviors • Provide reminders • Modify the task or task demands • Alter the physical arrangement • Withdraw from the individual • Remind use of alternative routine • Prompt the alternative routine • Praise engagement on the alternative routine
Peak	• Physical aggression • Self-abuse • Property destruction • Tantrums • Hyperventilation	Response	• Physically restrain the student (as allowed by your district) • Clear the room • Give a time-out • Get emergency assistance

TABLE 4 Phases, Behaviors, and Interventions of the Escalation Cycle

Phase	Behavioral Indicator	Intervention Stage	Strategy
De-Escalation	• Confusion • Attempts to reconcile • Withdrawal behaviors • Responsive to concrete directions • Denial of serious incident	Follow-Up	• Praise return to normal activities • Debrief with the student, if appropriate
Recovery	• Willingness to resume routine, especially tasks that do not require interaction • Subdued behavior • Reluctance to talk about/denial of behavior	Follow-Up	• Focus on normal routine • Praise appropriate behavior • Rehearse problem-solving routine • Provide easier, individual work

Strategies by Stage

As indicated in the table, each stage correlates with strategies the teacher can employ to help meet the stage's goal to break the chain of destructive behavior.

Strategies for Stage 1: Prevention The intent of all of these practices is to increase the likelihood that the student will be productively and successfully engaged in the class and school activities. In this way, appropriate behavior may be maximized and inappropriate behavior minimized. As we have discussed throughout this book, it is critical that the school as a whole and the classroom are positive, predictable environments with clear expectations. A schoolwide social skill curriculum must be taught that focuses on effective problem solving, anger management, impulse control, and empathy (e.g., the Second Step program). The social skills must be practiced by students and reinforced daily by all staff members. In addition, the physical design of the classroom needs to be carefully considered (Colvin, 2002; Colvin & Lazar, 1997). Careful planning of classroom organization and scheduling is essential (Chapter 11), and appropriate academic placement of students will maximize their chances for success.

Strategies for Stage 2: Interruption In this stage, strategies are designed to catch the problem behaviors at their onset, that is, to interrupt the behavioral chain so that the problem behaviors do not worsen or escalate. The teacher can defuse the situation when a problem behavior is likely to occur. For example, Johnny spends Wednesdays with his verbally abusive father. Every Wednesday afternoon, he becomes more and more agitated and usually escalates just before school is out. The teacher could talk to Johnny and acknowledge that it must be difficult to go home with Dad and ask if Johnny would like to spend time on the computer the last hour of school on Wednesdays. If Johnny leaves school in a calm manner, he can probably better tolerate some of his father's inconsiderate words. Depending on his age, he can be taught assertive and calm responses to his father's behavior.

Additional examples of managing escalating behavior can be seen in a video program featuring Geoff Colvin titled, *Defusing Anger and Aggression* (1999). The video provides examples and solutions for behavior that is off task, challenging, confrontational, defiant, disrespectful, or intimidating. In addition, it deals with behavior characterized by agitation, depression, and avoidance.

Strategies for Stage 3: Response When the student's behavior has reached levels where the personal safety of staff, students, and the involved student becomes a serious concern, crisis response is needed. Strategies for this stage are designed for safety first.

A plan must be in place to respond to a crisis situation. During a calm time, all students must be taught "room clear" procedures. These procedures (and all other expected behaviors) should be recorded on a standard lesson plan (see Chapter 6) and taught and practiced on a regular basis, just like a fire drill. During a room clear, all students except the escalating student should quickly and in an orderly fashion leave the room and go to a safe place (e.g., library, cafeteria, or playground). The escalated student stays in the room with supervision until the de-escalation phase occurs or until help arrives. Procedures on how and who to call for help (e.g., principal, crisis response team, security, police) must be clearly defined and easily available. In addition, legal requirements or school district policies on safety must be followed.

Strategies for Stage 4: Follow-Up Follow-up is needed after the student displays crisis behavior or initiates an escalation cycle, whether the behavior was exhibited, prevented, or avoided. The intent is to review the situation, identify triggers, evaluate responses, and make provision in the planning for future events. The team must decide if **Functional Behavioral Assessment** (FBA; see Chapter 16) and **Positive Behavior Support Plan** (PBS Plan; See Chapter 17) modifications are needed and who will be responsible. An excellent resource for conducting a functional assessment and developing PBS Plans is the book *Why Johnny Doesn't Behave: Twenty Tips for Measurable BIPs* (Bateman & Golly, 2003). A debriefing with the student and perhaps the parents might be necessary. When meeting with the student, ask if he or she understands what lead to the situation, what would help him or her avoid a similar situation in the future, and clarify any consequences that may be delivered.

Colvin's Approach to Defusing Escalation

Our colleague, Geoff Colvin, offers an excellent strategy for responding to escalation and provides a step-by-step approach to responding to student behavior that defuses, rather than escalates, the behavior. Figure 35 summarizes his general approach. Notice that this approach aligns with many best practices presented in *Best Behavior:* lesson plan components, positive reinforcement, the predictable sequence response, and strategies discussed in this chapter. We recommend that you review the material in this chapter in detail and remember that your response to escalation will be unique to each student. If you are to become skilled at responding to escalating behavior patterns, you will need to be aware of assumptions you may hold that interfere with a calm, businesslike approach, and acknowledge that your behavior often will be the difference between a dangerous, disruptive escalation and a return to expected school and classroom routines. The choice is yours!

FIGURE 35 Colvin's Approach to Defusing Escalation

If a student shows signs of escalation:

- Stop and think.
- Restate the expected behavior and bring other students on task.
- Recognize other students for acceptable behavior.
- Speak privately and acknowledge agitation calmly.
- Isolate, ignore, or offer support to the escalating student.
- Give the student a positive choice. (e.g., "You can either get back to work or go to the office.")
- Step away and give the student time to respond ("I will give you a chance to think about it."), unless it is an emergency.
- If the student complies, recognize and acknowledge cooperation.
- If the student continues to escalate, implement the preplanned consequence or school emergency procedures, as appropriate (e.g., room clear, get other adults).

Printed with permission by Walker, Colvin, and Ramsey. 1995. *Antisocial Behavior in Schools: Strategies and Best Practices*. Pacific Grove, CA: Brooks/Cole Publishing

---

Adult Assumptions Revisited

At the start of this chapter, we identified some problematic assumptions that get teachers and other adults into trouble during escalation cycles. Think about the behaviors you will need to learn, practice, and exhibit under duress—escalation cycles are hard on everyone!

Working backwards this time, think about the behaviors you will need to exhibit for the most successful management of escalation cycle phases and for the most successful outcomes for your students. Then, identify some assumptions you could hold that would support these types of behaviors. Fill in the chart provided. A couple of examples have been filled in.

Activity: Identifying Adult Assumptions That Can Lead to Helpful Behaviors

Potentially Helpful Teacher Behaviors	Helpful Assumption
Intervene early in the cycle.	I can improve my response to escalation.
Teach "room clear" during calm phases to all students. Initiate a "room clear" when required.	I need to establish and maintain student safety.
	My attention is a powerful reward.
	Remaining calm is how I can best role-model for my students.
Provide alternative behaviors to replace those in the escalation cycle.	

CHAPTER 16

Thinking Functionally About Behavior

The Benefits of Thinking Functionally

We have examined a variety of ways to organize your school and classroom to prevent problem behaviors. These systems are designed for *all* students (Tier I). You have also seen that, for *some* children, even the best preventive strategies will not work at all times and interventions are needed. We will now explore a way to support the *few* individual students (Tier III supports) who exhibit behavior that our lower levels of intervention do not address. These behaviors often challenge our resources and skills. To support these students, we will need to think functionally about their behavior—think about how the behavior functions to meet the student's needs.

Why Some Consequences Don't Change Behavior

Some traditional behavior management strategies, such as corrective consequences or simple reinforcement, are not effective in changing chronic and intractable behavior problems. This is because they are not logically linked to the causes (what sets it off) and functions (why it works for the student) of the behavior(s). In other words, the consequences being administered (whether positive or negative) are not having an effect on the problem behavior because its cause remains unaddressed, because the consequences are still acceptable to the student, or because a hidden need or want is being met.

For example, if José is using noncompliance to get out of completing a seatwork task, sending him to a time-out will not change the behavior because he is getting out of doing the work anyway! A better

OBJECTIVES

- ▶ Clarify why it is important to "think functionally" when addressing problem behavior

- ▶ Define Functional Behavioral Assessment (FBA)

- ▶ List the outcomes of a complete FBA

- ▶ Discuss when and how to conduct an FBA

- ▶ Detail the information to be gathered and assessed in a comprehensive and effective FBA

method for José might be to ignore the minor noncompliance and tell him that he will not be allowed to go to lunch until the seatwork is finished. We also would make sure that the seatwork task is of appropriate difficulty and is interesting, and we could perhaps offer a positive consequence for acceptable work. Identifying the true causes and functions of problem behavior is the work of this chapter. Once these true relationships can be established, a plan can be made to help the student learn more productive and positive behaviors. The plan can effectively change either the causes or the outcomes to affect behavior choices. Student needs usually can't be changed, but they often can be met in a number of ways.

The Function of Behavior

A process called Functional Behavioral Assessment (FBA) can be helpful in developing effective and positive behavior support plans (Crone & Horner, 2003; O'Neill et al., 1997; Scott et al., 2005). The function of a behavior is to address a student need. The true needs a student has may include gaining attention, asking for help, or requesting a break from school work. These needs may be conscious or unconscious and are revealed by carefully observing what the student "gets" from the behavior. It is possible that the student needs both an adjustment in the level of the work and an increased level of positive adult attention for positive behaviors, such as effort. One function of the FBA is to correctly apply consequences, both positive and negative, that will affect the behavior.

> Commonly, the function of behavior is to either gain adult or peer attention or to escape from tasks that are perceived as too hard or too easy.

The Cause of Behavior

Another function of the FBA is to identify and remove academic causes, or triggers, of the behavior. Effective positive behavior support plans include adapting the curriculum, instruction, and environment to individual student needs. Instruction is defined as how you teach, curriculum is defined as what you teach, and environment is defined as where you teach, meaning the precise physical environment in which you teach. Details on adapting these will be covered in Chapter 18.

Thinking Functionally: Addressing the True Causes and Functions of Behavior

In this chapter, you will learn how to use FBA to define problem behaviors, identify the adult or peer responses that tend to support or maintain them, and hypothesize about predictors or causes. We will learn to use our functional assessment information to develop behavior support plans in Chapter 17. Thinking functionally about a student's problem behaviors gives a simple road map to developing effective support plans that are logically linked to the reason(s) why students misbehave and, therefore, have a better chance of effecting positive behavioral change.

In order to get you thinking about a problem you would like to assess and solve, use the following space to briefly reflect on a student who exhibits problem behaviors.

Reflection

Thinking Functionally about Behavior

Student's First Name: _____

Grade: _____

Problem behaviors you see:

Places and times where the behaviors are likely to occur:

What would you like the student to do instead of the problem behaviors?

What Is Functional Behavioral Assessment?

FBA is a process of identifying the events that predict and maintain patterns of problem behavior. This includes both causes and functions. A simple FBA can be used relatively quickly for most students. All teachers should think functionally about behavior and modify their instruction and positive reinforcement strategies according to their students' needs. Here is a sample of what a teacher may consider for this FBA.

Question: Why is the student behaving this way? What can I do to change this behavior?

Background/Observations: Conduct an FBA.

Hypothesis: Develop a Summary Statement.

Create a Test: Write a Behavior Support Plan (Chapter 17).

Observe and Record: Note results, a decrease or increase in behavior.

Analysis and Conclusion: Did the behavior decrease? Was the Summary Statement correct?

Ask More Questions: Repeat as needed if the behavior didn't decrease.

Some students will require a very detailed analysis, commonly referred to as a Functional Behavior Analysis (O'Neill, et al., 1997), which is also referred to as an FBA. This type of formal FBA, however, is seldom required and should be conducted by a trained professional (e.g., school psychologist, behavior specialist). Federal special education law specifies the use of a "functional behavior assessment" in a specific manner, to be used to determine if a behavior is a manifestation of a student's disability. In this chapter, we will not detail these specific procedures. Instead, we will use functional-behavior assessment procedures in a more general sense, to be used by any teacher to think functionally about behavior.

When we think functionally about behavior, we don't first look for the source of the problem in the student's disability, home life, or other possible factor that is simply out of our control (e.g., the student is hyperactive or "acts this way because his parents are not helping at home"). Although these factors can clearly affect the student's performance, we need to look instead at those factors that we can control in the school setting (instruction, curriculum, and environment). We try to figure out what student need is being met (e.g., attention, avoidance) by the misbehavior.

What Are the Outcomes of an FBA?

In order to develop a logical and effective student support plan, you need to achieve four critical outcomes from the functional behavioral assessment. Although the process may look simple, it can be quite challenging, depending on the particular problem behavior being investigated. The key outcomes of an FBA follow.

1. Clearly define the challenging behaviors in observable and measurable terms.

2. Identify the events, times, and situations when the behaviors occur.

3. Identify the consequences that maintain the behaviors.

4. Develop a summary statement about the function of the problem behaviors.

FBA involves collecting information in order to make a summary statement about what sets off the behavior and what consequences (adult or peer responses) are maintaining them. In other words, what makes the behavior work for the student (what needs are being met)?

When Should You Conduct an FBA?

Designing an individualized behavior support plan can be time consuming and will require regular adjustments and data collection to support decision making (see Chapter 17 for more details). Because of the time demands, you should reserve functional behavior assessments for those students in your class who are not responding to your classroom management systems. These are the *few* students needing Tier III supports (see Chapter 3). However, we should think functionally about all behavior!

Assure that your classroom is a positive, predictable environment. This means that your expectations are clear and have been taught (use the following activity to assess your classroom practices). A sample list of expected classroom behaviors might include:

- Follow directions the first time given.
- Use personal space.
- Walk at all times.
- Use indoor voices.
- Ask for help appropriately.
- Use appropriate language.
- Work with voices off.

We recommend that a range of classroom management and group interventions (such as the Green/Red Card Game described in Chapter 14) be implemented to reduce the problem behavior before beginning FBA. When a student is chronically referred to the office for behavior problems, however, a functional behavioral assessment is indicated to build an effective support plan.

Activity: Self-Assessment of Classroom Practices			
Are the following practices in place in your classroom?	**Yes**	**No**	**Comment**
Can your student do the tasks you require? The tasks must not be too difficult or too boring.			
Your positive-to-negative interaction ratio for a student is 4 : 1.			
You are using descriptive noticing: "I noticed . . . I saw . . ." **Not:** "It makes me happy when you . . . I am disappointed when you . . ." This is not about teacher feelings!			
Your reinforcement is about paying attention to the things you want to see and hear from your students.			
You're staying out of power struggles: Use the words "regardless" and "nevertheless."			
You give short, clear directions. No excessive teacher talk!			
You only call on a student who has a hand raised without talking out.			
You ignore minor talk-outs.			
You frequently praise the student doing the right thing.			
You minimize attention for minor inappropriate behaviors.			

Thinking Functionally Is a Continuous Process

Functional behavioral assessment should be the central component of your behavior support planning. This means that the FBA is a continuous process, as student behaviors change over time. Sometimes, when behavior support plans solve one problem, new problems emerge. These new problems involve the use of limited resources (e.g., teacher time, incentives, and materials) and require new planning or changes to the plan. By continuing the FBA process, you will be gathering information in order to make decisions about the efficiency and effectiveness of the plan. Ongoing data collection is used to refine support plans. Refinements may include fading the plan or changing the schedule of reinforcement. FBA is not intended or suited for diagnostic labeling. It seeks to interrupt negative behavior cycles and replace unsuccessful behaviors with successful ones. Educators find it useful because assistance for problems is not driven by eligibility for special education. Instead, assistance is provided based on need alone.

Functional behavior assessment not only helps in the development of effective and efficient support plans, but it also helps us avoid errors in our attempts to encourage behavior change. The danger of making problem behavior worse is very real. We have all seen instances of children having tantrums in order to gain a treat, or children who behave aggressively in order to avoid a task (who are then sent to the corner for their behavior). In each case, the presumed solution actually reinforces the problem behavior because it meets the underlying need for either attention or avoiding an unpleasant task.

Conducting a Functional Behavior Assessment

There are three major methods for conducting a functional assessment:

1. Interviews

2. Direct observation of the student

3. Testing a hypothesis

We do not recommend the third method of assessment unless it is accompanied by expert supervision; we recommend only interviews and direct observation for classroom use.

We have found that conducting an interview of the teacher(s) involved is an efficient and effective method for assessing the behavior of most children. We also recommend that you confirm, clarify, or amend your interview information by directly observing the student. Interviews and direct observation will help you identify the major information needed to complete the FBA, upon which you will later build a support plan.

FBA Interview

The FBA interview format that is included and explained below was designed to allow teachers to view problem behavior from a functional perspective. A functional perspective examines what environmental features may be maintaining the problem behavior. Moreover, it allows teachers to identify predictors of problems, thus allowing them to target limited resources in a more efficient manner. Last, it looks at the outcomes the student experiences when the behavior is exhibited.

The following items are components of this interview and are included on the form provided at the end of this chapter.

Student Name, Grade, Date, and Staff Member Reporting Each of these items is useful for record keeping.

Student Profile We have found that it is important to ask teachers to list the strengths or positive attributes of the student. Focusing on only negative behavior is counterproductive. Also, the positives are useful in identifying recognition and reward opportunities.

Antecedents (Triggers) and Setting Events Antecedents also shed light on when the behavior does and does not occur. For example, a directive given by a teacher in a harsh tone may be an antecedent to the student talking back. You may be able to predict that, with no directive or with a private directive (spoken so only the student can hear), the behavior will not occur. Another antecedent for problem behavior may be an assignment that is difficult for the student. When the student is given simple work, she works on it without exhibiting the behavior.

> An FBA should be conducted for a single routine or time of day, rather than for everything the student does during the entire school day.

Setting events may happen long before the behavior occurs but may affect the likelihood of its occurrence. Identifying setting events can help identify when a problem behavior may occur. For example, if a student usually displays problem behavior on a certain day of the week, you may find that he stays with a relative in a particularly rowdy household or that the behavior happens when the student is tired or hungry. By identifying these factors, a teacher can address these needs, such as by using appropriate precorrection or by providing quiet time or snacks, thereby reducing the likelihood that the problem behavior will occur.

Problem Behaviors This section allows the teacher to identify the behaviors of concern in objective, concrete terms. Descriptors such as "stubborn" should be avoided and are not helpful. Describe what the behaviors look like or sound like (e.g., hitting, running, getting out of seat, yelling, whining, cussing, etc.). Similarly, frequency should be concrete, as should the specific consequences the student experiences as a result of the problem behavior.

Consequences and Function We have found it important to distinguish between what happens immediately after a problem behavior occurs from what is maintaining or keeping the behavior going. For example, a teacher may reprimand a student or give a warning for being off-task (consequence) but the function of the off-task behavior may actually be to avoid assigned school work.

FBA Hypothesis or Summary Statement

Once the interview process is complete, you will form some initial ideas about what sets off the behavior and define the behavior and its consequences. Now you are ready to form a hypothesis about the behavior and its maintaining consequences. We call this a *summary statement*.

A summary statement is simply the description of the pattern of antecedents or triggers, target behaviors, and consequences. It allows us to have a working theory about the function of a given behavior for an individual student, and it gives us a starting point to develop a positive behavior intervention plan. As was stated, this summary statement avoids ascribing the behavior to elements outside of the classroom or to untestable ideas or value judgments. Following are examples of correct and incorrect functional assessment summary statements.

Correct Summary Statements	Incorrect Summary Statements
Jenny (age 11) talks out in Mrs. Jones' science class when she hasn't had much attention from her peers in class. Mrs. Jones interrupts class to provide a reminder, and this attention from teacher and classmates maintains the behavior.	Jenny talks out in Mrs. Jones's class because she is unable to control herself.
Fred (age 13) is late to Mr. Smith's math class because he avoids work that is too difficult. Mr. Smith sends Fred to the office to obtain a tardy slip. Being able to leave class maintains Fred's avoidance behavior.	Fred is late to Mr. Smith's class because he doesn't care about schoolwork.
Melissa (age 8) pushes and kicks peers on the playground in order to escape other peers who are teasing her. Melissa is asked to sit on the "bench." Being removed from peers maintains the behavior.	Melissa pushes and kicks peers on the playground because she lacks anger management skills.
Maria (age 16) makes off-color jokes in class to gain attention from her peers. The teacher reprimands Maria in front of peers, who giggle and laugh. This reinforces Maria's need for attention.	Maria makes off-color jokes because she has poor role models at home and in the community.
Pierre (age 17) uses inappropriate language during science class to get adult and peer attention and to avoid doing the work that is boring to him. Pierre is sent to the "reflection room" to think about his inappropriate behavior. He continues to argue and use improper language while walking to the reflection room. His need for attention and work avoidance are being met.	Pierre uses inappropriate language because he is immature.

Although there may be some truth to the incorrect statements, they are not statements about the function of the challenging behaviors (what need is being met), and it is not possible to test whether these statements are true. These statements are called *attributions*, in which we infer causes for behavior. Whether accurate or not, they reflect things that we can't directly change and, therefore, will not be of use in our support plan. It is more productive to focus on what we can change, which are the classroom antecedents and consequences.

Without a hypothesis or educated guess based on interviews and direct observation, there is a serious risk for error in the eventual behavior plans. Even with an FBA, we could be wrong about the function of the behavior or about why the student keeps doing it in spite of our best efforts to change it. The positive behavior support plan is an opportunity for us to implement the FBA hypothesis, and we must be prepared to reanalyze, revise, and retry our work if our intervention doesn't change the behavior quickly. A real example illustrates this concept below.

Example   An FBA Revisited: Scott

Scott displayed violent behavior on a daily basis. When asked to do a language arts task, he tore his paper, threw his pencil, used profanity, and sometimes physically attacked his teacher. The FBA hypothesis was that he wanted teacher and peer attention. His behavior plan contained specific instructions on what to do when he acted appropriately: He earned classroom bucks, which could be spent on board games to play with his peers, or one-on-one time with his teacher. The plan also had specific instructions on what to do when he acted inappropriately: Upon refusal to comply with specific redirection requests from his teacher, Scott was put in an isolated area where the teacher would discuss the problem with him. When Scott continued to be verbally and physically aggressive, he was to be sent home for the remainder of the day. This plan was tried for several weeks until his parents refused to have him sent home day in and day out.

A more in-depth FBA was then conducted. Although it confirmed that Scott liked receiving attention from his teacher, peers, and parents when he acted out, the second FBA added a new hypothesis: Scott was trying to avoid language arts activities because they were too difficult. Scott was reevaluated and placed in an appropriate instructional group for reading, spelling, and writing. His schedule of reinforcement was increased so that he could earn classroom bucks much more frequently. The teacher role played with him the consequences if he didn't act appropriately: He was given a short, clear directive to either follow directions or go to the time-out room. There would be no processing or discussion about the problem behavior. He would not be sent home under any circumstances and would make up the time spent in time out during a preferred activity or after school. Scott quickly became more compliant and academically successful because his underlying need for instruction at an appropriate level had been met.

Consistency and Privacy

Keep in mind that simply developing a positive behavior plan based on an FBA doesn't change behavior. The plan must be implemented across the staff team. All adults dealing with the target student must be fully aware of how to interact with the student at all times.

This in no way threatens student confidentiality. When a student is placed on a special intervention plan, school personnel often express concern about sharing information and violating a student's privacy or confidentiality. Dr. Barbara Bateman has the following to say about this misconception concerning students with an Individualized Education Plan (IEP):

> Many concerns about violating a student's privacy or confidentiality by sharing necessary information among school personnel are simply misplaced. A legal exception exists specifically to allow this sharing, with or without parental consent. IDEA [Individuals with Disability Education Act] properly requires that IEPs be accessible to all school employees who have a legitimate educational interest in them (Bateman & Golly, 2003).

> Consistency in implementing the plan is crucial to its success.

When a positive behavior intervention plan has been developed for a student (whether on an IEP or not), it should be shared with all adults who need to know (e.g., teachers, assistants, playground and lunchroom supervisors, bus drivers). Consistency in implementing the plan is crucial to its success. Inconsistency can cause the inappropriate behavior to become more severe and more frequent.

Gather Information for the FBA

As we mentioned earlier, in order to develop an effective positive behavior plan, getting information is essential. The blank **Information to Develop an Individual Positive Behavior Plan** form at the end of this chapter provides an information-gathering tool. The purpose of this information gathering is to complete a working hypothesis (on the **Summary Statement** form provided). From the summary statement, the positive behavior plan will later be developed. (Specific steps and information on how to develop the positive behavior plan will be discussed in Chapter 18.) Figures 36 and 37 show examples of a completed behavior plan and its accompanying summary statement. Following that are blank forms for teachers to use to conduct their FBAs.

Activity: **Plan for Information Gathering and**
Summary Statement Development

- Choose a student with a chronic challenging behavior.
- Gather as much information as possible using the **Information to Develop an Individual Positive Behavior Plan** form in Figure 38 (see Figure 36 for a sample).
- Reach a consensus about the information gathered with others who work with this student.
- Develop a summary statement using the **Summary Statement** form in Figure 39. (see Figure 37 for a sample).

After the best guess has been made about each part of the summary statement, a positive behavior intervention plan can be developed. The next chapter will provide you with the necessary tools to carry on with this important work.

FIGURE 36   Information to Develop an Individual Positive Behavior Plan (Sample)

Student Name: _Siefke_ _____ Grade: _4_ _____

Reported by: _Nico Johnson_ _____ Date: _____

1. Description of student:

   - What are the strengths (e.g., academic, artistic, personal)? _positive, friendly, artistic_ _____

   - What does the student like to do (e.g., read books, play guitar, draw, do puzzles, ride skateboard, use computer)?
     draw, snacks, trinkets _____

   - Who does the student like (e.g., particular peer, principal, staff member)? _Mr. B. (5th grade teacher) and Scott Staals_

   - What food/drinks does the student like? _ice cream, hamburgers, lemon soda_ _____

   - What is home life like? _dad is in jail, Siefke lives with working mom, no siblings_ _____

2. Present level of functioning:

   - Which academic areas (e.g., reading, math, social studies) are easier for the student? _below grade level on reading and_
     math but making progress _____

   - Which academic areas are difficult for the student? _receptive and written language_ _____

   - How is the student being helped in these areas? _Siefke is getting help from the resource room in all academic areas_

   - What kind of social/behavioral problems does the student have? _Siefke blurts things out impulsively and constantly_
     interrupts the teacher _____

3. Describe the problems:

   - What do they look/sound like (e.g., hitting, cussing, running away)? _talks out_ _____

   - Where do the problems occur (e.g., playground, cafeteria, classroom, locker area, before or after school)?
     in the classroom _____

   - Who is usually around when the problem happens (e.g., teacher, assistant, peers)? _classroom teachers_ _____

   - What time of day does it usually happen? _during instructional time_ _____

4. What typically happens when the student gets into trouble? _the teacher tells him not to interrupt_ _____

5. How often do these problems take place? _every day_ _____

   When as much as possible of the above information has been gathered, the following summary can be made:

   - **Setting Events:** Things that are going on at home or before the student gets to school that may have an effect later in the day
     (e.g., home stress, fight with parents/peers, lack of sleep, medication). _dad's in jail_ _____

   - **Antecedent:** What typically makes the student act inappropriately (e.g., a direction, task, person)?
     teacher presence during class time _____

   - **Problem Behavior:** What does the student typically do that is inappropriate (e.g., talk back, whine, run away)?
     he talks out _____

   - **Consequence:** After the incident, what typically happens (e.g., send to office, time-out, parent contact, scolding)?
     teacher tells him not to interrupt and to raise his hand _____

   - **Maintaining Function:** Why does the student misbehave (e.g., to get attention, to have power/control, to get out of doing
     a task)? _Siefke wants adult attention_ _____

FIGURE 37 **Summary Statement (Sample)**

Setting Event (What might be happening at home or before school?)	Predictor (What sets student off?)	Problem Behavior (What does student do that is not appropriate?)	Consequence (What happens right after the inappropriate behavior?)	Maintaining Function (What does student want?)
dad's in jail	teacher is instructing	Siefke talks out and interrupts the teacher	teacher tells him to stop	adult attention

FIGURE 38 Information to Develop an Individual Positive Behavior Plan

Student Name: _____ Grade: _____

Reported by: _____ Date: _____

1. Description of student:

   • What are the strengths (e.g., academic, artistic, personal)? _____

   • What does the student like to do (e.g., read books, play guitar, draw, do puzzles, ride skateboard, use computer)?

     _____

   • Who does the student like (e.g., particular peer, principal, staff member)? _____

   • What food/drinks does the student like? _____

   • What is home life like? _____

2. Present level of functioning:

   • Which academic areas (e.g., reading, math, social studies) are easier for the student? _____

     _____

   • Which academic areas are difficult for the student? _____

   • How is the student being helped in these areas? _____

   • What kind of social/behavioral problems does the student have? _____

     _____

3. Describe the problems:

   • What do they look/sound like (e.g., hitting, cussing, running away)? _____

   • Where do the problems occur (e.g., playground, cafeteria, classroom, locker area, before or after school)?

     _____

   • Who is usually around when the problem happens (e.g., teacher, assistant, peers)? _____

   • What time of day does it usually happen? _____

4. What typically happens when the student gets into trouble? _____

5. How often do these problems take place? _____

   When as much as possible of the above information has been gathered, the following summary can be made:

   • **Setting Events:** Things that are going on at home or before the student gets to school that may have an effect later in the day (e.g., home stress, fight with parents/peers, lack of sleep, medication). _____

   • **Antecedent:** What typically makes the student act inappropriately (e.g., a direction, a task, a person)?

     _____

   • **Problem Behavior:** What does the student typically do that is inappropriate (e.g., talk back, whine, run away)?

     _____

   • **Consequence:** After the incident, what typically happens (e.g., send to office, time-out, parent contact, scolding)?

     _____

   • **Maintaining Function:** Why does the student misbehave (e.g., to get attention, to have power/control, to get out of doing a task)? _____

FIGURE 39 **Summary Statement**

Setting Event (What might be happening at home or before school?)	Predictor (What sets off student?)	Problem Behavior (What does student do that is not appropriate?)	Consequence (What happens right after the inappropriate behavior?)	Maintaining Function (What does student want?)

CHAPTER 17

Building Positive Behavior Support Plans for Individual Students

Designing Effective Behavior Support Plans

Positive behavior support planning is the process of taking the information collected through the Functional Behavior Assessment (FBA) process (Chapter 16) and turning it into a logical and effective plan. The general goal of the plan is to replace the problem behavior with more positive behaviors. As educators, we can thoughtfully alter certain features of the student's environment in order to produce or encourage positive behavior change. In the FBA process, these features are referred to as setting events, antecedents, and consequences. You learned about these in the previous chapter on thinking functionally about behavior.

In addition, when developing a behavior support plan, we must always consider the resources we have available. Specifically, these include the people and time that can be devoted to teaching the student and arranging the environment. For effective implementation, these resources must be identified, allocated, and scheduled (D. Crone, Hawken, & Bergstrom, 2007).

Figure 40 presents the big ideas about behavior supports.

FIGURE 40 **Big Ideas about Positive Behavior Supports**

- Understand why problem behavior works for the student (FBA).
- Change external elements: ICE (Instruction, Curriculum, and Environment).
- Make problem behaviors irrelevant, ineffective, and inefficient.
- Teach a new, more positive way to behave.

OBJECTIVES

▶ Understand the logical link between functional assessment results and positive behavior supports

▶ Describe the components of an effective behavior support plan

▶ Discuss what adults can do to bring about change in student behavior

▶ Learn to make problem behaviors irrelevant, ineffective, and inefficient by teaching replacement behaviors

▶ Practice developing a customized behavior plan

Linking the Plan to the FBA

As we discussed in Chapter 15, adult responses should not be based on what the teacher thinks is aversive or rewarding but on what actually changes the behavior. For example, if you keep a student in for recess for a behavior problem and the problem doesn't get better, then the student may not mind staying in for recess. If the student is acting out at recess to avoid peers (whining, pushing people away), then recess inside may not extinguish the behavior but could make it worse. Or, if a student is talking out in class for teacher attention and the consequence for this behavior is the teacher talking with the student outside the classroom, then once again, the behavior will probably persist. You know when you've found an effective response when you see a change in behavior. For this reason, keeping a record of the behavior after the plan is in place is essential. It is critical to provide a logical link between the function of student behavior and the positive behavior support strategy. As we have shown, if we don't understand why the behavior works for the student and what need is being met, we may choose strategies that actually reinforce the problem rather than reduce it.

> If you have to do the same thing over again and behavior continues, then the plan is not working.

Changing External Elements

Changes can be made to the learning context in order to support students in using positive behaviors. The acronym ICE is a useful reminder that a positive behavior support plan looks at ways to modify the Instruction (how you teach), the Curriculum (what you teach), and Environment (where you teach). Changing instructional practices, curriculum, and the environment are ways to address the antecedents and setting events that are prompting the problem behavior. Chapter 18 provides specific examples on how to adapt curriculum to prevent problem behaviors. The following chart gives a few examples of ICE elements.

Instruction	Rather than just having students read instructions from a book, provide a teacher-led direct instruction lesson.
Curriculum	Give extra practice for errors you anticipate before instruction.
Environment	Use a whiteboard or overhead projector to keep students focused.

Making Negative Behaviors Less Useful

A behavior support plan should make a student's negative behaviors irrelevant, ineffective, and inefficient (Crone, et al., 2007; Crone & Horner, 2003; O'Neill, et al., 1997). For example, if a student talks out to get attention, then teach the student to seek attention more appropriately. By giving the student attention when he raises his hand and not when he calls out, you have made the problem behavior irrelevant and ineffective. If the new behavior works better for your student (he gets attention more quickly), then the old behavior has become inefficient. This learning takes time, so it is important to reinforce even small changes in behavior.

Teaching a Better Way

The student needs to know a replacement behavior to use to get his or her needs met (behavior function). Simply telling a student to "stop" doesn't give him or her options and may actually promote noncompliance. It is much easier to do something than to not do something. This is the function of the schoolwide and classroom expectations: They are positive statements of expected behavior, rewarded with positive reinforcement and recognition. Similarly, *some* individuals will need extra support in these behaviors (reteaching or more reinforcement) or will need other specific positive behaviors to use. For example, an individual plan could include the positive behavior of taking a walk around the room or to the drinking fountain when angry, instead of yelling or throwing things. The replacement behaviors should align with schoolwide and classroom rules and behavior expectations and with the school's prosocial and antibullying curriculum. In addition, they must be behaviors that will work for both the student and the adults.

> **Positive, Not Punishing**
> Say: "Would you like to choose and earn?" rather than, "If you don't, you will lose."

Intervention Strategies by Behavior Function

Please take a moment to review Table 5 to understand the link between behavioral function and selection of a support strategy. Listed in the table are intervention strategies to address the two main functions of student behavior: attention seeking and avoidance. If the function of the behavior is to obtain attention or a tangible reward, then the teacher should use the strategies listed to teach positive alternatives to getting attention or obtaining tangibles. If the function of the behavior is to escape or avoid an instructional demand or undesirable situation, then appropriate strategies will decrease the student's need to escape or avoid the undesirable situation and will increase the desirability of the expected behavior.

The process of implementing selected interventions will be simplified and faster if the school has a standardized intervention program that can be implemented with minor adjustments. The point system and behavior cards at the end of this chapter can be modified based on the needs of the school and the student. The particular consequences (positive and negative) of the points earned can be varied by student; the forms just help capture data about what was earned.

TABLE 5 Tiered Interventions by Function

	Function of Behavior: Obtain Attention or Tangible Reward	Function of Behavior: Escape/Avoid as a Result of Instructional Demand or Undesirable Situation
Universal Interventions (*all* students)	• Recognize students for following school behavior expectations. • Ignore minor problem behaviors in classrooms and common areas; notice others for correct behavior. • Teach the students an acceptable alternative to the problem behavior that addresses their need. • Provide class-wide rewards for following school behavior expectations.	• Recognize students for compliance with instructions. • Teach students to ask for help rather than acting-out when instruction is too difficult (be responsible). • Adapt instruction so that it is at the student's instructional level: not too easy, not too hard. • Recognize or reward students when they use the desired behavior (be respectful). • Initially remove or reduce demands and then gradually reintroduce them. • Provide class-wide rewards for working hard, completing tasks, and so forth.
Selected and Targeted Interventions (*some* students)	• Reteach the student an acceptable alternative to the problem behavior that addresses the need. • Briefly deny access to the activity or tangible (time-out). • Briefly remove or restrict the student from your or another student's attention (time-out). • Provide a school-based adult mentor who will coach and reinforce the student for appropriate behavior. • Have students "check in" with a behavior card with each teacher during the day. • Use an individual-token economy, earning points for acceptable behavior. • Teach peers to ignore the problem behavior of the student.	• Avoid using time-out for escape-motivated students. • Reteach the student to ask for help, rather than acting out when instruction is too difficult (be responsible). • Use an individual-token economy, earning points for acceptable behavior (e.g., asking for help). • Adapt instruction to meet the student's needs (instructional level, learning style, interest, or other individual needs). • Provide additional instruction in difficult subjects. • Recognize or reward the student for desired behavior. • Initially remove or reduce demands and then gradually reintroduce them. • Provide the student with the opportunity to earn rewards for the class or group. • Interrupt and redirect the student to task. • Teach students to self-manage work completion so that they don't get behind.

If universal interventions (Tier I) have been implemented with integrity and some students still aren't responding, then a Tier II intervention can be implemented that involves the entire class but focuses specifically on the students who need extra support. The main idea here is that the entire class receives intermittent reinforcement but that the focus students receive planned, predictable reinforcement (see the example below).

EXAMPLE **Planned, Predictable Reinforcement**

The teacher makes a large motivational chart. This can be an object like the outline of a sheep, a butterfly, a tree, a car, or a train, or it can be an outline of a scene, such as a garden, a racetrack, the solar system, or some other thematic scene.

For the objects, the sheep for example, have a large bag with cotton balls and a glue stick in a designated place. When individual students are doing the right thing, ask them to go put a cotton ball on the sheep. When the expected behavior is being exhibited (e.g., following directions), ask the target student(s) to put a cotton ball on the sheep in a predictable schedule (for example, every 10 minutes). The target student earns cotton balls on a predictable schedule, while the other students earn them intermittently. When the entire sheep is covered in cotton balls, there will be a special activity for the entire class.

This reinforcement activity serves several purposes. First, it doesn't single out the focus student, but it provides a high frequency of reinforcement. Second, it provides *all* students with positive movement. Last, it reminds the teacher to focus on positive behavior.

Developing a Customized Plan

Guided by the critical design elements discussed earlier, you are now ready to implement a customized plan for a student. Implementing a plan includes putting the behavior support plan on paper, carrying it out, and tracking results for review and revision. There are a number of forms to help guide you in completing these steps. First, you have the FBA (developed in Chapter 16), which identified the problem behavior, its function,

Behavior Plan	Plan elements overview
10-Point Support Plan	Plan details, responsible parties, deadlines
Individual Student Plan	Version is given to the student
Individual Student Point Chart	A data table for recording points earned (when using a point system)
Student Point Card	A card the student carries to classes and home to track points

and other aspects of the student and the situation. In this chapter, you can add to the FBA using the supports listed in the chart provided here.

A good plan will address the big ideas of positive behavior support, as listed in the box at the beginning of the chapter. It will have procedures for increasing the desired behavior, including positive consequences, and ICE alterations. It will also include procedures for responding to inappropriate behavior. Think about ways to prevent the behavior, how to teach and acknowledge the expected behavior, and how you and others will respond when the problem behavior occurs. The forms listed above will help you organize those thoughts as we move through the chapter.

Many behavior support plans fail because they aren't explicit enough about how to implement the intervention and about who will be responsible for what. It is necessary to clearly specify who is involved and how the behaviors need to be taught and changed. Again, this involves adults changing their behavior first. For example, for one student, the problem behavior is talking-out, and the student has been explicitly taught to raise a hand quietly instead of talking-out. If the teacher is not committed to completely ignoring talk-outs and reinforcing the student when she is quiet, then the plan will fail. All adults involved must know exactly what to do, how to do it, and when. Should the teacher give a reward after the student has an outburst and suddenly becomes quiet? Should the student be rewarded in all classes or in just a select few classes where the problem is the most acute? These are questions that must be answered before the plan gets implemented. The adults must also agree to make the necessary changes in their own behavior so that the plan is carried out as intended.

The Behavior Plan

The behavior plan is a natural extension of the FBA. Thus, some of the questions on the Behavior Plan form will be familiar. Whether the form provided in this chapter is used or whether the team creates its own, the teacher or the team needs to answer the following questions.

1. What are the student's strengths? What does the student do well? Is he or she successful in certain social settings? What subject area might he or she be successful at? What are the problem behaviors?

2. What do you think is the purpose of the behavior (attention, avoidance, or escape)?

3. What do we want the student to do?

4. How will we teach the desired behavior?

5. What are you willing to do to help the student (point card by period, feedback on 15-minute timer)?

6. How often are you willing to provide feedback to the student's guardians, and in what way (daily, weekly, e-mail, written, point card)?

7. What can the student earn?

8. What happens if the student displays unacceptable behaviors?

9. How will the plan be measured?

10. How long will the plan be tried before it is re-evaluated?

Figure 41, **A Behavior Plan for Siefke**, uses the information provided in Chapter 16 to create a behavior plan. An excellent resource for more examples and specific behavior plans is *Why Johnny Doesn't Behave: Twenty Tips and Measurable BIPs* by Barbara Bateman and Annemieke Golly (2003).

FIGURE 41   A Behavior Plan for Siefke

Student Name: _Siefke_ _____ Age: _10_ ___ Grade: _4_ ___ Date: _1/11/12_ ___

What are the student's strengths (e.g., social, academic, other)? _positive, friendly, artistic_ _____

What are the problem behaviors? _Siefke blurts things out impulsively and constantly interrupts the teacher._

What do we want the student to do? _Siefke needs to raise his hand in class to get permission to talk._

How will we teach the desired behavior? _The teacher will role play with Siefke how to raise his hand appropriately._
The teacher will demonstrate the acceptable and unacceptable ways of how and when to raise his hand for
permission to talk.

What can the student earn? _Siefke can earn a star each time he raises his hand quietly and at an appropriate time._
When he has earned his goal of 20 stars, he can spend 2 minutes talking to the teacher about a subject of his choice.

What happens if the student displays unacceptable behavior? _The teacher will not pay attention (planned ignoring) to_
Siefke when he talks out or interrupts.

How will the plan be measured? _The teacher will collect data on how quickly Siefke reaches his goal of raising his hand_
20 times. The teacher will also collect data on how often he talks out without raising his hand.

How long will the plan be tried? _The teacher will keep track of Siefke's talk-outs and when he quietly raises his hand._
The plan will be evaluated in 1 week.

Data collection: _The teacher tracks both talk-outs and hand raises. The plan will be evaluated in 1 week. We hope to see_
the talk-outs decrease and the hand raises increase.

Siefke's data:

Date	Hand raises	Talk-outs	Comments
Oct 5	ⵏⵏ II	ⵏⵏ	
Oct 6	ⵏⵏ II	III	
Oct. 7	ⵏⵏ ⵏⵏ	I	Earned 2 minutes with teacher.
Oct. 8	ⵏⵏ ⵏⵏ ⵏⵏ		Earned 2 minutes with teacher.
Oct. 9	ⵏⵏ ⵏⵏ II		No talk-outs all morning. Earned 2 minutes with teacher.
Oct. 12	ⵏⵏ III		No talk-outs all day. Earned 10 minutes with Mr. B.

Follow-up: This is a common problem and a simple plan. The critical ingredient is the role playing to teach Siefke how to
perform appropriately. After I demonstrate the skill, Siefke needs to demonstrate the skill several times during role play
with lots of positive feedback from me. Too often, it is assumed that the child knows how to perform but chooses not to
do so.

   If Siefke's talk-outs decrease significantly, then the plan can be allowed to fade out. For example, after 5 days, if he has
no talk-outs in the morning, he can earn 2 minutes of talking to me (he loves adult attention). After 1 week, if he has had
no talk-outs all day, he can earn 10 minutes with Mr. B. (his favorite teacher) during recess. I must continue to give Siefke
opportunities to gain teacher attention appropriately and reinforce him intermittently when he is doing well. For example,
once in a while I may say, "Siefke, you are being so respectful by raising your hand when you want my attention. Would you
like to walk with me when we go out to recess and talk with me for a while?"

Activity: Questions about Your Student with Challenging Behaviors

Think of a student with challenging behaviors. You may want to use the one for whom you created the FBA in the last chapter. Use the following form and answer the questions as completely as possible using Figure 41 as a model.

Student Name: _____ Age: _____ Grade: _____ Date: _____

What are the student's strengths? _____
_____

What are the problem behaviors? _____
_____

What do we want the student to do? _____
_____

How will we teach the desired behavior? _____
_____
_____
_____
_____

What can the student earn? _____
_____
_____
_____
_____

What happens if the student displays unacceptable behavior? _____
_____
_____
_____
_____

How will the plan be measured? _____
_____
_____
_____

How long will the plan be tried? _____
_____
_____
_____
_____

Planning the Details

Now that you have gathered information on your student, you are ready to assign tasks to the implementation team, which will include the classroom teacher(s) for the specific student, those staff members assigned to the planning team, and the parent, as appropriate. The implementation team consists of the student's teachers and aides, and may include other staff, including administrators, who interact with the student regularly. For consistency in implementation, others who interact with the student will be informed of the plan (this may include bus drivers, cafeteria workers, librarians, or others). The **10-Point Support Plan** form that follows has been helpful and effective when teams use it to execute a positive behavior plan.

10-Point Support Plan

Activity	Person Responsible	Implementation Due Date	Completed
1. Clearly define expected behaviors. (What do you want to see; what do you want to hear?)			
2. Teach or role play expected behaviors.			
3. Develop a menu of rewards. (What does student want to work for?)			
4. Meet with the student to discuss reward system (point system, consequences, carrying the card, etc.).			
5. Develop a point system.			
6. Develop consequences (e.g., bottom line).			
7. Develop data collection/progress-monitoring system.			
8. Develop implementation time line, including regular intervals to review progress, and make program modifications.			
9. Set next meeting date.			
10. Share plan with guardians, as needed.			

Developing Consequences

When developing consequences for an individual student, keep in mind that what reinforces (or punishes) one person may do the opposite for another. The proof that you have selected well will be in the results, but thoughtful consideration is a good start! Review the following resources.

- Schoolwide reinforcers in Chapter 7.
- Classroom-level reinforcers in Chapter 14.
- What you have learned about the student in the FBA.
- Appropriate interventions by behavior function (Table 5).

Different students will need different reinforcers and schedules of reinforcement.

Ideas for immediate reinforcers:

- Student receives a schoolwide token for each period.
- Student receives two tokens for a successful day, one token for a mostly successful day.
- Student colors in part of a picture that depicts something of interest.
- When all parts have been colored in, the student earns a privilege.

Ideas for delayed reinforcers include trading tokens for privileges, such as:

- Eating on the stage.
- Getting in line first.
- Passing out papers in class.
- Pet or feed the class pet.
- Sitting in a special chair.

Communicating the Plan with the Student

The sample **Individual Student Plan** that follows can be adapted for individual students. Refer to Figure 42 for a sample point chart for tracking progress if points are used and to pages 266–268 for sample point cards that the student, teachers, and family members may all use to track points.

In the following example, points are added or taken away as consequences. A warning about removing points as a negative consequence: Usually, losing points has the effect of refocusing the student on the desired behavior and earning points. Occasionally, however, there might be a student who will escalate when points are removed or taken away. In this case, points should not be taken away but should simply not be awarded during the period when undesirable behaviors are exhibited.

> **Point Removal Causing Escalation**
>
> If point removal leads to escalation for a student, simply omit points rather than removing them.

Individual Student Plan

Behavior Goals:

1. Follow directions.

    • When a teacher asks me to do something, I will do it.

2. Be safe.

    • I walk quietly and safely in classrooms, hallways, and breezeways.

3. Be responsible.

    • I raise my hand and wait for permission to talk.

4. Be respectful.

    • I keep my hands, feet, objects, and inappropriate comments to myself.

Positive Consequences:

I will:

• Receive positive attention from adults and students.

• Receive 2 points per period if my behavior is acceptable.

• Earn the privilege to participate with the rest of the class throughout the day.

• Earn special activities at school (e.g., computer time, free time).

• Earn special activities at home (e.g., special story, visit from friend, movie, or favorite treat).

Negative Consequences:

I will receive:

• Minus 1 point: Warning for behavior change.

• Minus 2 points: If my behavior does not change, the privilege to be part of the group will be lost, and I must report to the desk in the back of the room.

If my behavior is disruptive, I must go and work in the back of another classroom or another designated quiet place. The teacher or principal will make this decision.

_____   _____
Student   Teacher

_____   _____
Date   Date

Tracking Results

Next, a system needs to be prepared ahead of time so that data can easily be tracked from the first day of implementation. This is part of the 10-Point Support Plan. Results will be needed to assess the plan and improve upon it.

An example was given of a tracking chart at the end of Siefke's Behavior Plan, that was customized to the specific data to be tracked: hand raising and calling out. Feel free to create such a chart for your plan. If you elect to use a point system as part of your consequences and measurement plans, however, review Figure 42, the example for Jessica, to see how a point plan can be used and the kind of data it provides. This form is generally for teacher or adult tracking and use. Use the blank **Individual Student Point Chart** at the end of this chapter to measure behaviors for students who have a point system as a part of their behavior plans.

Another tracking device is the **Student Point Card**. This allows the student to have the tally, which can then travel through classes during the school day, and it will allow him or her to be able to take it home. This provides feedback to the student, communication among staff, and information to the home. This may be a choice to make a little later in implementation or in conjunction with initial implementation. If this is the only tracking device, make sure that the data are captured so that the team can review and assess the plan. We have provided samples of Student Point Cards. A point card might be developed for schoolwide use (Chapter 7) for ease of implementation, as the consequences associated with different amounts of points would still be customized to the student (as must be, to address the function of that student's behavior).

To modify the school's generic point card to meet the needs of individual students and teachers, the following procedures are recommended, which align with the steps presented in this chapter. These details should be included in the Behavior Plan (as appropriate) and in the 10-Point Plan.

1. Teacher and PBIS Team Actions

   a. The teacher meets with one of the PBIS team members (e.g., counselor, principal, behavior specialist).

   b. The team member interviews the teacher regarding the specific child's issues (see FBA).

   c. The team member and teacher discuss whether a self-management procedure (see Chapter 18) or a point card would be appropriate.

   d. The teacher and team member personalize the generic point chart (see examples provided).

   e. Teacher and team member decide when to evaluate the card system chosen.

2. Teacher and Student Meeting

   a. The teacher meets with the child, explains the point chart, and asks the child to pick the color of the card.

   b. The teacher and child discuss how the card should be carried (e.g., plastic pouch like a name tag, in pocket, pinned to clothing).

   c. Teacher and student discuss what privileges will be earned and tie them into the schoolwide system (e.g., schoolwide tokens).

   d. If the schoolwide token system is not reinforcing, ask the student how else rewards should be earned (e.g., coloring spots on the chart, or coloring parts of preferred-interest item, such as windows on an airplane or train, parts of dinosaur, solar system, rock star, musical instrument, insects).

3. Home Communication

   a. Guardians are informed of the card procedure.

   b. Guardians are asked how they want to receive a copy of the card each day (e.g., fax, e-mail, paper copy).

   c. Guardians are encouraged to provide positive comments to the child for doing well.

   d. Guardians are encouraged not to discuss the card when things didn't go well. They are asked to simply say: "You can try again tomorrow," and not punish the child at home.

For any plan in which the student is the carrier of the tally, adults will write with pen (to prevent sabotage, e.g., erasing, changing).

FIGURE 42   Individual Student Point Chart (Sample)

Student Name: _Jessica_   Date: _Jan. 10–Jan 15_

Period	Monday	Tuesday	Wednesday	Thursday	Friday	Total
7:50–8:25 Opening	2	2	2	2	2	10
8:25–9:25 Reading	2	2	2	2	2	10
9:25–10:10 P.E.	0	1	0	0	1	2
10:10–11:00 Computer	2	2	2	2	2	10
11:00–11:20 Language	0	2	2	1	2	7
11:20–11:40 Lunch	2	2	2	2	2	10
11:40–11:55 Recess	2	2	2	2	2	10
11:55–12:15 Social Studies	2	2	2	0	1	7
12:15–1:00 Math	0	0	1	0	1	2
1:00–1:55 Science	2	2	2	2	2	10

Note: The number of points, 0, 1, or 2, was awarded for accomplishments during each period. Jessica can earn 10 maximum points for each period, for a total of 100 points. The agreement made with Jessica was as follows: 70–80 points, earn 20 minutes of extra computer time; 81–90 points, earn 30 minutes of extra computer time; 91–100 points, earn lunch with a friend in the classroom. The chart shows that Jessica earned 78 points for the week of January 10. She earned 20 minutes of extra computer time.

Reviewing and Revising the Plan

Remember that behavior support planning is a continuous process and that it is normal to experience glitches with your plan initially.

After implementing the plan according to the time line, evaluate the plan using the data collected and see if any changes need to be made. Most students who need to increase positive behavior and decrease inappropriate behavior respond well to a clear and concise plan that meets their individual needs.

Remember that if student behavior hasn't changed, you haven't correctly identified either the function of the behavior or consequences that matter to the student. This may require returning to redo the FBA. Also, look for patterns of improvement and variations under different circumstances, such as time of day, class or content area, day of the week, and so forth, for areas of further investigation and growth. For example, the points on Jessica's card show that she is having a more difficult time during P.E. and math, as she earns fewer points then. The teacher or team needs to analyze what might be happening during that time and make changes to help Jessica be more successful during those periods.

Depending upon the needs of the child, the intervals for reinforcers may need to be adjusted. Some children may change their behavior for a weekly reinforce, as in the Jessica example. Children with severe behavior problems may require daily, or even more frequent, reinforcement.

Individual Student Point Chart

Student Name: _____   Date: _____

Period	Monday	Tuesday	Wednesday	Thursday	Friday	Total

Student Point Card Example 1

Student Name: _____ Date: _____

- Be respectful.
  - Work without distracting others.
- Be responsible.
  - Complete school work on time.

_____ Is homework completed?

Time of Day	Work Without Distracting Others	Complete Classwork
Before Recess 8:00–10:05		
Before Lunch 10:05–12:35		
After Lunch 12:35–2:10		

Positive comment from teacher:

Student Point Card Example 2

Student Name: _____ Date: _____

- Be safe.
  - Keep hands, feet, and objects to yourself.
- Be respectful.
  - Listen when others are talking.

Positive Reinforcement:

- Student will receive verbal reinforcement and thumbs-up tickets. Ten thumbs-up tickets may be traded in for a golden ticket.
- Student will earn special privileges at home and at school.

Area/Time	Being Safe	Listening
8:00–8:30 Warm-Up		
8:30–9:15 Math		
9:15–9:30 Recess		
5 ☺ = Thumbs-Up Ticket	Total =	Total =

Teacher likes to use smiley faces.

Card will be faxed to mom each day.

Uncle will reinforce student when criteria have been met (he earns time on computer to play games).

Uncle will not discuss why smiley faces weren't earned. Uncle will simply say, "You can try again tomorrow."

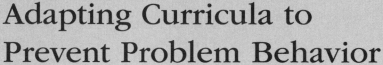

CHAPTER 18

Adapting Curricula to Prevent Problem Behavior

3
Individual Student Supports

Background: Poor Instruction Means Poor Behavior

One of the principal reasons why students misbehave in school is because instruction is too difficult or poorly adapted (Crone & Horner, 2003; O'Neill, et al.,1997). In fact, avoiding instruction or tasks that are too difficult, too easy, or poorly matched to students' ability is one of the most common reasons why students present challenging behavior in schools.

Teachers may think that adapting curriculum and instruction is very complicated or time consuming, but this does not have to be the case! Effective teachers can adapt or differentiate instruction for *all* students by using good problem-solving techniques. Good problem solvers can quickly identify the issue, generate alternative solutions, and try one or two to see if they work. In the case of preventing problem behavior, we recommend the process of "try and test," rather than investing a lot of time in complicated (but rarely sustainable) behavioral strategies, such as intricate token economies, behavioral contracts, or exclusion from the classroom. Curriculum adaptation can maximize success and participation for students who are not getting the lesson content or not learning important skills from lessons that are designed for most students in the class (Cole et al., 2000).

Following are some assumptions about curriculum adaptation.

- Poorly adapted instruction is aversive to the student and leads to behavior problems and poor outcomes for both the classroom and student.
- Therefore, we have to meet the student at his or her current level of performance for best learning and management outcomes.

OBJECTIVES

▶ Describe classes of curriculum adaptation that can prevent problem behavior

▶ Outline a process for adapting curricula and instruction

▶ Develop and adapt a classroom lesson to prevent problem behavior

- Poorly adapted instruction is difficult or boring from the student's perspective. Difficult or boring instruction is aversive, and this can promote problem behavior, resulting in either too much behavior (errors, acting out) or not enough behavior (inaccurate, poor quality, social withdrawal, or lack of effort).

There is immense pressure on teachers today due to federal and state requirements for academic achievement. This can create a drive for a "one size fits all" or a "teach to the test" mindset and practice. For the best educational practice, it is clear that we need to meet the students at their current levels of performance and build toward longer term objectives. If we shoot too high or aim too low, then both the teacher and the student will be frustrated.

> Adaptations for schoolwide discipline (SWD) will need to be incorporated into the IEP, and the adaptation strategy is intended to work for every educator.

A Better Fit for All

Differentiation is widely understood to mean adapting content, process, or product (output) to meet the individual needs of students. The student needs are understood to vary in terms of readiness, interest, and learning profile for any given curricular area or skill set. This becomes increasingly important with the wide diversity of learners in our increasingly inclusive classrooms.

Matrix of Adaptations

Deschenes, Ebeling, and Sprague (1994) developed a simple model for quickly developing adaptations to curricula and instruction for academic success using a matrix for increasing academic success (Cole, et al., 2000; Deschenes, et al., 1994). We have expanded and reorganized this matrix to increase behavioral success, and we will review its basic strategies and then practice using them. Table 6 provides definitions and examples of curriculum adaptations. Review each one carefully and think about how you would use the strategy to adapt the curriculum for one of your students. Later, you will be asked to select and apply the strategies for a particular student.

TABLE 6　Classes of Curriculum Adaptation

Change the Context	Change the Presentation	Change Behavior Expectations or Consequences
Precorrect Errors Give extra practice for errors you anticipate before instruction.	**Task Difficulty** Adapt the skill level, problem type, or rules to increase accuracy (> 75%).	**Time to Complete** Adapt the time allotted and allowed for learning, task completion, or testing.
Level of Participation Adapt the extent to which a learner is actively involved in a task or activity.	**Task Size** Adapt the number of items that a learner is expected to complete or master.	**Output Method** Adapt how the learner can respond to instruction.
Alternate Goals Adapt the goals or expectations while using the same materials.	**Input Method** Adapt the way instruction is delivered to the learner.	**Increase Rewards for Acceptable Behavior** Make exhibiting expected behaviors more valuable than committing errors or other problem behavior.
Substitute Curricula Provide different instruction and materials.	**Level of Support** Increase the amount of personal assistance provided to the learner.	**Remove or Restrict** Take away desired objects or activities when problem behavior is observed.

The examples below show how teachers approached each of the curriculum adaptations listed in the chart.

Change the Context

- **Precorrect Errors**
  - Before instruction begins, Tamara asks Mitch to sit down and practice the rules of staying in a seat and keeping hands and feet to yourself.
  - Jana tends not to participate, so before instruction starts, the teacher reminds Jana that she will call on her and may even let her know the question ahead of time. This way, Jana can prepare her answer.

- **Level of Participation**
  - Pam is very shy about raising her hand in class, so the teacher allows her to write down the answer on a card. She is less anxious and does not act out during lectures.
  - Kristina has lots of good ideas and can dominate a classroom discussion. The teacher asks her to keep a tally of how many responses she and others have to see if she uses her fair share of time. The teacher also promises to call on Kristina after a few others have had a chance to share.

- **Alternate Goals**
  - In social studies, Ceci is expected to locate just the states while others locate the capitals as well. When she is successful, she makes fewer bids for peer attention during cooperative group activities.
  - Mitch already knows the states and capitals in social studies, so he is expected to select three activities from a tic-tac-toe sheet with choices related to the topic, such as creating a timelines, listing economic factors, or writing about a state motto.

- **Substitute Curricula**
  - John is in high school and at risk for dropout. He is introduced to a self-directed curriculum based on a computer. He can see his accomplishments clearly and is very motivated to earn high school credits.
  - Anna is advanced in math, so her teacher brings in a higher level textbook for extensions and also uses a nationwide competitive online math program to support Anna's problem-solving skills.

Change the Presentation

- **Task Difficulty**
  - Jeff is allowed to use a calculator to figure math problems to decrease difficulty and his motivation to escape the task. His teacher gradually increases the difficulty and allows him to practice problems without the calculator.
  - Liam learns quickly and is bored easily, so the teacher makes sure to have some problems lined up for each lesson that allow for creative thinking.

- **Task Size**
  - Joe has difficulty completing the entire social studies assignment, so his teacher allows him to complete half to maintain his motivation for learning.
  - Nina is advanced in math but has trouble focusing, so her teacher allows her to complete only half of the problems. However, her teacher selects the questions with higher level thinking skills.

- **Input Method**
  - Tom has a hard time tolerating morning circle, and he often gets up and runs away. He is allowed to stay at his desk and learn about the schedule for the class that day.
  - François is in an ELL program, so his teacher provides vocabulary words ahead of time and also puts words with images for concepts, such as *rotation* and *revolution,* on the wall for content areas (such as science).

- **Level of Support**
  - José is given a peer tutor for extra practice in reading grade-level material.
  - Dallas has individual learning contracts for content areas in which he has high background knowledge, and he completes these independently.

Change Behavior Expectations or Consequences

- **Time to Complete**
  - Stephen can complete his seat work with few errors, but it takes him longer than other students. His teacher gives him extra time, and he doesn't lose any credit.
  - Ben completes his work quickly and accurately, so he has independent study time, allowing him to read content-related fiction books (or other enriching works) in the specific content area.

- **Output Method**
  - Leslie will often use inappropriate words when asked to speak in front of the class without notes. Her teacher allows her to write her comments and read them instead.
  - Jack is a resistant writer if the product must be hand written, but he loves technology. He is allowed to publish his writing work using a computer and multimedia presentations.

- **Increase Rewards for Acceptable Behavior**
  - Even though Kindle hates to complete math worksheets and often tosses them on the floor, she will complete them if she can earn 5 extra minutes of recess on Friday.

- **Remove or Restrict**
  - George has difficulty with botany facts but can do the work if he is motivated. He and his teacher agree that he will lose 5 minutes of lunch any day he refuses to complete the daily quiz.

Seven Steps for Adapting Curricula and Instruction

Deschenes et al. (1994) outlined seven simple steps for adapting curricula to support inclusion. We have adjusted these steps to address behavioral support issues. Each of the 12 curriculum adaptation strategies defined in Table 6 can be used in the sixth step below for adapting curricula and instruction in a variety of combinations to make instruction more tolerable (even enjoyable), thereby preventing problem behavior from occurring.

1. Select the subject area.

2. Select the topic.

3. Identify the goal for most learners.

4. Develop the lesson plan for most learners.

5. Identify learners who will need adaptations in curricula or instruction.

6. Choose an appropriate mix of adaptations.

7. Evaluate the effectiveness of the adaptations.

Activity: **Planning for Adaptations in Your Classroom**

The following form, **Adapting Instruction to Minimize Problem Behavior and Maximize Student Success**, includes space to plan the seven steps for adapting curricula and instruction, and to use the matrix to select types of adaptation. This type of planning can be done for curricular areas, for particular curricular units, or for specific lessons, as needed. Keep in mind that, although this form is simplified for recording purposes, it is not simplified in its actual process. Each student's specific behavioral needs must be considered by the teacher, and having the PBA or behavioral plan for each such student at hand will assist in this.

Teachers have found this simple problem-solving process to be quick and effective in reducing mild behavioral problems. The curriculum adaptation strategy can be used prior to implementing the more complex and formal functional behavior assessment process, and results may actually inform it.

Choose a student, a lesson, or a unit that is coming up. Use the forms to plan for adaptations to improve outcomes for your students.

Adapting Instruction to Minimize Problem Behavior and Maximize Student Success

1. Select the subject area (and grade level) to be taught.

   ○ Reading   ○ Math   ○ Science   ○ Social Studies   ○ Writing

   ○ Music   ○ Health   ○ P.E.   ○ Art   ○ Other (specify): _____

   Grade Level: _____

2. How will the lesson be taught (in one day)? _____

   What is the format (e.g., whole class, small group, individual)? _____

   _____

   What will students do?

   ○ Permanent products (e.g., worksheets)

   ○ Listen

   ○ Seatwork

   ○ Cooperative group activity

   ○ Other (specify): _____

3. Describe the instructional plan for most learners. List learner objectives and activities.

   _____

   _____

   _____

   _____

4. Identify the student who will need adaptations in the curriculum or instructional plan in order to reduce problem behavior and enhance learning and participation.

   Student Name: _____

5. Provide a summary statement regarding the student with problem behavior (see Chapter 16).

When the predictor happens	Student performs (behavior)	In order to get/avoid (attention, the task, etc.)

Adapting Instruction to Minimize Problem Behavior
and Maximize Student Success (continued)

6. Now use the 12 types of adaptations as a means of thinking about some ways you could adapt what or how you teach to support this learner for this lesson. Try to put one idea in each box. Some strategies may overlap.

Precorrect Errors	Task Difficulty	Time to Complete
Level of Participation	Task Size	Output Method
Alternate Goals	Input Method	Increase Rewards for Acceptable Behavior
Substitute Curriculum	Level of Support	Remove or Restrict

7. Evaluate your adaptation. After using the process, it will be helpful to reflect on the following questions regarding your curriculum or instructional adaptation.

   a. Will this adaptation improve the level of participation in class for the student?

   b. Is this adaptation the least intrusive (i.e., least interfering) option?

   c. Will this adaptation give the student a variety of options, or will the same adaptation be used for all activities

      (e.g., always do, less problems)?

   d. Does the adaptation ensure an appropriate level of difficulty for the student?

   e. Can the student use this adaptation in other classes or activities?

8. Conclusions

   _____

   _____

   _____

   _____

   _____

   _____

   _____

Strategies for Adapting Curriculum

Here is a list of various activities, strategies, or approaches that can further assist you in adapting curriculum for the different kids in a given classroom.

- Tic-tac-toe or choice boards.
- Extensions menu.
- Compaction (opposite of extended time).
- Enrichment (menu: included for tiered intervention and in contracts for individual students, and so forth).
- Cooperative learning, groups (heterogeneous support groups, homogeneous interest groups), jigsaw, and literacy circle.
- Tiered lessons/centers (tiered reading materials, response requirements, depth of knowledge/Bloom's), different points of entry.
- Centers/stations (access to curriculum through multiple modalities and learning styles).
- Supports (word walls, vocabulary previews, graphic organizers, teacher notes, earmuffs or carrels to block distractions, visual reminders on cards or taped to desk).
- Student learning contracts, agendas, portfolios, or orbital studies.
- Problem-based learning; real-world problems; service projects; simulations; and discovery-based, hands-on, open-ended tasks.
- Metacognition and self-assessment.
- For support: mentors, vertical teaming, or older study buddy.

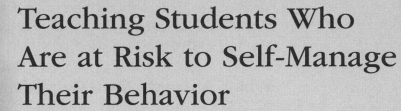

CHAPTER 19

Teaching Students Who Are at Risk to Self-Manage Their Behavior

Benefits of Self-Management

We hope that our students will become self-directed, intrinsically motivated learners. Intrinsic motivation is motivation from the inside and is related to interest, satisfaction, accomplishment, pride, or other positive feelings (Cameron & Pierce, 1994). When a student is intrinsically motivated, there is a decreased need for external reward; this creates greater independence, or self-direction, in learning and, indeed, in life (Katz, 1997). This helps the students harness the dynamo of their own energy in the pursuit of their self-interest in academia and other areas.

There are many benefits for the student who can self-manage. Teachers value compliance to reasonable requests, students who are prepared for class, and students who do their best to complete assigned work (Bradshaw, Tandon, & Leaf, 2011; Walker, Ramsey, & Gresham, 2004). They value this because it makes it easier to provide a safe environment for *all* students to achieve academic and social learning success. It also makes it easier for teachers to teach. Students who are good managers of their behavior can also learn to manage their own learning (to the extent the teacher is comfortable with!).

Safe, respectful, and responsible students learn to self-manage their behavior. Thus, the schoolwide and classroom behavior management components you already have in place provide important support for *all* your students. Likewise, students who self-manage are more safe,

OBJECTIVES

- ▶ Describe the purposes and benefits of teaching self-management

- ▶ Describe the core features of self-management programs

- ▶ Illustrate how to design and teach a self-management program

Benefits of Student Self-Management:
- Better social outcomes (peer and teacher relationships).
- Learning to manage their own learning (academic outcomes).
- Better classroom management (be safe, be responsible, be respectful).

respectful, and responsible. However, there are *some* students who will need additional support to access this cycle of self-management and its resulting rewards. This chapter will help you motivate these children to increase their success in behavior self-management.

Which Students Need Help Learning Self-Management?

The self-management method can be used as a universal or Tier II intervention. Students who have difficulty managing their behavior may be observed being told:

- What to do.
- How to do it.
- When to do it.
- When not to do it.
- If they did it correctly or not.

Often, when behavioral problems persist, we tend to "rein in" in an effort to control students, get them engaged in the learning process, and get them back on track to compliance. This response assumes that the student alone needs to solve the problem, that it is within his or her ability to do so, that more of the same solution is required, and (sometimes) that increased negative consequences will accomplish this. For these students, constant direction or correction from adults may create a situation that promotes escape in the form of problem behavior, withdrawal, or lack of motivation.

Other students may simply lack the skills of self-management and will need to be taught these skills. If we are to help our students achieve self-control and intrinsic motivation, then we will need to teach those students with problem behavior to respond more independently and to manage their behavior and school work. We should not assume that they know how to do this or that they purposely are not managing their own behavior. Instead, we need to teach them skills, allow time for practice, and support steps toward success.

What Is Self-Management?

With a little help from the teacher, a student who is a good self-manager is able to identify problems to be solved, distinguish alternative behaviors, and arrange contingencies to change those behaviors. For example, the student may identify the problem to be solved as not getting work done or not being prepared for class. The alternate behaviors that the student considers are

> Mistakes are opportunities to reteach, as opposed to punish.

working without interruption for 15 minutes or using a checklist to assure that all materials are ready for class. The rewards that the student receives may include the enjoyment of a job well done, access to the computer, or free time after work completion.

Why Teach Self-Management?

Teaching self-management has multiple practical benefits, as mentioned earlier, including benefits in the classroom. It is an effective curriculum adaptation for many problems, and it is a way to make thinking overt, so you can teach the student to think aloud or on paper at first and then fade into independent performance. This models both the specific positive behavior being taught and the higher level skill of metacognition (or thinking about thinking). Self-management is an excellent way to replace adult-mediated behavior, thus minimizing teacher–student conflicts over the control of a situation or task. Self-management also promotes independence now and in the future and teaches positive social behavior. Last, self-management routines can minimize interactions during classroom routines, reducing noise and distraction in the classroom.

Setting Up a Self-Management System in Your School or Classroom

There are a number of schoolwide and classroom-based practices already covered in this book that support the development of self-management. For example, posting expectations, classroom motivational rewards (such as token systems), and prosocial and antibullying curricula help—as do specific techniques. These can include strategies like playing the Red/Green Card Game discussed in Chapter 14, which is a classroom-level support for behavior self-management.

Some schools choose to design a schoolwide self-management approach to guide students who need additional, or Tier II, behavior supports (Due et al., 2005; Hawken, MacLeod, & Rawlings, 2007). In these systems, the self-management strategy involves providing a behavior report card that students carry with them throughout the day (compare this to the student point cards discussed in Chapter 17). Some youths check in with a school adult in the morning and the afternoon, and others may check in with an adult during each class period or transition. Teachers and school staff members rate behaviors by routine or classes. This increases positive contact with adults and provides information on how the young person is doing throughout the day. Data on individual youth performance are summarized weekly, and success is determined based on the performance data.

A generic report card, form, or other method for students to record their behavior can be created for use and reuse both schoolwide or in the classroom, with room to customize for each student. Use the checklist forms provided later in this chapter as template ideas.

Self-Management Components

There are four major self-management components:

1. Self-monitoring
2. Self-recording

3. Self-evaluating

4. Self-delivery of reinforcement

Each is defined, with examples, in the following sections.

Self-Monitoring: What Am I Doing Right Now?

Self-monitoring is the first step in self-management. The student learns to discriminate between correct and incorrect performance of skills or behaviors. For example, a student may count the number of problems completed on a math worksheet or the number of times he or she talks out in class. The student learns to do this without being told or recognized by the teacher. Self-monitoring may be prompted by external (cues, checklists) or internal (thoughts) events.

Self-monitoring assumes that the student can differentiate between expected or desired behavior and other behaviors. If the difference has not been taught as a schoolwide or classroom expectation, then it will need to be. Use the school lesson plan format to develop and deliver the lesson (Chapter 6).

Also, though it may sound simplistic, many students may not be aware of their behavior and may need to learn to observe themselves when they are performing acceptable and unacceptable behavior. For example, students who talk out of turn in class often may not be aware of the frequency or volume of their talk-outs. They may also not understand how this impacts their behavior. We generally recommend that an external cue (such as a computer sound) or checklist (provided later in this chapter) be used initially to simplify monitoring and compliance to the routine.

Self-Recording: Keeping Track of What I Am Doing

In self-recording, the student notes what she or he is doing or that a behavior or task has been performed. The most common method is a type of paper-and-pencil checklist, although a device, such as a golf counter, can be used. For many of us, the date book or task list is a great example of a self-recording device.

Recording Methods

- Checklist (form)
- Tally (index card, sticky note)
- Planner, date book, to-do list
- Golf counter

Initial Improvement Versus Long-Term Improvement It is commonly demonstrated in research that taking data on oneself has reactive effects; that is, once you start paying attention to a behavior and counting or recording it, you may do less of the behavior for a while. Unfortunately, this reactivity usually wears off unless there is some form of prompting or a source of reward for continuing to count (e.g., "I get better and stay better.") For example, an adult attempting to quit smoking may count the number of cigarettes smoked in a day in an effort to use less tobacco. For a few days, this might work, but without some motivation, the effect will be short lived. In the classroom, we may ask a student to count talk-outs, but this habit will soon fade unless all of the self-management components are put into place. This focuses our attention on the need for the next step: self-reward. Do not be satisfied with the temporary improvement of reactivity; instead, help create longer-lasting skills and habits for the success of your student.

Take a moment to complete the following reflection. Relate your experiences with behavior management to those you will use for your students.

Reflection

Self-Management

1. What behaviors have you self-monitored?

2. What are ways that you self-record in your life?

3. How do you keep track of your daily tasks or long-term projects?

4. What rewards do you give yourself for completion, progress, or success?

5. How do you promote self-management in your classroom now?

Setting Up Self-Recording The following steps illustrate the process for setting up self-recording.

1. Identify a specific behavior (e.g., talking out in class).

2. Detect whether the behavior has occurred (provide the student with a definition of talking out, and demonstrate examples and nonexamples).

3. Record the behavior over time.

Self-Evaluating: How Did I Do?

In the self-evaluation step, the students evaluate their behavior in relation to a criterion, determining if the behavior is correct or appropriate according to the criteria you have set. This is the toughest step!

Let's revisit the talking-out example: Whether the student does or does not talk out in class, at the end of an interval (2 minutes, for example), the student must judge whether the behavior occurred or not and evaluate his or her performance. This judgment provides the basis for self-recording and, later, for the self-delivery of a reward. An adult will need to review self-evaluation frequently

> **Self-evaluation is the toughest step!**
> - Criterion based
> - Student assessed
> - Teacher reviewed—only after student's self-assessment

with the student to assure honesty, model accuracy, and ensure rewards only for positive behavior. However, be aware that the most important step in teaching self-evaluation is to let the student self-evaluate before an adult gives any feedback!

Self-Delivery of Reinforcement: What Is My Reward for Doing It?

The most satisfying step in self-management is to deliver a reward or recognition to yourself! Self-delivered consequences are the same as any others and may include tangible or material rewards, self-praise, moving onto the next step or activity, or simply checking off a job well done. (One way to determine if simply checking off a task is a reward is to ask others if they have ever put a task on their list and checked it off after it was done!) Rewards can include those identified at the school or classroom level (classroom rewards were developed in Chapter 14), or they may include others that are specific to the student. Remember that a reward is only truly a reward if it increases the expected behavior for the student in question.

Possible Rewards

- Student self-delivers coins or tokens upon completion of tasks or items.
- Student self-delivers stickers or stars on the chart.
- Student colors in a piece of a goal chart (see Chapter 14 for more on goal charts).
- Student analyzes performance records (e.g., homework completed, fewer talk-outs) and takes some free time (under agreement with the teacher).
- Student delivers a praise statement to him or herself (you can have the student premake index cards with statements to support this).
- Student asks for feedback from the teacher by raising hand (teacher knows to come over and recognize the accomplishment).
- Student writes a note about the success to home, to the principal, to a mentor, or in a success journal.

Building a Self-Management Routine for Your Students

Now that you have the basics, you can begin building self-management systems for your students. The big steps follow.

1. Select a behavior that needs changing (you can decide this yourself or negotiate with the student).

2. Select an alternative behavior that either replaces or competes with the behavior that needs changing. For example, raising a hand is a replacement for talking out; staying in the seat competes with getting out of the seat.

3. Teach the student to self-monitor (become aware of) the behavior. Use the lesson plan format you developed in Chapter 6 (this includes components such as giving a rationale, showing examples and nonexamples, and practicing using role play).

4. Determine or design a method for recording the behaviors, and teach the student how to use it (see Chapter 14).

5. Coach the student in self-monitoring and recording initially. If you see the student engaging in the target behavior, wait briefly and then remind him or her to record the event. If the student records independently and correctly, recognize the student.

6. Set a criterion for rewards that is reachable, and teach the student to track progress. For example, staying in the seat 9 out of 10 intervals during seatwork could meet the criterion for five minutes of extra recess. You may need to start with smaller gains and work toward increases in expected behavior in either frequency or length of time. Develop endurance.

7. Decide upon a recognition, reward, or a schedule for these with increasing rewards for increasing success. Make sure the reward fits the student.

8. You can decide if you want your student to self-deliver a reward or just ask for it when the criteria are met. The sample self-management forms include a place for a guardian signature. This is a great way to incorporate a delayed reward at home for the child, as well as to communicate successes to home.

Activity: Design a Reporting Form

The following **Self-Management Checklists (1–4)** are samples that you can adapt for use in your classroom (the first checklist is a blank checklist that you can fill in to reflect your unique situation). Take a look at how they are set up, and then use the development steps outlined in this chapter to build a system for one of your students. In the forms with "yes or no" in the box, each "yes" can be counted as a point either for a behavioral contract (e.g., if you earn 80% of the points, you get five minutes of extra recess) or for progress monitoring (you can add up the number of points earned per day or per period and plot them on a simple graph).

Self-Management Checklist

Student Name: _____ Date: _____

Behavior Goals:

1. _____

2. _____

3. _____

Recording method (select one): ○ Tally of Positive ○ Write "Yes" or "No"

Teacher: Allow student to rate his or her behavior first. Then, initial if you agree.

Period	Goal 1: _____ _____	Goal 2: _____ _____	Goal 3: _____ _____	Teacher Initial
Morning Check-In				
1.				
2.				
3.				
4.				
5.				
6.				
7.				
Afternoon Check-Out				
Total				

Criteria for Reward:

_____

Reward:

_____   _____
Guardian Signature   Date

Self-Management Checklist 1

Student Name: _____ Date: _____

Behavior Goals:

1. Arrive on time.

2. Complete work.

3. Stop and listen.

Allow student to rate his or her behavior first. Then, initial if you agree.

	Arrive on Time	**Complete Work**	**Stop and Listen**	**Teacher Initial**
Morning Check-In	Yes / No	Yes / No	Yes / No	
Math	Yes / No	Yes / No	Yes / No	
Reading	Yes / No	Yes / No	Yes / No	
Social Studies	Yes / No	Yes / No	Yes / No	
Lunch	Yes / No	Yes / No	Yes / No	
Language Arts	Yes / No	Yes / No	Yes / No	
Music	Yes / No	Yes / No	Yes / No	
Science	Yes / No	Yes / No	Yes / No	
Afternoon Check-Out	Yes / No	Yes / No	Yes / No	
Total	/9	/8	/9	/9

Reward:

_____   _____
Guardian Signature   Date

Self-Management Checklist 2

Student Name: _____ Date: _____

Behavior Goals:

Follow directions in class.

Allow student to rate his or her behavior first. Then, initial if you agree.

	Stop and Listen	Repeat Direction	Ask for Help	Start Right Away	Finish on Time	Teacher Initial
Morning Check-In	Yes / No	Yes / No	Yes / No	Yes / No	Yes / No	
Math	Yes / No	Yes / No	Yes / No	Yes / No	Yes / No	
Reading	Yes / No	Yes / No	Yes / No	Yes / No	Yes / No	
Social Studies	Yes / No	Yes / No	Yes / No	Yes / No	Yes / No	
Lunch	Yes / No	Yes / No	Yes / No	Yes / No	Yes / No	
Language Arts	Yes / No	Yes / No	Yes / No	Yes / No	Yes / No	
Music	Yes / No	Yes / No	Yes / No	Yes / No	Yes / No	
Science	Yes / No	Yes / No	Yes / No	Yes / No	Yes / No	
Afternoon Check-Out	Yes / No	Yes / No	Yes / No	Yes / No	Yes / No	
Total	/9	/9	/9	/9	/9	/9

Reward:

_____   _____
Guardian Signature   Date

Self-Management Checklist 3

Student Name: _____ Date: _____

Behavior Goals:

Solve problems without getting angry.

Allow student to rate his or her behavior first. Then, initial if you agree.

Define Problem	Teacher Rating	Teacher Rating	Teacher Initial
State what I need.	Yes / No	Yes / No	
Generate alternative solutions.	Yes / No	Yes / No	
Choose a solution.	Yes / No	Yes / No	

Evaluate the choices:
    How do I feel?
    How do others feel?
	Yes / No	Yes / No	

Did it work?	Yes / No	Yes / No	
Total	/5	/5	/5

Reward:

_____   _____

Guardian Signature   Date

Self-Management Checklist 4

Student Name: _____ Date: _____

Behavior Goals:

Finish five math problems and then raise hand.

Allow student to rate his or her behavior first. Then, initial if you agree.

Problem 1	Problem 2	Problem 3	Problem 4	Problem 5	Teacher Initial

Reward:

_____   _____
Guardian Signature   Date

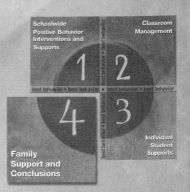

SECTION 4

Family Support and Conclusions

CHAPTER 20

Working with Families and the Community for *Best Behavior*

Background: One Last System for *Best Behavior*

So far, we have shared the following major systems of support for *Best Behavior* implementation:

- Schoolwide and Common Area (Chapters 1–10).
- Classroom (Chapters 11–14).
- Individual Student Supports (Chapters 15–19).

Now we need a system for communicating and collaborating with families and the community!

The Interrelation of School and Home Behavior Supports

Implementing and sustaining an organized, schoolwide system for providing behavior supports and teaching social behavior is the foundation for effective efforts towards preventing problem behavior in schools. In addition to the direct benefit it has on student behavior in school, such a system creates the context for school-based efforts to support effective parenting (Pas, Bradshaw, & Hershfeldt, 2011; Stormshak, Connell, & Dishion, 2009; Walker et al., 2008, Winter).

When school personnel have a shared vision of the kind of social behavior and environment they want to promote, they are in a position to inform and collaborate with families in creating the same kind of supportive environment at home and in the community. When educators are clear about how to use rules; positive reinforcement; and mild, consistent consequences to support positive behavioral development, they are better able to communicate these and coordinate their efforts with those of caregivers.

As a result, caregivers will know more about their children's behavior in school and will be able to provide the same types of supports and consequences that the school is providing. In the same manner, caregivers can provide valuable input regarding the features of support plans that are feasible and acceptable from their perspective.

Schools and families must be partners in supporting and socializing students. Without caregiver collaboration, school behavior gains may be limited to that setting (Walker, Ramsey, & Gresham, 2004). Caregiver and community support can significantly increase the effectiveness of any school intervention (Buhs, Ladd, & Herald, 2006). Figure 43 illustrates how family and community involvement intersects with all the other systems of *Best Behavior.*

> Schools with thoughtful and effective behavior systems can support better behavior at home, too.

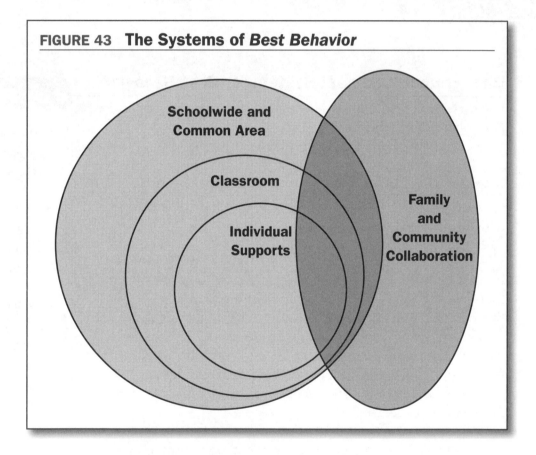

FIGURE 43 **The Systems of *Best Behavior***

Schoolwide and Common Area

Classroom

Individual Supports

Family and Community Collaboration

Why Involve Families?

As teachers and educators, we are frequently asked the question, "What is the most frustrating aspect of your job?" The answer is often, "Dealing with caregivers." But caregivers are not creatures from another planet who don't want to cooperate with us. Many teachers are caregivers themselves. We must try to stand in the shoes of caregivers when working with students. We must remember that caregivers know their children better than anyone and are with them many more hours a week than teachers. Caregivers are the most important teachers of the child. On the other hand, teachers are experts at knowing and teaching curricula. We need to remember that the main goal of caregivers and teachers is to help the child be as successful as possible both academically and socially. The information in this chapter can be used as a resource when working with caregivers. Many of the practices may also be helpful for other adults working with children.

Having caregivers as cooperative partners is very beneficial to a child's progress. The information provided here can be shared with all the significant adults in a student's life. Many children spend a majority of their waking hours in the presence of adults other than their caregivers. Daycare providers, babysitters, grandcaregivers, aunts, uncles, neighbors, or older siblings may be primary caregivers. In this chapter, we will refer to all adult caregivers as "caregivers" and all school staff members as "teachers."

Caregivers have been shown to be natural helpers, especially when included as partners in the process of schooling. We know it won't work for everyone, but increases in cooperation between families and schools are linked to improved school success (Pas, et al., 2011). Using the prompt provided, please reflect upon your opinion about family involvement.

Students need optimum support to be successful in school, so adding any resources can benefit everyone. We also know that when caregivers are informed, involved, and supportive when things go well, it will be easier to problem solve when things do not go well. Last, the federal special education law (IDEA-IA) requires meaningful caregiver participation! Systems that accommodate special education can be expanded to benefit all students. There are a number of stakeholders in student success, all aiming for the same goal, as seen in Figure 44. Each is an important resource in attaining that goal.

What is the common goal?
- Student success!
- Every caregiver wants his or her child to be successful at school.
- Every teacher wants each student to be successful.
- Communities need successful children and youths.

Reflection

Raise Student Achievement

What is the best way to raise student achievement? Consider the options below:
- Lengthen the school day.
- Decrease class size.
- Increase caregiver involvement.
- Is there a place for all three?

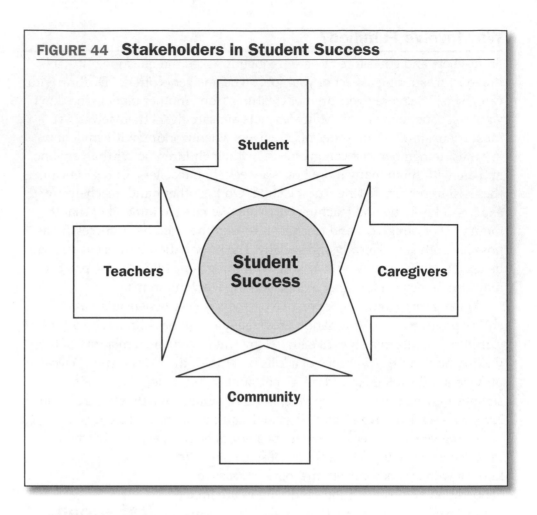

FIGURE 44 Stakeholders in Student Success

Challenges to Family Involvement

Many of us may say to ourselves, "I wish I had more cooperation from some families. How can I do my job when there is so much happening to students away from school?" On the other hand, caregivers and community members often report that they are not clearly informed. In addition, many caregivers may have had negative school experiences themselves and are reluctant to work with school personnel.

The first contact with a caregiver or family member typically happens due to discipline, when there is a problem with the student. This is not a great way to invite caregivers to work with us! We have also observed that school personnel are not sufficiently knowledgeable about local family support resources and intervention approaches to determine what would be best for a particular concern, child, or family. We are rarely able to follow up to ensure that help was received or even know what kind of help to suggest.

> "My son doesn't behave at school during the day . . . why would I bring him back here at night?!"
>
> Quote from mother while participating in a PTA meeting

When working with students who display challenging behaviors, remember that caregivers have had to deal with their child for many hours a day for many years and have dealt with many teachers. Teachers often blame caregivers for unacceptable student behavior, while caregivers often blame teachers for not giving their child needed help. Yet, both parties want the best for the child. Caregivers, even ineffective ones, want their child to be successful at school. Many children have wonderfully supportive caregivers who value the importance of being respectful, responsible, and safe in school.

The suggestions provided in the following section will help establish cooperation with many caregivers. Unfortunately, many students have unsupportive, chaotic home environments, and school is a safe haven for them. In spite of our best efforts to communicate with all caregivers, some will not be reached.

Remember, however, that you must never punish children for having ineffective caregivers. In such cases, teachers are often the only consistent and respectful adult in a child's life. By being clear, consistent, and respectful, teachers can make a huge difference in the lives of even the most disadvantaged students.

The reproducibles at the end of this chapter may help in your discussions with caregivers about how they can work with their children at home to develop and strengthen the skills of communication, cooperation, limit setting, problem solving, and confidence building. Some caregivers may never have had exposure to this type of information.

How Do We Get Families Involved?

We realize that gaining greater family involvement can be challenging, but there is ample research to suggest that a few simple strategies can help us (Crick, Ostrov, & Werner, 2006):

- Keep caregivers informed.
- Open the door for parenting education.
- Support more effective parenting practices.
- Promote positive caregiver-child interactions.
- Improve student success and self-esteem.

The research on family involvement suggests that the following factor increases the chances of caregivers "being positively involved with the school" (Buhs, Ladd, & Herald, 2006): when the caregiver perceives that his or her involvement is welcomed and common at the school.

This "welcome the caregiver" perception can take the form of:

- General school invitations (e.g., formal invitation to have lunch with student, school performances, project fares).
- Specific invitations from the child (e.g., come to my school, help me with my homework).
- Specific invitations from the teacher (e.g., here's what's going on in class now, here's how you can help).

What Specific Roles Can Families Fill?

Caregivers may think that they are expected to volunteer in the classroom. This is actually beyond the capacity of many families, due to work schedules and other demands. Therefore, it should not be the primary goal of a caregiver-involvement initiative. The first focus is to support the child's schoolwork at home (e.g., provide a place to do homework, monitor homework, check backpack and communication from the school, regularly check the school's website). Following is a list that provides a nice summary of ways caregivers can become involved and how a school can encourage these involvements (Crick, et al., 2006).

- Parenting
  - Help all families establish home environments that support children as students.
- Communicating
  - Design effective forms of school-to-home and home-to school communications about school programs and children's progress.
- Volunteering
  - Recruit and organize caregiver help and support.
- Learning at home
  - Provide information and ideas to families about how to help students at home with homework and other curriculum-related activities.
- Decision making
  - Include caregivers in school decisions, thereby developing caregiver leaders and representatives.
  - Identify and integrate resources and services within the community.

Figure 45 translates these general role categories into specific opportunities that are commonly available at schools.

FIGURE 45 Examples of Family Involvement at Schoolwide Level

- Include a caregiver on the PBIS team.
- Include caregiver volunteers in classroom activities (e.g., party planners, creating materials for the class, displaying work, field trips).
- Include caregiver volunteers in schoolwide activities (e.g., fundraisers, activities, events).
- Train caregiver volunteers to be effective in the classroom (e.g., instructional help, leading small groups, holding interventions).
- School- or caregiver-sponsored support or advisory groups (e.g., parent-teacher associations, parenting support groups).
- Design specific events to meet the needs of your school's families and community (e.g., specific service projects, speakers, fundraisers).

What Do Families Need from Schools?

Caregivers consistently tell us what they want, and we have listed these specific requests here.

- To hear from the teacher at the beginning of the year (and regularly thereafter).
- To know specific expectations for the student.
- To learn about problems before they get out of hand.
- To have general information about what is going on at school.
- To hear good things about their child!

The strategies outlined or detailed here will address each of these needs, thus encouraging a positive relationship with the family and laying the base for good communication and effective collaboration.

Communication Strategies for Teachers

A lack of effective communication too often causes a lack of cooperation between caregivers and teachers. By providing caregivers with a copy of school and classroom expectations, routines, and schedules and by requesting a signed verification after reading them, teachers initiate the first step to effective communication. Inviting caregivers into the classroom, making positive phone calls, and sending e-mail messages and notes before problems occur establishes positive communication.

Often, caregivers learn about what is going on at school only from their child's report card. If caregivers can hear or see firsthand how your classroom is organized, how you have taught expectations, how you interact with all students, and how much work and effort you put into making the classroom a positive and predictable environment, then they will understand their child's reports more clearly. Some caregivers have had negative school experiences, may view teachers as intimidating, or have been contacted by the school only when there was a problem. When caregivers do need to get involved because of a problem, it is much easier if good communication was already established. Inviting caregivers to school assemblies and activities when students perform is another way to encourage caregivers to become involved in a positive way. Both of these allow the caregivers to have a positive context for any issues that arise.

A simple solution (and not the only one!) is to regularly communicate with and invite all families to participate in *Best Behavior* activities and other school functions. To flesh out this simple solution with more detail on communication rules, teachers should try to follow these DOs and DON'Ts.

DO	DON'T
• View caregivers as allies. • Communicate clearly and frequently. • Let caregivers know when the child is doing well. • Realize that some caregivers have had negative school experiences. • Empathize with caregivers. • Listen to caregivers. • Use humor. • Remember how you would like to be treated as a caregiver.	• View caregivers as enemies or blame them for child's behavior. • Assume what caregivers should know. • Call only when there is a problem. • Assume that caregivers don't care or don't want to take responsibility. • Assume that your concern is the only thing caregivers are dealing with. • Assume that you have all the answers, or know all the facts. • Make mountains out of molehills. • Treat caregivers as if they were from another planet.

While all of this may seem like a lot of new tasks and responsibilities, we have found there are a few simple things we can do to get the caregiver-involvement ball rolling! Figure 46 shows strategies to accomplish this. Some of these may be part of the schoolwide varied reinforcement plan from Chapter 7. Sample forms and formats for many of these communications are at the end of this chapter.

FIGURE 46 Positive Family Communication Practices

	Calendar-Specific Items	All Year Long
Early in Year	Letter of introduction and welcome. Find out caregiver communication preference (e-mail, phone, text, notes in backpack, or planner). Establish positive contact as early as possible. Example: Send home a positive note or e-mail at the beginning of the school year, such as, "John had great ideas during science class." Provide caregivers with copies of: • School and classroom expectations. • Routines and schedules. • Individual student expectations. Request verification (signature) on communications.	• Establish an open-door policy for visits to your classroom. Invite caregivers to come and visit the classroom anytime. • Provide a regular classroom calendar or newsletter (paper and on the website, where it's accessible to community). • Maintain a caregiver communication log. • Good News Notes: Routinely send home positive notes about your students (e.g., "Lucy asked great questions in English class today."). • Inform caregivers of small accomplishments (e.g., bringing notebooks to class consistently, asking for help appropriately, and helping peers). • Make positive comments on student papers and assignments (e.g., "You wrote topic sentences with at least three supporting sentences, Carmen. Good for you!"). • Provide opportunities for students to call home to report a positive occurrence. • Keep data to show caregivers the positive changes in student behavior and academics. Well-organized graphs speak louder than words. • Keep up a home /school communication sheet. • Keep things light.
Midyear	Midyear: Caregiver Satisfaction Survey	
End of Year	End of Year: Caregiver Satisfaction Survey Provide a celebration of student successes, such as: • Closure event • Portfolio of works	

Develop Your Communication System

In this chapter, we have provided you with a variety of ideas and a rationale for the critical importance of encouraging and strengthening family involvement in *Best Behavior* systems. We suggest that you build your family communication system using the following examples as models.

Best Behavior Letter of Information for Families—Model

Best Behavior is an approach used at our school to support students' success. This information sheet describes what *Best Behavior* is, how it is used at our school, and how you can get involved in *Best Behavior* to help your student succeed.

What is *Best Behavior*?

Best Behavior is an approach for supporting students' academic success by making schools more safe, predictable, and supportive of *all* students. It is based on over 40 years of scientific research and work in schools and is used in thousands of schools across the country. Through *Best Behavior*, we put routines in place that help *all* students be successful with their behavior. We consider all of the things (both positive and negative) that might affect students and their behavior in school. Through *Best Behavior*, we also pay attention to understanding why a student may be showing challenging behaviors at school, and we then create a personalized strategy to help that student succeed.

How Is *Best Behavior* used in our school?

Best Behavior uses strategies that are respectful and tailored to each student's strengths, behavior, and learning and communication style. The strategies are focused on helping the student control negative behaviors, have positive social interactions, develop friendships, improve communication skills, and develop school success skills in a healthy, nurturing environment.

    Best Behavior offers different levels of support to students and their families. First, for *all* students in our school, we set the following behavioral expectations: *Be Safe, Be Respectful, and Be Responsible*. We regularly teach what these expectations mean, and we recognize and reward students when these expectations are followed. We also focus on positive adult supervision in common areas, such as hallways, the lunchroom, and recreational areas.

    Some students require additional teaching and ongoing support in order to develop and maintain socially appropriate behavior. This level of support that *Best Behavior* offers identifies the child's needs that are met by the challenging behaviors that interfere with his or her learning. After we study these behaviors and get an understanding of them, we develop a positive behavior support plan to teach more appropriate behaviors that will meet these needs. We also teach positive ways to cope with stresses, such as peer conflicts or academic difficulties, that can affect learning.

How do caregivers get involved?

If your child is having some behavioral, social, or emotional difficulties that are interfering with school success, then he or she could benefit from *Best Behavior*.

What we discover at school is shared with caregivers, and we encourage students to practice these new skills and behaviors both at home and at school to strengthen them. We have learned that, the more these behaviors are practiced, the sooner the child will experience better learning and positive relations with teachers and other students. You can help your child benefit by consistently noticing his or her efforts to demonstrate positive behaviors and by partnering with our school to ensure your student's success.

Letter of Introduction—Model

Dear Caregivers,

Welcome to our school and classroom! I am looking forward to the school year and getting to know each of you and your child.

You are welcome to leave a message for me at school (phone #) or e-mail me (XXXXX@XXX.net), and I will try to get back to you in the same day.

At _____ school, we are safe, respectful, and responsible. During the first few weeks of school we will explain and teach expected behaviors to students across the whole school. I will send home notes reminding you to discuss good behaviors with your child.

Respectfully,

Teacher Name

Sample Classroom Calendar

April

Monday	Tuesday	Wednesday	Thursday	Friday
13	**14**	**15**	**16**	**17**
Math Lab Be respectful in the cafeteria. Read Chapters 1 and 2—Social Studies textbook. Study spelling words. Classwide good-behavior drawing.	Study spelling words. Homework: math worksheet 1	Study spelling words. Homework: read Chapter 1 of *Moby Dick.*	Study spelling words.	Spelling test

Sample Classroom Newsletter

Riverview Tigers Are Safe, Respectful, and Responsible!

We are off to a good start this year. We have all learned to use the cafeteria and playground appropriately, and all classroom routines have been taught and reviewed.

Ask your child to tell you what being respectful on the playground means, and encourage her or him to keep up the good work!

Research shows the importance of caregiver encouragement of school work, so please talk with your child daily about the required work, and schedule a set time for homework every day.

New Activity

We are preparing for our field trip to the planetarium by reading books on astronomy. You can support your child by talking about the stars, space, and so forth. I will be sending home some caregiver tips on Wednesday to help you.

Student of the Week

Our student of the week this week is Maria Gomez. Her classmates will thank her each morning for being safe, respectful, and responsible!

Caregiver Orientation Night

On September 29, we will have our first open house, and you are encouraged to come and learn about all of the new things your child is doing. Childcare will be provided for no charge to encourage your attendance!

From: Mrs. Jones

Sample Home/School Communications

Many teachers frequently send positive notes to caregivers. This can be done via e-mail, regular mail, or the child's backpack. The note should focus on the child's good behavior, academic work, or homework. This works most effectively when preprinted postcards including the teacher's name and contact information are made available by the school to every teacher.

Teachers may also send home a record of what the student did during the day and what is expected in terms of homework. This form provides an opportunity for caregivers to respond. The sample on p. 305 shows how this could look.

Good-News Note or Postcard

Name: _____

Date: _____

I am sending this good-news note home because your child has been

Safe _____

Respectful _____

Responsible _____

Demonstrating good behavior in school is a key to success, and we all appreciate it! Be sure to let your child know how proud you are!

Sincerely,

Daily Home/School Communication Sheet (Sample)

Today is: _____

1st Period: Math with Ms. Jones in Room X03.

2nd Period: English with Ms. Jones in Room X03.

3rd Period: P. E. with Mr. Wesson in the Gym.

4th Period: Computers with Mrs. Byte in Room 210.

LUNCH: (Best Buddies and Interact every other Tuesday in Room X02).

5th Period: Reading with Ms. Elmer in Room X03.

6th Period: Social Studies with Ms. Elmer in Room X03.

Homework/Comments.

Parent Signature: _____

Caregiver Comments/Questions:

Caregiver Communication

The following pages are reproducibles that support caregivers in specific skills that are consistent with the teacher practices in *Best Behavior*. In addition, your school's curricula for prosocial skills or for antibullying behaviors may provide ideas for caregiver-skill newsletters.

Communication

When your child communicates information about what has been going on at school, it gives you a chance to share in your child's successes and help with any problems. Children provide information in many ways: talking, drawing, showing, and even teaching. Caregivers can teach their children to share from the very first day of preschool and should make it a daily practice. Caregivers need to teach and use specific communication skills to have more in-depth sharing sessions. If these daily sessions are routinely done in a comfortable place at the same time, they will continue throughout the child's entire school career. The following suggestions may help.

DO
• Offer undivided attention.
• Have a quiet place.
• Make eye contact.
• Get comfortable.
• Ask specific questions.

DON'T
• Talk about school when you're upset.
• Ask your child about school when you're busy.
• Interrupt your child when he or she is talking to you.
• Correct how your child shares information or does the activities.

Cooperation

Cooperation helps children avoid problems. Children who cooperate tend to be more successful and happy in school and in the world. Encouraging cooperation in your child doesn't mean stifling individuality. On the contrary, children who cooperate are better able to adapt and express themselves appropriately. The following suggestions will make it easier for your child to cooperate with your requests.

DO

- Be close to your child.
- Make eye contact.
- Use a neutral tone.
- Make one request at a time.
- Be specific.
- Provide positive feedback. Use sentences like, "I noticed . . . , I see . . . "
- Catch your child doing the right thing.

DON'T

- Be in another room.
- Yell or use an angry tone.
- Phrase a request as a question.
- Ask too many things at once.
- Be vague.
- Use sarcasm.
- Make a mountain out of a molehill.

Limit Setting

When expectations (such as getting out of bed, going to bed, eating routines, chores and homework, the use of appropriate language, visiting friends, and telephone privileges) are clearly explained, taught, and reinforced, it's easier for children to make choices about their behavior. Caregiver limits keep children safe and healthy until they achieve independence and the ability to keep themselves safe and healthy. The more clear and consistent your expectations are, the safer the child will feel.

Caregivers need to pay attention and continually let their child know when rules are followed and state clear consequences when rules are violated. Consequences may include removing privileges (e.g., telephone, TV watching, visiting friends), time-out (e.g., time in a quiet room, loss of time with friends or car), or restitution (e.g., yard work, house cleaning, loss of allowance). When you impose consequences, you should do so in a calm, neutral voice without yelling or using harsh words or lecturing. Even if the child begins to resist your request, keep your tone even. It will help to keep you in control of your emotions, and it will also be an example of self-control for your child. The following suggestions should help you set limits effectively.

DO
• Use a neutral tone.
• Use mild consequences.
• Provide encouragement.
• Be consistent.
• Know where your child is.
• Know who your child is with.

DON'T
• Yell or use an angry tone.
• Make empty threats or have too many rules.
• Call your child names.
• Change your rules when you feel like it.
• Allow your child to go places that you have no information about.
• Allow your child to go to someone's house if you haven't checked with the adults in charge.

Problem Solving

A problem is the difference between what is observed or what happens and what is expected or wanted. If caregivers incorporate problem-solving strategies from very early on, children will be able to use these skills and improve on them for the rest of their lives.

Caregivers can help children find a place to start working on a problem so that they can see the possibility of a solution. For example, when Nico is having a hard time building a tower with blocks, his dad helps him start by making the base stronger. This gives Nico a plan to begin. Saying, "Haven't you figured out how to put that together yet?" or "What's wrong? Can't you figure that out? It's so easy," doesn't offer Nico a starting place. The following suggestions should allow you to help your child problem-solve effectively.

DO
• Target the situation, not the person.
• State the problem in a neutral way.
• Try perspective-taking.
• Look for a win/win situation.
• Guide your child.
• Break the problem into manageable parts.
• Prompt your child. Ask questions that lead to solving problems.

DON'T
• Label the person.
• Blame others.
• Always want to be right.
• Give all the solutions.
• Attack the whole thing all at once.
• Criticize your child.

Confidence Building

Regardless of whether or not you live with your child, it's important that you maintain a positive relationship with the child. A positive relationship gives your child a stable environment in which to grow so that you are one of the people your child can depend on. The time to begin building on a positive relationship and your child's self-confidence cannot start too early. Caregivers' messages build children's beliefs about who they are and what they can do in life.

When children are experiencing problems getting along, they are usually receiving a lot of negative messages from others. They don't feel good about themselves. Caregivers can help by pointing out their children's good ideas, positive attributes, and appropriate behaviors. Daily attention for appropriate behavior can help children through difficult times at school and with friends.

It is harder to be positive with children who are going through a tough period. Also, it is more difficult to provide positive feedback and compliments to discouraged children. It may take time to figure out ways of encouraging children that are comfortable for both you and your child. The following suggestions can help you build your child's confidence.

DO

- Look for daily positive behavior.

- Try to have positive communications outnumber negative ones.

- Offer opportunities to try new skills.

- Build on what your child does well.

- Make time for your child.

- Do things your child likes to do.

- Ask for your child's ideas and help.

DON'T

- Compare your child with another child.

- Use sarcasm with positive feedback.

- Take over your child's activities.

- Focus the most attention on things your child doesn't do well.

- Require mastery or perfection.

- Criticize.

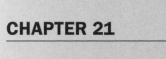

CHAPTER 21

Planning to Sustain and Improve Your Success with *Best Behavior*

Family Support and Conclusions

Best Behavior: The Big Picture

We have covered a lot of material regarding effective positive behavior interventions and support methods for the whole school, classroom, individual students, and families. It is critical to not view *Best Behavior* as a set of tricks, but rather as an integrated, sustainable system of supports for students, yourself, and your colleagues. In this chapter, you will take some time to reflect on how you will use your new skills and knowledge at your school.

For change to be effective, you need to be able to embed training and support for your colleagues and students across the school year. When training or coaching your peers, be sure to include theory, modeling, and practice as we have shown you here. Last, you should allow for team-based planning for implementation.

The PBIS Team's Ongoing Role

As your PBIS team progresses, members can take on the role of coaches and trainers and provide technical assistance on new methods, co-teach expected behavior lessons, or observe or coach colleagues. Plan to allocate the resources required in order to support activities and groups that are important to your school's implementation:

- Consider approving release time for observing or coaching, staff meeting time for discussion and planning, and the provision of follow-up training (see Chapter 2 for additional information).
- Provide coaching and training to the instructional assistants who work with some of your neediest students. Consider holding a staff

OBJECTIVES

- ▶ Review the overall goals and content of *Best Behavior*

- ▶ Provide ideas for solutions to common problems

- ▶ Develop personal and program goals for your next steps in the journey to implementing *Best Behavior* in your school

meeting just for instructional assistants at least once a month to provide training, coaching, and problem-solving discussion.

Provide targeted training to people who work for the transportation department so that the services students receive are seamless from home to school and back home again (**http://www.pbis.org/school/primary_level/ bus_drivers.aspx**). Alignment with school behavior expectations and reinforcement systems is important, and any special procedures for students with challenging behavior must be coordinated with the school.

- Additional support needs for your school may include external evaluation services or consultation, training and consultation from outside experts regarding new or complicated behavior support planning problems or new interventions, and coordinating family support or training with community agencies (Fixsen, Naoom, Blase, Friedman, & Wallace, 2005).

Last, we suggest that you return to the ***Best Behavior* Self-Assessment Survey** that you completed in Chapter 4. Review the goals you developed and the action steps you set out there. This review and planning step will help you to strategically plan and implement your program.

Reflection

Self-Assessment and Goal Review

Think about the following questions as you review your ***Best Behavior* Self-Assessment Survey** and related goal from Chapter 4.
- Would you have different responses to the self-assessment after completing your initial study of *Best Behavior*?
- Do your goals need any modification?
- Can you add any new action steps to accomplish your goals?

Responding to Challenges

As with any change or maintenance of a comprehensive system, challenges will arise. These may range from individual staff member buy-in, to implementation, to weaknesses in systemic practices, or to meeting school-specific needs. The regular activities of the PBIS team and the systems described in *Best Behavior* will help you identify and correct such issues. Some of the more common ones are listed for you here.

Staff Buy-In

As you are well aware, schools have a hard time getting some staff members to adopt, implement, and maintain effective practices. Research suggests that a strategy for influencing school personnel to adopt a research-based practice should have the following elements.

- **Collaboration:** A collaborative process that empowers school staff with knowledge, shared vision, and choice (Gottfredson et al., 2000).
- **Relevance:** Clear and persuasive articulation of information (e.g., school rules, ODR procedures) and linking of advocated practices to valued outcomes to inform and motivate school staff (Gilbert, 1996; Rogers, 2002).
- **Trailblazers:** Utilization of the social influence process of early adopters and opinion leaders to increase motivation (Webster-Stratton & Taylor, 1998).
- **Commitment:** Overcoming psychological barriers (e.g., unpleasantness associated with change or feelings of burnout) through commitment to valued action despite distress.
- **Professional Supports:** Consultation and technical assistance in establishing appropriate systems and structures (Mihalic & Irwin, 2003).

Postimplementation Doldrums

Sometimes we hear the following from teachers and/or administrators: "We got a good start on implementation, but now it's not working."

The perception of "not working" is created when the staff members are working hard, yet problems are still occurring. Keep in mind that, even with a very highly developed program, problems will still occur. When people perceive failure, it's important to go back to the basics of *Best Behavior*:

- Are the behavior expectations clear (Chapter 5)?
- Have the students been taught using the critical lesson plan components (Chapter 6)?
- Are the students being frequently noticed for doing the right things (Chapter 7)?

The most common breakdown is that adults are noticing undesirable behavior at a much higher rate than they are noticing desired behavior. The second most common problem is that the students have forgotten what they are expected to do because it has not been reviewed or retaught recently. To address this, the PBIS team needs to meet; review the expectations, procedures, and lesson plans; set a plan to remind everyone of the schoolwide and classroom expectations; and notice and reinforce desired behavior. For change to happen, desired or successful behaviors must

> **4:1 Rule** Adults need to engage in four times as many positive interactions as negative interactions with every student.

replace undesirable and unsuccessful behaviors. It is adult attention to desired behaviors that produces this result.

PBIS Team Effectiveness

Sustainability is the result of an effective team. The schoolwide PBIS team needs to meet at least monthly to monitor behavioral data and promote the ongoing review of expectations and schoolwide positive reinforcement efforts. Figure 47 first appeared in Chapter 1; we have now added the PBIS team as the core sustaining the cycle.

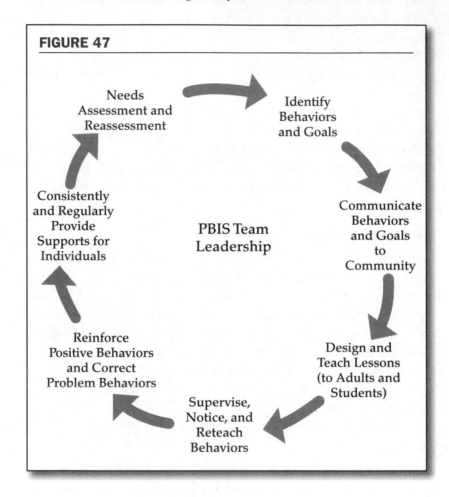

FIGURE 47

Schools with more advanced systems will also implement specialized teams to consult on Tier II and Tier III behavioral support interventions. These will include staff members with more advanced training or skills and understandings of *Best Behavior* procedures. They will consult with other staff members to design more individualized support systems based on the schoolwide positive behavioral support system. This support may involve classroom observations, functional behavioral assessment (Chapter 16), and individualized behavioral support planning (Chapters 17–19). It is common for members of this team to include the principal, school counselor, school psychologist, and special education teachers, as well as interested and skilled general education teachers.

Common Problems and Solutions

Our experience has shown that certain problems are common in implementation and maintenance. These are presented here, along with the strategies and program components of *Best Behavior* that will help address the problems.

Schoolwide

One common problem is when behavior incidence reports or office referral patterns don't show the complete picture.

Problem	Solution
Descriptions of student behaviors are extravagant, emotion-laden, and lacking in specific information.	Staff members need to be trained on how to write descriptions of behavior that are neutral, accurate, and clear.
Some staff members are reluctant to write behavior reports for a variety of reasons. Therefore, behavior data may be incomplete or inaccurate.	The individuals designing the support plan must gather additional information through observation and by interviewing staff members who work with the student.

Common Areas

Problem	Solution
Common areas are a likely place for a variety of misbehaviors.	The expectations for common areas need to be frequently reviewed. Some schools call these booster shots. This review needs to occur following holidays, prior to anticipated disruptive events (e.g., Halloween, Valentine's Day), and whenever spikes in undesirable behavior are noticed or anticipated (see Chapter 6).

Individual Student Supports

Problem	Solution
When the schoolwide program has been implemented with fidelity, there will still be students who require additional support.	Some of these students will require only minor additional interventions (Tier II); others may require very carefully designed individualized intervention programs (Tier III). All of these interventions are based on the schoolwide teaching and reinforcement plans. They are simply implemented at an increasing level of detail and sophistication.

Tier II Supports

Problem	Solution
How to develop more intensive supports when the program for *all* students doesn't meet the needs of an individual student or a group of students.	A fully developed system will have available interventions that may be easily selected for students that need more support. These interventions may include small group reteaching of expectations and/or academic skills and simple behavior support plans that can be implemented without intensive evaluation (see Chapter 16).
Teachers are experiencing frustration or parents are expressing concern over a particular student.	Consider a Tier II intervention.

Tier III Supports

Problem	Solution
A very few students have extreme behaviors. Also, other, more easily implemented interventions (Tier II) have failed for a student.	More intensive support will start with more intensive planning (see Chapters 16 and 17). These students may be reacting to academic failure, lack of social skills, or chronic stress. They will require carefully performed functional behavior assessments and careful program planning (including curriculum adaptations, Chapter 18) to help them be more successful. Possible adjustments to their behavior support plans will include adjustments to academic demands, shortening of intervals for reinforcement, and more frequent review of expectations. Expert assistance is likely to be required for this planning. The school should identify people with the skills necessary to provide this assistance.

Problem-Solving Steps

What happens when a teacher has a problem that he or she cannot solve alone? A first step is always to consult with grade-level team colleagues. If the problem exceeds the capacity of this team, then the school must have resource people in place (e.g., PBIS team members, mentor teacher, counselor, behavior support person, school psychologist, special education teacher, or principal) who the teacher can go to and depend on for support in designing positive behavioral interventions.

The following steps can be adapted to fit your school's context and resources.

1. Teacher seeks support from appropriate staff member (PBIS team member or identified support person).

2. The teacher schedules an interview with that staff person.

   a. Staff person obtains an FBA via an interview with the teacher.

   b. Together, they complete the FBA, which identifies the problem areas.

   c. Together, they create a tracking and rewards system (modify the point card template, or other) to fit the needs of the child and teacher.

3. Staff person or teacher interviews the child to find out which reinforcers will, indeed, be reinforcing (e.g., likely to increase desired behavior).

4. The teacher and the staff person meet with the student to model the desired behaviors and explain the plan.

5. Share the plan. If guardians are able to be involved in reinforcing the desired behavior, then share the plan with them. Share the plan and the behavior being addressed with other school adults, as appropriate.

6. The teacher (and others, as indicated) implements the plan.

7. After 1 week of implementation, the teacher and the supportive staff person meet again to discuss how the plan is going.

   a. If it is not working, then the expectations may need to be retaught, the reinforcer may need to be changed, and/or the frequency of the descriptive noticing may need to be increased.

   b. If it is working, then the plan is continued.

Envisioning Success

As you envision success, think about the following ways to make it happen.

- Next steps: specify some actions you will take in your work. Be willing to live your values and suppress troubling or difficult thoughts and feelings, even though the next steps might be hard or challenging.
- Write down some specific actions that everyone will take (changing or adding a practice).
- Define how we will know when it's in place and working (an outcome measure).

Conclusion

Best Behavior systems and strategies can be summarized in three clear principles:

1. Staff members agree to a common set of expected prosocial behaviors.

2. These expectations are carefully taught and reviewed.

3. Desired behaviors are systematically noticed and reinforced.

The entire school behavior support system is based on these three principles. Interventions simply become more sophisticated and intensive as the needs of the students increase. Without a fully implemented schoolwide system, individualized interventions are difficult to implement and are less effective. With a fully implemented schoolwide system, individualized interventions are often not even needed.

When challenges arise, return to the basics: clarify the expectations, reteach, and notice desired behavior!

The *Best Behavior* Message

This book describes a schoolwide system for positive behavior support and the implementation steps used to build both a positive schoolwide social culture and the capacity to support individual students with more intense behavioral needs. The major messages are that (a) problem behavior in schools is both a significant social challenge and a barrier to effective learning, (b) traditional "get tough" strategies have not proven effective, (c) the foundation for all behavior support in schools begins with establishing a positive social culture by defining, teaching, and rewarding appropriate behaviors, (d) additional behavior support procedures based on behavior analysis principles are needed for children with more intense behavior support needs, and (e) school personnel are demonstrating both the ability to collect and use quality improvement data systems and the value of those systems for improving schools.

Controlled research studies are in progress to examine the effects of SWPBIS with greater precision and control, and current evaluation results are encouraging. Schools throughout the country are demonstrating the ability to adopt and implement SWPBIS practices with fidelity (Bradshaw, 2008; Horner et al., 2004; Horner et al., 2009). When schools adopt SWPBIS practices, they report reductions in problem behavior, improved perceptions of school safety, and improved academic performance. Schools also report that establishing a positive social climate is proving more effective in their implementation of individual, wrap-around support for students with high behavior support needs (Eber et al., 2009).

This progress is encouraging. Schools are able to improve and demonstrate that change is linked to valued student outcomes. If these gains are to become important at a national scale, then additional research is needed to demonstrate experimentally controlled effects, strategies for improving efficiency, and strategies for supporting sustained implementation.

> " Children are likely
> to live up to what
> you believe of them. "
>
> —Lady Bird Johnson

Closure Activity: Countdown to Change

Please take a few minutes to reflect on the ideas, questions, feelings, and actions that you will take as a result of reading *Best Behavior*.

Reflection

New ideas I've gotten:	Actions I'm going to take:
Questions that have been raised in my mind:	Feelings I've experienced:

Please complete the following with your PBIS team.

List three goals for the remainder of the year:

1. _____

2. _____

3. _____

- What will you accomplish?

- When will you meet these goals by?

List what you and your school need:

- Specialized Assistance (coaching and expert assistance):

- Training and Staff Development:

- Materials and Tools (books, videos, additional examples):

Other:

Bibliography

Agatston, P. W., Kowalski, R., & Limber, S. (2007). Students' perspectives on cyberbullying. *Journal of Adolescent Health, 41*(6), 559–560.

Atlas, R. S., & Pepler, D. J. (1998). Observations of bullying in the classroom. *Journal of Educational Research, 92*(2), 86–99.

Bauer, N. S., Lozano, P., & Rivara, F. P. (2007). The effectiveness of the Olweus bullying prevention program in public middle schools: A controlled trial. *Journal of Adolescent Health, 40*(3), 266–274.

Becker, W., & Engelmann, S. (1978). Systems for basic instruction: Theory and applications. In A. Catania & T. Bringham (Eds.), *Handbook of applied behavior analysis: Social and instructional processes* (pp. 325–378). New York, NY: Irvington.

Biglan, A., Hallfors, D., Spoth, R., Gottfredson, D., & Cody, C. (in press). *Effective strategies for nurturing successful development in school settings*: United States Department of Education.

Biglan, A., Holder, H. D., Brennan, P. A., & Foster, S. L. (2004). *Helping adolescents at risk: Prevention of multiple problem behaviors.* New York: Guilford.

Biglan, A., Metzler, C. W., Rusby, J. C., & Sprague, J. R. (1998). *Evaluation of a comprehensive behavior management program to improve school-wide positive behavior support.* Eugene, OR: Oregon Research Institute and University of Oregon.

Blonigen, B. A., Harbaugh, W. T., Singell, L. D., Horner, R. H., Irvin, L. K., & Smolkowski, K. S. (2008). Application of economic analysis to school-wide positive behavior support (SWPBS) programs. *Journal of Positive Behavior Interventions, 10*(1), 5–19. doi: 10.1177/1098300707311366

Bradshaw, C. P. (2008). Impact of school-wide positive behavioral interventions and supports (PBIS) on the organizational health of elementary schools. *School Psychology Quarterly, 23*(4), 462–473.

Bradshaw, C. P., Mitchell, M. M., & Leaf, P. J. (2010). Examining the effects of schoolwide positive behavioral interventions and supports on student outcomes. *Journal of Positive Behavior Interventions, 12*(3), 133–148. doi: 10.1177/1098300709334798

Bradshaw, C. P., O'Brennan, L. M., & McNeely, C. A. (2008). Core competencies and the prevention of school failure and early school leaving. *New Dir Child Adolesc Dev, 2008*(122), 19–32. doi: 10.1002/cd.226

Buhs, E. S., Ladd, G. W., & Herald, S. L. (2006). Peer exclusion and victimization: Processes that mediate the relation between peer group rejection and children's classroom engagement and achievement? *Journal of Educational Psychology, 98*(1), 1–13.

Cameron, J., & Pierce, W. D. (1994). Reinforcement, reward, and intrinsic motivation: A meta-analysis. *Review of Educational Research, 64*(3), 363–423.

Cole, S., Horvath, B., Chapman, C. D., Deschenes, C., Ebeling, D., & Sprague, J. (2000). *Adapting curriculum and instruction in inclusive classrooms: A teacher's desk reference* (2nd ed.). Bloomington, Indiana: Institute for the Study of Developmental Disabilities.

Colvin, G. (1993). *Managing acting-out behavior: A staff development program to prevent and manage acting-out behavior.* Eugene, OR: Behavior Associates.

Colvin, G. (1999). *Defusing anger and aggression* [motion picture]. Eugene, OR: IRIS Educational Media.

Colvin, G., (2002). *Defusing anger and aggression: Safe strategies for secondary school educators* [video]. Eugene, OR: IRIS Media.

Colvin, G., & Lazar, M. (1997). *Effective elementary classroom: Managing for success.* Longmont, CO: Sopris West Educational Services.

Colvin, G., Sugai, G., Good, R., & Lee, Y. (1997). Effect of active supervision and precorrectinon transition behaviors of elementary students. *School Pscyhology Quarterly, 12*(4), 344–363.

Crick, N. R., Ostrov, J. M., & Werner, N. E. (2006). A longitudinal study of relational aggression, physical aggression, and children's social-psychological adjustment. *Journal of Abnormal Child Psychology, 34*(2), 127–138.

Crone, D. A., & Horner, R. H. (2003). *Building positive behavior support systems in schools: Functional behavioral assessment.* New York: Guilford Press.

Crone, D., Hawken, L., & Bergstrom, M. (2007). A demonstration of training, implementing and using functional behavioral assessment in 10 elementary and middle school settings. *Journal of Positive Behavior Interventions, 9*(1), 15-29.

Darch, C. B., Kame'enui, E. J., & Crichlow, J. M. (2003). *Instructional classroom management: A proactive approach to behavior management* (2nd ed.). Upper Saddle River, NJ: Prentice Hall.

David-Ferndon, C., & Hertz, M. F. (2009). A CDC issue brief for researchers. *Electronic Media and Youth Violence*. Retrieved from http://www.cdc.gov/violenceprevention/pdf/Electronic_Aggression_Researcher_Brief-a.pdf

De Pry, R. L., & Sugai, G. (2002). The effect of active supervision and precorrection on minor behavioral incidents in sixth grade general education classroom. *Journal of Behavioral Education, 11*, 255–267.

Deschenes, C., Ebeling, D., & Sprague, J. R. (1994). *Adapting curriculum and instruction in inclusive classrooms: A teacher's desk refrence*. Bloomington, IN: Institute for the Study of Developmental Disabilities.

Domitrovich, C. E., Bradshaw, C. P., Greenberg, M. T., Embry, D., Poduska, J. M., & Ialongo, N. S. (2010). Integrated models of school-based prevention: Logic and theory. *Psychology in the Schools, 47*(1), 71–88. doi: 10.1002/pits.20452

Due, P., Holstein, B. E., Lynch, J., Diderichsen, F., Gabhain, S. N., Scheidt, P., Currie, C., and the Health Behavior in School-Aged Children Bullying Working Group. (2005). Bullying and symptoms among school-aged children: International comparative cross sectional study in 28 countries *European Journal of Public Health, 15*(2), 128–132.

Dweck, C. S. (1975). The role of expectations and attributions in the alleviation of learned helplessness. *Journal of Personality and Social Psychology, 31*(4), 674–685. doi: 10.1037/h0077149

Eber, L., Hyde, K., Rose, J., Breen, K., McDonald, D., & Lewandowski, H. (2009). *Completing the continuum of schoolwide positive behavior support: wraparound as a tertiary-level intervention handbook of positive behavior support*, 671–709: Springer US.

Elias, M., Zins, J., Weissbert, R., Frey, K., Greenberg, M., Haynes, N., . . . Shriver, T. (1997). *Promoting social and emotional learning: Guidelines for educators*. Alexandria, VA: Association for Supervision and Curriculum Development.

Emmer, E. T., Evertson, C., & Worsham, M. E. (2000). *Classroom managment for elementary teachers* (5th ed.). Needham Heights, MA: Allyn & Bacon.

Fixsen, D. L., Naoom, S. F., Blase, K. A., & Wallace, F. (2007). Implementation: The missing link between research and practice. *APSAC Advisor, 19*, 4–11.

Fixsen, G., Naoom, S. F., Blase, K. A., Friedman, R. M., & Wallace, F. (2005). *Implementation research: A synthesis of the literature*. Tampa, FL: University of South Florida, Louis de la Parte Florida Mental Health Institute, The National Implementation Research Network (FMHI Publication #231).

Garbarino, J., Bradshaw, C. P., & Vorrasi, J. A. (2002). Mitigating the effects of gun violence on children and youth. *Future Child, 12*(2), 72–85.

Gilbert, T. F. (1996). *Human competence engineering worthy performance, tribute edition*. Silver Spring, MD: International Society for Performance Improvement.

Glasgow, R. E., Vogt, T. M., & Boles, S. M. (1999). Evaluating the public health impact of health promotion interventions: The RE-AIM framework. *American Journal of Public Health, 89*(9), 1322–1327.

Gottfredson, G. D., Czeh, E. R., Cantor, D., Crosse, S. B., & Hantman, I. (2000). *National study of deliquency prevention in schools*. Ellicott City, MD: Gottfredsgon Associates.

Grossman, D. C., Neckerman, H. J., Koepsell, T. D., Liu, P., Asher, K. N., Beland, K., Rivara, F. P. (1997). Effectiveness of a violence prevention curriculum among children in elementary school: A randomized controlled trial. *Journal of the American Medical Association, 277*(20), 1605–1611. doi: 10.1001/jama.277.20.1605

Hagan-Burke, S., Ingram, K., Thier, K., Lewis-Palmer, T., Garrett, U., Derickson, E., et al., (2002). *School-wide discipline research synthesis: A review of the literature*. Manuscript in Preparation.

Hawken, L. S., MacLeod, K. S., & Rawlings, L. (2007). Effects of the behavior education program (BEP) on problem behavior with elementary school students. *Journal of Positive Behavior Interventions, 9*, 94–101.

Hofmeister, A., & Lubke, M. (1990). *Research into practice: Implementing effective teaching strategies*. Boston: Allyn & Bacon.

Horner, R. H., Todd, A. W., Lewis-Palmer, T., Irvin, L. K., Sugai, G., & Boland, J. B. (2004). School-wide evaluation tool (SET): A research instrument for assessing school-wide positive behavior support. *Journal of Positive Behavior Interventions, 6*(1), 3–12.

Horner, R. H., Sugai, G., Smolkowski, K., Todd, A., Nakasato, J., & Esperanza, J. (2009). A randomized control trial of school-wide positive behavior support in elementary schools. *Journal of Positive Behavioral Interventions, 11*, 133–144.

Huesmann, L. R., & Guerra, N. G. (1997). Children's normative beliefs about aggression and aggressive behavior. *Journal of Personal Social Psychology, 72*(2), 408–419.

Irvin, L. K., Horner, R. H., Ingram, L. K., Todd, A. W., Sugai, G., Sampson, N., & Boland, J. (2006). Using office discipline referral data for decision-making about student behavior in elementary and middle schools: An Emperial investigation of validity. *Journal of Positive Behavior Interventions, 8*(1), 10–23.

Irvin, L. K., Tobin, T. J., Sprague, J. R., Sugai, G., & Vincent, C. G. (2004). Validity of office discipline referral measures as indices of school-wide behavioral status and effects of school-wide behavioral interventions. *Journal of Positive Behavior Interventions, 6*(3), 131–147. doi: 10.1177/10983007040060030201

Kame'enui, E. J., Carnine, D. W., Dixon, R. C., Simmons, D. C., & Coyne, M. D. (2002). *Effective teaching strategies that accommodate diverse learners.* Upper Saddle River, NJ: Pearson Education, Inc.

Katz, M. (1997). *On playing a poor hand well: Insights from the lives of those who have overcome childhood risks and adversities.* New York: Norton.

Kellam, S. G., Mayer, L. S., Rebok, G. W., & Hawkins, W. E. (1998). Effects of improving achievement on aggressive behavior and of improving aggressive behavior on achievement through two preventive interventions: An investigation of causal paths. In B. P. Dohrenwend (Ed.), *Adversity, stress, and psychopathology* (pp. 486–505, 567). New York, NY: Oxford University Press.

Knoff, H. M. (2007). *Teasing, taunting, bullying, harassment, and aggression: A school-wide approach to prevention, strategic intervention, and crisis management.* New York, NY: Haworth Press.

Knoff, H. M., & Batsche, G. M. (1995). Project ACHIEVE: Analyzing a school reform process for at risk and underachieving students. *School Psychology Review, 24*(4), 579–603.

Lafferty, J. A. (2007). Sugar and spice and everything nice? A contemporary review of girls' social and aggressive behaviors, *PsycCRITIQUES. 52*(20), 2007.

Lambert, S. F., Bradshaw, C. P., Cammack, N. L., & Ialongo, N. S. (2011). Examining the developmental process of risk for exposure to community violence among urban youth. *J Prev Interv Community, 39*(2), 98–113. doi: 936139246 [pii] 10.1080/10852352.2011.556558

Latham, G. I. (1992). *Managing the classroom environment to facilitate effective instruction.* Logan, UT: P & P Ink.

Lewis, T. J., Colvin, G., & Sugai, G. (2000). The effects of precorrection and active supervision on the recess behavior of elementary school students. *School Psychology Quarterly, 23*(2), 109–121.

Loeber, R., & Farrington, D. (2001). *Child delinquents.* Los Angeles: Sage.

Maag, J. W. (2001). Rewarded by punishment: Reflections on the disuse of positive reinforcement in schools. *Exceptional Children, 67*(2), 173.

Marzano, R. J., Pickering, D. J., & Pollock, J. E. (2001). *Classroom management that works.* Alexandria, VA: Association for Supervision and Curriculum Development.

Mayer, G. R. (1995). Preventing antisocial behavior in the schools. *Journal of Applied Behavior Analysis, 28*(4), 467–478. Retrieved from http://dx.doi.org/10.1901%2Fjaba.1995.28-467

Mayer, G. R., & Butterworth, T. (1995). A preventive approach to school violence and vandalism: An experimental study. *Personnel and Guidance Journal, 57*(9), 436–441.

Mayer, G. R., & Sulzer-Azaroff. (1991). Interventions for vandalism. In G. Stoner, M. R. Shinn, & H. M. Walker (Eds.), *Interventions for achievements and behavior problems* (pp. 559–580). Silver Spring, MD: National Association of School Psychologists.

McCloud, C., & Messing, D. (2006). *Have you filled a bucket today?* Northville, MI: Ferne Press.

McDonald, J., & Stoker, S. (2008). *Bully-proofing for high schools.* Longmont, CO: Sopris Learning.

Menard, S., Grotpeter, J., Gianola, D., & O'Neal, M. (2008). *Evaluation of bullyproofing your school: Final report* (N. C. J. Service, Trans.): U.S. Department of Justice.

Mihalic, S. F., & Irwin, K. (2003). Blueprints for violence prevention: From research to real world settings—Factors influencing the successful replication of model programs: *Youth Violence and Juvenile Justice, 1*(4), 307–329.

Nafpaktitis, M., Mayer, G. R., & Butterworth, T. (1985). Natural rates of teacher approval and disapproval and their relation to student behvior in intermediate school classrooms. *Journal of Educational Psychology, 77*(3), 362–367.

Nelson, J. R. (1996). *Designing predictable and supportive school environments: Bringing order to schools.* Spokane, WA: Cyprus Group.

Nishioka, V., Coe, M., Burke, A., Hanita, M., & Sprague, J. (2011). *Student-reported overt and relational aggression and victimization in grades 3–8.* (Issues & Answers Report, REL 2011–No. 114). Washington, DC: U.S. Department of Education, Institute of Education Sciences, National Center for Education Evaluation and Regional Assistance, Regional Educational Laboratory Northwest. Retrieved from http://ies.ed.gov/ncee/edlabs.

O'Donnell, J., Hawkins, J., Catalano, R., Abbott, R., & Day, L. (1995). Preventing school failure, drug use, and delinquency among low-income children: Long-term intervention in elementary schools. *American Journal of Orthopsychiatry, 65,* 87–100. doi: http://dx.doi.org/10.1037%2Fh0079598

Olweus, D. (1993). *Bullying at school: What we know and what we can do.* Oxford, England: Blackwell.

O'Neill, R. E., Horner, R. H., Albin, R. W., Sprague, J. R., Newton, S., & Storey, K. (1997). *Functional assessment and program development for problem behavior: A practical handbook* (2nd ed.). Pacific Grove, CA: Brookes/Cole.

Pas, E. T., Bradshaw, C. P., & Hershfeldt, P. A. (2011). Teacher- and school-level predictors of teacher efficacy and burnout: Identifying potential areas for support. *Journal of School Psychology, 50*(1), 129–145. doi: S0022-4405(11)00055-0 [pii] 10.1016/j.jsp.2011.07.003

Patterson, G. R. (1982). *Coercive family process*. Eugene, OR: Castalia.

Patterson, G. R., Reid, J. B., & Dishion, T. J. (1992). *Antisocial boys*. Eugene, OR: Castalia Press.

Reid, J. B., & Patterson, G. R. (1989). The development of antisocial behaviour patterns in childhood and adolescence. *European Journal of Personality, 3*(2), 107–119.

Rogers, E. M. (1995). *Diffusion of innovations*. New York, NY: The Free Press.

Rogers, E. M. (2002). Diffusion of preventive innovations. *Addictive Behaviors, 27*(6), 989–993. Retrieved from http://dx.doi.org/10.1016%2FS0306-4603%2802%2900300-3

Ross, S. M., Horner, R. H., & Stiller, B. (2011). *Bully prevention in PBIS: Elementary school version*. Eugene, OR: Education and Community Supports: University of Oregon.

Scott, T. M., McIntyre, J., Liaupsin, C., Nelson, C. M., Conroy, M., & Payne, L. (2005). An examination of the relation between functional behavior assessment and selected intervention strategies with school-based teams. *Journal of Positive Behavior Interventions, 7*(4), 205–215.

Shores, R. E., Wehby, J. H., & Jack, S. L. (1999). Analyzing behavior disorders in classrooms. In A. C. Repp & R. H. Horner (Eds.), *Functional analysis of problem behavior: From effective assessment to effective support* (pp. 219–237). Pacific Grove, CA: Wadsworth Publishing Company.

Skiba, R. J. (2002). Special education and school discipline: A precarious balance. *Behavior Disorders, 27*(81–97).

Skiba, R., & Peterson, R. (2000). School discipline at a crossroads: From zero tolerance to early response. *Exceptional Children, 32*, 200–216.

Smith, S. G., & Sprague, J. R. (Writers). (2004). *Play by the rules*. In I. M. Inc. (Producer). Eugene, Oregon.

Smith, S., & Sprague, J. R. (Writers). (2004). *Systematic supervision: Creating a safe and positive playground*. In I. Iris Media (Producer). Eugene, Oregon.

Spaulding, S. A., Irvin, L. K., Horner, R. H., May, S. L., Emeldi, M., Tobin, T. J., & Sugai, G. (2010). Schoolwide social-behavioral climate, student problem behavior, and related administrative decisions. *Journal of Positive Behavior Interventions, 12*(2), 69–85. doi: 10.1177/1098300708329011

Sprague, J. R., & Golly, A. (2005). *Best behavior: Building positive behavior supports in schools*. Longmont, CO: Sopris West Educational Services.

Sprague, J. R., & Walker, H. M. (2005). *Safe and healthy schools: Practical prevention strategies*. New York, NY: Guilford Press.

Sprague, J. R., Cook, C. R., Wright, D. B., & Sadler, C. (2008). *RTI and behavior: A guide to integrating behavioral and academic supports*. Horsham, PA: LRP Publications.

Sprague, J. R., Walker, H. M., Golly, A., White, K., Myers, D. R., & Shannon, T. (2001). Translating research into effective practice: The effects of a universal staff and student intervention on indicators of discipline and school safety. *Education and Treatment of Children, 24*(4), 495–511.

Sprague, J., Sugai, G., & Walker, H. (1998). Antisocial behavior in schools. In S. M. Watson & F. M. Gresham (Eds.), *The handbook of child behavior therapy*. New York: Plenum Press.

Stormshak, E. A., Connell, A., & Dishion, T. J. (2009). An adaptive approach to family-centered intervention in schools: Linking intervention engagement to academic outcomes in middle and high school. *Prevention Science, 10*(221–235).

Sugai, G. (2007). Promoting behavioral competence in schools: A commentary on exemplary practices. *Psychology in the Schools, 44*(1), 113–118.

Sugai, G., & Horner, R. (2010). School-wide positive behavior support: Establishing a continuum of evidence-based practices. *Journal of Evidence-Based Practices for Schools, 11*(1), 62–83.

Swearer, S. M., & Cary, P. T. (2007). *Perceptions and attitudes toward bullying in middle school youth: A developmental examination across the bully/victim continuum*. New York, NY: Haworth Press.

Taylor-Greene, S., Brown, D., Nelson, L., Longton, J., Gassman, T., Cohen, J., et al., (1997). School-wide behavioral support: Starting the year off right. *Journal of Behavioral Education, 7*, 99–112.

Tobin, T., Sugai, G., & Colvin, G. (in press). *Using discipline referrals to make decisions*. NASSP Bulletin.

Vernberg, E. M., Jacobs, A. K., & Twemlow, S. W. (1999). *The peer experiences questionnaire: A survey to assess bully-victim-bystander experiences in schools*. Unpublished manuscript: University of Kansas, Lawrence.

Walker, H. M. (1995). *The acting-out child: Coping with classroom disruption* (2nd ed.). Longmont, CO: Sopris West Educational Services.

Walker, H. M., & Sylwester, R. (1998). Reducing students' refusal and resistance. *The Council for Exceptional Children, 30*(6), 52–58.

Walker, H. M., & Walker, J. E. (1991). *Coping with noncompliance in the classroom : A positive approach for teachers*. Austin, TX: Pro-Ed.

Walker, H. M., Colvin, G., & Ramsey, E. (1995). *Antisocial behavior in school: Strategies and best practices*. Pacific Grove, CA: Brooks/Cole.

Walker, H. M., Horner, R. H., Sugai, G., Bullis, M., Sprague, J., Bricker, D., & Kaufman, M. J. (1996). Integrated approaches to preventing antisocial behavior patterns among school-age children and youth. *Journal of Emotional and Behavioral Disorders, 4*, 194–209. Retrieved from http://dx.doi.org/10.1177%2F106342669600400401

Walker, H., Ramsey, E., & Gresham, F. (2004). *Antisocial behavior in school: Evidenced-based practices*. Florence, KY: Cengage.

Walker, H., Seeley, J., Small, J., Golly, A., Severson, H., & Feil, E. (2008, Winter). The First Step to Success program for preventing antisocial behavior in young children: Update on past, current and planned research. *Report on Emotional & Behavioral Disorders in Youth, 8*(1), 17–23.

Walker, H., Sprague, J., Perkins-Rowe, K. A., Beard-Jordan, K.Y., Seibert, B., Golly, A., . . . Feil, E. (2005). The first step to success program: Achieving secondary prevention outcomes for behaviorally at-risk children through early intervention. In M. H. Epstein, K. Kutash, & A. Duchnowski (Eds.), *Outcomes for children and youth with behavioral and emotional disorders* (2nd ed.). Austin, TX: Pro Ed.

Wang, J., Iannotti, R. J., & Nansel, T. R. (2009). School bullying among adolescents in the United States: Physical, verbal, relational, and cyber. *Journal of Adolescent Health, 15*(4), 368–375.

Webster-Stratton, C., & Herbert, M. T. (1994). *Troubled families—problem children: Working with parents: A collaborative process*. Chichester, England: Wiley and Sons.

Webster-Stratton, C., & Taylor, T. K. (1998). Adopting and implementing empirically supported interventions: A recipe for success. In A. Buchanan & B. L. Hudson (Eds.), *Parenting, schooling and children's behavior: interdisciplinary approaches* (pp. 127–160). Brookfield, VT: Ashgate.

Zins, J. E., & Ponte, C. R. (1990). Best practices in school-based consultation. In A. Thomas & J. Grimes (Eds.), *Best practices in school psychology II* (pp. 673–694). Washington, DC: National Association of School Psychologists.

Photo Credits